GW00597423

The Treasury and Social Policy

Transforming Government

General Editor: **R. A. W. Rhodes**, Professor of Politics, University of Newcastle

This important and authoritative series arises out of the seminal ESRC Whitehall Programme and seeks to fill the enormous gaps in our knowledge of the key actors and institutions of British government. It examines the many large changes during the postwar period and puts these into comparative context by analysing the experience of the advanced industrial democracies of Europe and the nations of the Commonwealth. The series reports the results of the Whitehall Programme, a four-year project into change in British government in the postwar period, mounted by the Economic and Social Research Council.

Titles include:

Nicholas Deakin and Richard Parry
THE TREASURY AND SOCIAL POLICY
The Contest for Control of Welfare Strategy

B. Guy Peters, R. A. W. Rhodes and Vincent Wright
ADMINISTERING THE SUMMIT
Administration of the Core Executive in Developed Countries

Martin J. Smith
THE CORE EXECUTIVE IN BRITAIN

Kevin Theakston
LEADERSHIP IN WHITEHALL

Kevin Theakston (*editor*)
BUREAUCRATS AND LEADERSHIP

Patrick Weller, Herman Bakvis and R. A. W. Rhodes (*editors*)
THE HOLLOW CROWN
Countervailing Trends in Core Executives

Transforming Government
Series Standing Order ISBN 0–333–71580–2
(*outside North America only*)

You can receive future titles in this series as they are published by placing a standing order. Please contact your bookseller or, in case of difficulty, write to us at the address below with your name and address, the title of the series and the ISBN quoted above.

Customer Services Department, Macmillan Distribution Ltd, Houndmills, Basingstoke, Hampshire RG21 6XS, England

CARLTON LODGE
Nursing and Residential Home plc

Accounts Office:
No.1 Battersea Square,
Battersea,
London SW11 3PZ
Tel: 071 924 3026
Fax: 071 924 2559

With Compliments

The Treasury and Social Policy

The Contest for Control of Welfare Strategy

Nicholas Deakin
Honorary Professor of Social Policy
University of Birmingham

and

Richard Parry
Senior Lecturer in Social Policy
University of Edinburgh

Foreword by R. A. W. Rhodes

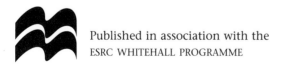

Published in association with the
ESRC WHITEHALL PROGRAMME

E·S·R·C
ECONOMIC
& SOCIAL
RESEARCH
COUNCIL

First published in Great Britain 2000 by
MACMILLAN PRESS LTD
Houndmills, Basingstoke, Hampshire RG21 6XS and London
Companies and representatives throughout the world

A catalogue record for this book is available from the British Library.

ISBN 0–333–75245–7

First published in the United States of America 2000 by
ST. MARTIN'S PRESS, INC.,
Scholarly and Reference Division,
175 Fifth Avenue, New York, N.Y. 10010

ISBN 0–312–23020–6

Library of Congress Cataloging-in-Publication Data
Deakin, Nicholas.
The treasury and social policy : the contest for control of welfare strategy /
Nicholas Deakin and Richard Parry.
p.   cm.
Includes bibliographical references and index.
ISBN 0–312–23020–6 (cloth)
1. Public welfare—Great Britain.   2. Social service—Great Britain.   3. Great
Britain—Social policy.   4. Great Britain. Treasury.   I. Parry, Richard, 1953–
II. Title.

HV245 .D3476   1999
361.941—dc21

99–049498

This book is printed on paper suitable for recycling and made from fully managed and sustained
forest sources.

10   9   8   7   6   5   4   3   2   1
09   08   07   06   05   04   03   02   01   00

Printed and bound in Great Britain by
Antony Rowe Ltd, Chippenham, Wiltshire

Contents

List of Tables and Figures

Tables

Figures

General Editor's Foreword: Transforming Government

There are enormous gaps in our knowledge of the key actors and institutions in British government. We cannot do simple things like describing the work of ministers of state, permanent secretaries, and their departments. Also, there have been large changes in British government during the post-war period, such as: the growth of the welfare state; the professionalization of government; the consequences of recession; the effects of New Right ideology; the impact of the European Union; the effects of new technology; the hollowing out of the state; and the new public management with its separation of policy and administration. We do not know how these changes affected British government. And we cannot understand the effects of these changes by focusing only on Britain. We must also analyze the experience of the advanced industrial democracies of Europe and the Commonwealth.

To repair these gaps in our knowledge and to explain how and why British government changed in the post-war period, the Economic and Social Research Council mounted the Whitehall Programme on 'The Changing Nature of Central Government in Britain'. This series on 'Transforming Government' reports the results of that four-year research programme. The series has five objectives.

- Develop theory – to develop new theoretical perspectives to explain why British government changed and why it differs from other countries.
- Understand change – to describe and explain what has changed in British government since 1945.
- Compare – to compare these changes with those in other EU member states and other states with a 'Westminster' system of government.
- Build bridges – to create a common understanding between academics and practitioners.
- Dissemination – to make academic research accessible to a varied audience ranging from sixth-formers to senior policy-makers.

The books cover six broad themes:

- Developing theory about the new forms of governance.

- The hollowing out of the state in Britain, Europe and the Commonwealth.
- The fragmenting government framework.
- The changing roles of ministers and the senior civil service.
- Constitutional change.
- New ways of delivering services.

Nicholas Deakin and Richard Parry explore the ways in which the Treasury's roles and relationships with other departments have changed by examining in some detail its links with social policy departments. In Chapter 2 they describe the Treasury's search for more effective ways of carrying out its functions. We see the rise and fall of PES (the public expenditure survey) and the 'Treasury under the Tories' again. The system in 1983 is seen as 'unsystematic and politically contingent', with little effective purchase on social policy. Chapter 3 documents how, under the (then) Chancellor Nigel Lawson, the Treasury developed a new technical repertoire. The shift from cash to volume public expenditure planning undermined PES. It gave the Treasury 'a more secure basis for controlling the public sector' and fuelled fears in the social policy departments they would be punished with cuts in their running costs if they did not meet their spending targets.

Chapters 4 and 5 are devoted to the internal reform of the Treasury. The *Fundamental Review of Running Costs* (1994) (otherwise known as the Heywood report) not only streamlined the organization but also sought a thorough re-examination of its working style and culture. Thus, there was to be a shallower hierarchy with responsibility for the Treasury's links to departments and discussions about spending devolved to team leaders at Grade 5. Spending divisions were to be more proactive, strategic with each team reviewing the trade-offs and options available, and responsive to their customers, the departments. In theory at least, the adversarial role was in the past but the strategic role admitted the Treasury into departmental policy development. It intervened on cross-cutting issues as arbitrator and facilitator, causing fears the Treasury had too much power.

Chapters 6 to 8 explore the Treasury's changing role and departmental fears through revealing interviews with key actors. The familiar distinction between guardians (of the public purse) and advocates (of expenditure) is too simple but there are important cracks in the Treasury–department links wonderfully captured in the following quote. There is:

a view which I think the rest of British government should stand firmly against, that they see themselves as getting out of the detail and operating at a strategic level across every strategic issue that government faces. They see themselves actually as a holding company for the British government, with a lot of operating companies, being controlled by the 'Hanson head office' who will check them mostly on numbers, but will also have an overall sort of company strategy which will be capable of affecting every aspect of life, and they think they are capable of doing that, and they could not be more wrong. If they came out and said that was what they were about, loudly, they would have met with a sort of fierce response, but I do think that is what they think they're about, and as I say, it would be disastrous if they were allowed to get away with it. They've got enough power as it is . . .

So, Deakin and Parry conclude, the Treasury seeks 'more control over less' but there is a gap between its wish to intervene and its capacity to do so. Money lies at the heart of government. The Treasury is strong and getting stronger. But it lacks the staff, expertise and analytical ability to intervene effectively in substantive social policies. It needs a refit so it can exercise its influence in a more systematic and informed way.

There have been many fine books on the Treasury. Hugh Heclo and Aaron Wildavsky's *The Private Government of Public Money* (Macmillan, 1974) is a classic of modern political science. Colin Thain and Maurice Wright's *The Treasury and Whitehall* (Clarendon Press, 1995) is a monumental and exhaustive study of the planning and control of public expenditure. Inevitably Nicholas Deakin and Richard Parry's book will be compared with its distinguished predecessors, but they can hold their heads high. It is a fine addition to the canon. Of course a series editor would say that, wouldn't he? But just because I am the editor of the series, I do not lose all judgement. They combine Thain and Wright's grasp of detail with Heclo and Wildavsky's eye for the telling quote. The result is both authoritative and readable, technically up-to-date but accessible. Above all, it communicates the feel of what it is to like to work for the Treasury and what it is like for a department to deal with the Treasury. Their book is a major addition to the Whitehall Programme's series.

Newcastle upon Tyne   R.A.W. RHODES
Director, ESRC Whitehall Programme, and
Professor of Politics, University of Newcastle

The ESRC Whitehall Programme had published four books in the 'Transforming Government' series by March 1999:

Rhodes, R.A.W., Weller, P. and Bakviss, H. (eds), *The Hollow Crown* (London: Macmillan, 1997)

Smith, M.J., *The Core Executive in Britain* (London: Macmillan, 1999)

Theakston, K., *Leadership in Whitehall* (London: Macmillan, 1999)

Theakston, K. (ed.), *Bureaucrats and Leadership* (London: Macmillan, 1999)

It had also published six books outside the series:

Bradbury, J. and Mawson, J. (eds), *British Regionalism and Devolution* (London: Jessica Kingsley, 1997)

Day, P. and Klein R., *Steering but not Rowing? The Transformation of the Department of Health: A Case Study* (Bristol: The Policy Press, 1997)

Lowe, R., *The Welfare State in Britain* (London: Macmillan, 1999)

Rhodes. R.A.W., *Understanding Governance: Policy Networks, Governance, Reflexivity and Accountability* (Buckingham: Open University Press, 1997)

Rhodes, R.A.W. and Dunleavy, P. (eds), *Prime Minister, Cabinet and Core Executive* (London: Macmillan, 1995)

Sergeant, J. and Steele, J., *Consulting the Public: Guidelines and Good Practice* (London: Policy Studies Institute, 1997)

Preface and Acknowledgements

This book originally grew from our dissatisfaction with some common stereotypes of the Treasury's role in British government. Academics and practitioners in our own field, social policy, generally held a conspiratorial view of Treasury attitudes and behaviour that sometimes bordered on the paranoid. Despite the existence of a series of heavyweight academic studies of the Treasury that put its activities in a more objective perspective, that view persisted. We felt that the Treasury's performance could and should be seen in a different light, looking at the impact that its actions and location at the centre of British government has had on the shape and development of social policy but without prior prejudice.

The advent in 1995 of the Whitehall research programme, negotiated by the Economic and Social Research Council with the Cabinet Office, provided us with the opportunity to do so. We owe a great debt to the Council for funding our project and to the programme's academic director, Professor Rod Rhodes. His energy, enthusiasm and general sense of buoyancy have sustained us and our colleagues on the programme. Professor Ben Pimlott, as chair of the ESRC Committee supervising the programme, gave great encouragement, especially to our attempts to provide readable and challenging published output. The support for the programme and active participation in its discussions both formal and informal of successive heads of the home civil service, Sir Robin Butler and Sir Richard Wilson, set the tone for the programme from the outset. On a practical level, it helped us in the crucial task of securing access to the people we wanted to interview.

Our main debt of gratitude for help in writing this book is to the many civil servants in the Treasury and other departments who agreed to see us and talk to us about their work. Convention still requires that we do not name the other civil servants with whom we have had extended discussions. We completed thirty formal interviews with officials at a wide range of different grades. Almost all of them allowed us to record their words on tape; they have offered comments on the precise words we quote, but the use made of quotations from the interviews and the interpretation is our responsibility alone. We are very grateful to have been permitted to proceed in this way, which let us report our respondents' approach to key issues in their own words.

We hope thereby to have been able to convey some sense of the dynamism of the Treasury teams and of their leaders that we interviewed, fearlessly combative in argument, and of the reactions of the long-suffering departmental finance officers in the social spending departments who had to do business with them, who often unburdened their frustrations to us, sometimes almost in confessional style.

Two Treasury officials have had a public profile in the area of our work which we can acknowledge – Norman Glass, Deputy Director of Public Services, a member of the Economic and Social Research Council and a commentator on a paper we gave in 1996, and Sir Terry Burns, who before his retirement as Permanent Secretary in 1998 broke new ground for a senior official in giving thoughtful public lectures, including one on no less sensitive a subject than the transition to the Labour government.

One of the stipulations that grant holders in the Whitehall programme have had to meet is the requirement to feed back the findings of their research to the subjects of their inquiries. In December 1996, we were invited to speak to the Treasury Spending Directorate by its director, Robert Culpin. The entire staff turned up to hear us: to paraphrase President Kennedy, never has there been such a distinguished assemblage of brainpower on spending control since Gladstone dined alone. The Treasury's unique mixture of power and informality that even casual visitors can scent when they walk through the door at Great George Street was on luxuriant display in the discussion that took place that day.

A word on timing. Most of our interviews, which constitute the main but not the only source for our account, took place under the Major government. We are well aware that it can be suggested that some lines of criticism that we advance have already been dealt with by subsequent changes. Nevertheless, we felt it necessary to await the outcome of the 1997 Election before writing up our material and then had to wait for the Labour government to declare its hand on public spending through the Comprehensive Spending Reviews and Public Service Agreements. After the 1999 Budget and some other policy announcements at the end of the financial year, we hope we have hit a relatively calm period during which the ageing process of our book will not accelerate too fast, but by the time this is being read who knows what crises and cuts may have dashed the Treasury's perennial hope that, finally, everything is under reasonable control.

In the course of our study, we were assisted by an advisory group of retired senior officials – David Faulkner, Paul McQuail, Ian Penman and William Plowden – who provided wise advice at the outset and allowed us to try out some of our preliminary conclusions with them. We are most grateful for their help. Our secretarial tasks were lightened by Norma Macleod at Edinburgh and Sue Gilbert at Birmingham, to whom our gratitude also goes.

The writing and redrafting of this book was done equally by both of us, the order of our names on the title page being of alphabetical significance only. On a personal level, Nicholas Deakin would like to thank his nephews Phineas and Felix and niece Romola for their boisterous hospitality on those frequent occasions when work on this book took him to Edinburgh; and Richard Parry gratefully acknowledges the hospitality of Penny Clark in Oxford and Liz Davies in London that facilitated his visits in the opposite direction.

Parts of Chapter 3 draw upon the chapter 'Does the Treasury have a social policy?' we contributed to N. Deakin and R. Page (eds), *The Costs of Welfare* (Avebury, 1993). An earlier version of Chapter 9 appeared as 'The Treasury and New Labour's social policies' in the Social Policy Association's *Social Policy Review 10* (1998). Part of chapter 10 draws upon our end-of-award report to the ESRC.

Crown copyright material in the Public Record Office is reproduced by permission of the Controller of Her Majesty's Stationery Office.

The Economic and Social Research Council showed striking entrepreneurial skill in launching and sustaining this research programme, and our final acknowledgement is to them, mentioning as they would wish that they funded our research under grant number L 124 25 1004.

Birmingham and Edinburgh   NICHOLAS DEAKIN
                                              RICHARD PARRY

1
The Treasury: Images and Realities

Those who exercise financial power within the core executive of any modern government possess a special form of authority. Within the executive, financial decisions have an overriding force, since governments are now judged principally by their success or failure in managing the economy. As a result, the location where this authority resides becomes a pole of attraction for exceptionally energetic and talented people, both politicians and officials. When this location consists of one long-established department combining a number of related functions, ranging from financial, economic and taxation policies through public sector management to the supply side of social policy, there is an obvious potential for concentration of power. This is the present position of Her Majesty's Treasury and of its chief minister, the Chancellor of the Exchequer.

In the circumstances, it is hardly surprising that the Treasury has been the object of persistent attention from journalists and academics – economists by the content of the economic issues at stake, political scientists by the scent of power, and students of social policy by a search for explanations for the performance of the welfare state. Students of the core executive note the strength of the Treasury's resources: as Martin Smith says, 'the importance of its functions, the status of its ministers and the impact it has on all other departments uniquely places it to affect the operation of the core executive as a whole' (Smith, 1999: 145).

The pursuit of power

However, researchers who approach the Treasury, as we have done, in search of better understanding how this power is exercised, do

'Whitehall's Balliol', coined by a former Chancellor, Harold Macmillan, may not have been as kindly meant as those who repeat it seem to believe. When another former Treasury minister, Harold Lever, observed that moving from another department to the Treasury was like moving to the Savoy from a two-star hotel in the provinces he was articulating a view that most civil servants would recognize, even while rejecting it.

The Treasury's response to all this has traditionally been urbane self-deprecation. Peter Hennessy describes a department stuffed with Whiggish intellectual aristocrats, deflecting criticism with irony and 'the equanimity that comes from long familiarity' (1989: 396). It may be that outsiders will misunderstand their objectives. It may even be that what they are attempting to achieve will fail to achieve the right results, out in the 'real world'. Hennessy quotes, without attributing it, the lament by the former Treasury senior official Leo Pliatzky that pulling 'the levers of power' may be futile because it is never clear what the outcome of doing so will be. But even if their actions produce adverse results they can face the consequences – to be popular is not a realistic ambition for a Treasury official. 'My withers remain unwrung', Hennessy quotes one Assistant Secretary remarking in an exchange with a spending department in a simulated expenditure exercise (ibid.: 397). This, Hennessy remarks, is a department with iron withers – though even iron can be friable, when subject to extreme stress, as the Treasury has been at various points in the post-war period.

Treasury politicians

Over time, the Treasury's reputation has waxed and waned, as has the standing of its political head, the Chancellor of the Exchequer. Over the post-war period, the Chancellor has come to be one of the two key figures in any administration, though this was by no means always the case, as Roy Jenkins has shown in his study of earlier Chancellors (1998). The importance of the office was underlined in 1961 by the creation of the new senior post of Chief Secretary to the Treasury, the holder of which normally sits in the Cabinet, explicitly to help the Chancellor perform the key function of controlling public expenditure. Discharging this task successfully has increasingly come to be seen as a major performance indicator for any government.

In his comprehensive review of the performance of post-war

Chancellors of both parties, the former Labour Treasury minister Edmund Dell (1996) ruthlessly dissects the reputation of each politician that has held that office. Few escape censure in the detailed judgments that Mr Justice Dell hands down; but his general conclusions can be summarized in three sentences. First, nothing substantial can be achieved by a Chancellor without the support of the Prime Minister: a secure relationship sustained over time between the tenants of No. 10 and No. 11 Downing Street is vital for the tenure of both of them. Given that initial – and crucial – proviso, Chancellors are themselves responsible for the outcomes of their policies: it is idle to attempt to indict the Treasury as an institution for the failures of politicians. And finally the reputations of all Chancellors, flexible or iron, is built on sand; none of them leaves office with their reputations wholly intact (1996: 93, 346, 551).

It all seems rather different, of course, from the perspective of those who have actually done the job. Most post-war Chancellors have given us an account of their time in office and not surprisingly their versions of events and verdict on their own performance differ considerably. Some concentrate on the political aspects of their time in office to the exclusion of almost everything else (Hugh Dalton is the extreme case, but James Callaghan and R.A. Butler are not far behind); the Treasury as an institution features only in general terms, with a ritual obeisance to the image (Denis Healey, Geoffrey Howe). Roy Jenkins acknowledges the special role of the Treasury and gives his view of the culture he encountered there and even the occasional individual official (invariably, of course, 'exceptionally able'). But only one, Nigel Lawson, is prepared to describe the official half of the Chancellor's life in the Treasury with the same frankness as his political relationships. One constraint on memoir-writers is that the Treasury seeks to enforce the 'Radcliffe rules' against public discussion of the content of advice given by individual officials, leading to usually undiscussed gaps in what may have appeared to be frank memoirs. The rare contributions by a Chief Secretary (J. Barnett, 1982) and a Permanent Secretary (Wass, 1984) are similarly unrevealing.

So it would be fair to say that with the exception of Lawson, none of the accounts given by former Chancellors offer more than a lukewarm defence of the Treasury and its role at the centre of government. This must be set alongside a positive blizzard of criticisms from those politicians who held office in spending departments.

The 18 years of Conservative government, during which ministerial experience was widely distributed among all sorts and conditions of politician, produced a vast crop of memoirs, most of which have subsided rapidly on to the remainder shelves. But nearly all of them have in common the theme of legitimate ambitions thwarted and the source of their frustration is almost invariably identified as the Treasury. Among the bitterest of these is Norman Fowler's description of his dispute with the Treasury over pensions policy; and for this dispute we are for once in a position to set the departmental minister's account against that of the incumbent Chancellor, Nigel Lawson. This episode, to which we will return in due course, is in itself sufficient to justify the journalist Simon Jenkins' comment that:

> The gulf between the 'Downing Street culture' and the 'spending department culture' is one of the biggest in British politics. Yet it seldom attracts parliamentary, press or public attention or debate. (1995: 227)

Academic perspectives on the Treasury

Alongside the folklore and the autobiography, there is now a substantial specialist literature, which continues to grow, on the Treasury as an institution and its relationship to the rest of Whitehall. Explicitly social policy treatments are rare: Alan Walker's *Social Planning* (1982) set the tone of regarding the Treasury as an unsympathetic, controlling black box. An important contribution has been made by Howard Glennerster; his pioneering treatment of 'paying for welfare' has helped to relate social policy to other studies which modify the image of the Treasury as the unsleeping and ruthlessly efficient organization of the myth and substitute something much more complex. His statement that the Treasury has 'swung the rules of the game more and more effectively in its direction' is typical of this more analytical approach (Glennerster, 1997: 73).

The Treasury boasts an official biography in the New Whitehall series, ostensibly written by the former permanent secretary Lord Bridges but in fact largely ghosted by the young Peter Jay (1964). It has also attracted a professional historian in Henry Roseveare (1969), whose account is still invaluable for the early history and development of the Treasury's role through the nineteenth century, when it was still a relatively weak department and Chancellors did not enjoy that status that they now possess.

But the sequence of policy-based studies really begins with one which used access on a privileged basis to construct a convincing view of the Treasury culture at the point when a long period of Conservative government was just ending. Samuel Brittan's *The Treasury under the Tories* (1964), revised as *Steering the Economy* (1971) is an important chronicle of an era in which Treasury officials 'learned to react with almost Jamesian sensitivity to each other's every unspoken nuance' (1971: 471). Reflecting subsequently, Brittan (who had encountered serious problems in getting his manuscript cleared for publication) commented that the

> refrain about 'advice given by civil servants to ministers' being on a par with the confessional has recurred throughout my journalistic life. All talk of open government is so much hot air while the Whitehall line remains that officials will not give frank advice if it is liable to be reported. (1996: 11)

The next and still in many ways the most authoritative source is Heclo and Wildavsky's influential book *The Private Government of Public Money* (1974). It touched a whole generation of civil servants and is still mentioned spontaneously by serving officials as a source of enlightenment and stimulation. The picture of the Treasury as 'smart' and technically adept that it presents rests heavily on the view that the system for controlling public expenditure through medium-term planning of aggregate spending in real terms that was set in place in this period – PESC, of which much more later – represented a breakthrough in getting the rest of Whitehall to take on the Treasury way of thinking. The subsequent collapse of the PESC system has not invalidated either this general conclusion or the subtle portrait painted by Heclo and Wildavsky in their account of the 'Whitehall policy village'.

The exploration of the mutuality and trust that this image conveys gives Heclo and Wildavsky's book a quite different character to earlier studies. It shows a Treasury that proceeds by negotiating and by activating community networks within the village – including information exchanged through gossip or a quiet word in the Cabinet Office mess and a department acutely sensitive to the importance of meeting ministerial priorities. This is obviously easier to achieve in a small department with few executive responsibilities – especially one that is 'collegiate', where comparatively junior officials enjoy direct access to politicians in a way that does not exist elsewhere in Whitehall.

A more recent perspective on the Treasury's standing is provided in Thain and Wright's monumental study *The Treasury and Whitehall* (1995). Here again, the internal structures that they describe have already been radically altered; but the broad conclusions of their study stand, independent of structural changes. To over-simplify a complex argument, these are that the Treasury's power is severely circumscribed. It is the prisoner of events taking place on a wider stage; the overall health of the British economy at a time when it is uniquely open to developments in the wider global economic sphere and of changes in the political arena. As a result, the Treasury's scope for imposing its priorities in domestic negotiations with Whitehall partners is sharply restricted.

This restriction can be clearly illustrated in the failure to deliver over the past two decades on the Treasury's 'historic mission to restrain the growth of public expenditure'. This is because, except in times of

> acute economic or financial crisis, the Treasury cannot dictate to departments or impose its will upon them. Their relationships are interdependent; their room for discretionary manoeuvre mutually constrained. The paradigm of the politics of public spending at the heart of British central government is negotiated discretion. (Thain and Wright, 1995: 5)

Finally, a recent study by Richard Chapman, *The Treasury in Public Policymaking* (1997), reinforces this view of departments whose role is circumscribed by a number of constraints, old and new. Among them, he cites changes in the character of the civil service as a whole as a result of structural reforms of the 1980s and the hiving off of many executive functions into free-standing agencies, together with the changes in values that have taken place – the importing from the private sector of different approaches to management. One of the consequences of structural reform, Chapman suggests, has been the decline of the distinctive professional ethos of the public sector. All these changes, he argues, have imported a different emphasis into the roles the Treasury performs and its relationships and diminished the significance of its location at the heart of government. Heclo and Wildavsky's Whitehall policy village has been transformed by speculative development into a jerry-built suburban estate.

All in all, these accounts, taken together with the two radio programmes masterminded by Hugo Young and Anne Sloman in the 1980s, which gave the civil servants themselves and some ministers free rein to put their own version on record, show a Treasury of a different kind – less confident, far from omni-competent, even prone at times to self-pity. One explanation for the disparity between this portrait from a multiplicity of sources and the traditional public image may be to do with time lag. Many commentators have referred to differences between the immediate post-war period and the situation that developed from the early 1960s onwards. Denis Healey, who spent five exceptionally turbulent years in the Treasury (1974–9), told the BBC that:

> I would say that of all the departments the one that has the least coherent view of its role is the Treasury. It may have been true in the ten years after the war that all Treasury officials knew exactly how the country should be run, but in my experience none of them knows how. They're deeply divided on many of the central issues. (Young and Sloman, 1982: 25)

The approach of this project

Our own original approach to the question of the Treasury's role and its relationships with other government departments was through the study of the Treasury's interest in social policy. We wished to explore this particular theme because we believed that it would help to illuminate the search for power, through the examination of how Treasury attempts to exercise control in policy areas in which there had been a spectacular rise both in the volume of expenditure and in the public profile of the activities that government funds: health, education, and above all social security.

We also believed that there was a submerged theme in the basis on which the Treasury has approached these social policy issues, which had not received sufficient attention. In addition to the concern with implementing economic policy priorities and restraining public expenditure in aggregate, we argued that the Treasury might also have an interest in influencing the content of social policies (Deakin and Parry, 1993). In 1994, the then Permanent Secretary, Sir Terry Burns, observed that:

> The Treasury's interests are wider than just the aggregate level of spending and having control mechanisms to ensure that agreed

totals are not exceeded. Value for money, output and quality will always be important, as will suitable monitoring mechanisms to ensure that policies are fulfilled. (1994: 45)

And when the political will exists, the means to intervene are always present. In his account of his Chancellorship, Nigel Lawson asserts that:

> the Chancellor if he proceeds with care and caution, can affect the content and not merely the cost of other ministers' policies and in a limited number of carefully selected areas, generate the ideas which decisively affect the direction of government policy. (1992: 273)

He goes on to give a number of examples of areas in which he and his officials (at least, according to his account) influenced or even determined the outcome of new social policy initiatives.

In addition, we speculated that the changes in the structure and functions of central government – the 'fragmentation' referred to earlier – would have had a significant impact on the dynamics of the Treasury's outside relationships. Like Richard Chapman, we assumed that the breaking up of the Whitehall monolith through the separation of the policy and implementation functions and the creation of semi-autonomous agencies to perform many of the tasks previously carried out by departments would alter the nature of these relationships. Given that the implementation of the Treasury approach to public expenditure depends on the inculcation of common objectives, how far would these changes require new 'attitudes, arrangements and approaches' (Monck, 1993: 279) that go beyond those that have been effective in the past?

Finally, in these changed circumstances, we wanted to look at different ways in which the 'hollowness' at the centre of the executive might be filled up and the role that the Treasury might perform as a key player in any changes that take place. Past images of the Treasury and its 'heavy hand' are liable to provoke concern about the implications of giving the department a larger role in policy development, going beyond the temporary ambitions of individual Chancellors. Yet as the search for identifying better means of addressing 'cross-cutting' issues and devising new 'joined up' policies to deal with them continues, it is hard to see how the Treasury's claims for a wider role can be ignored.

The Treasury in the Whitehall research programme

The establishment of the Whitehall research programme by the Economic and Social Research Council, in conjunction with the Cabinet Office, gave us the opportunity to follow through these objectives. The programme can be seen as tangible evidence of an attempt, from the mid-1990s onwards, to open up the inner workings of the machinery of British government to closer scrutiny. Its particular value to researchers with an interest in the development of policy within Whitehall lies in the access it secured for those awarded grants under the programme to individual civil servants for discussion of current policy issues.

Our original intention was to cover a number of social policy programmes in which Treasury interest was likely to be especially close: health, education and social security. Social security was selected largely because of the sheer size of the programme; health because of its high political visibility and the level of public concern that it attracts and education both for these reasons and because of the more positive character of the Treasury's past relations with the Department of Education (as it then still was).

To this we added two further areas of interest. First, the 'territorial' departments (Scotland, Wales, Northern Ireland) because they represented a clear case of Treasury willingness to delegate a degree of control within fixed limits (both before and after the constitutional reform process begun in 1997). And, second, we wished to look at another form of delegation – the consequences of the creation of arm's length administrative bodies in certain social policy areas – civil service executive agencies and the NHS Executive. Did their appearance signal a change in the nature of Treasury control in these areas, with extended lines of command creating new semi-independent organizations, whose Chief Executives would develop different roles and thereby complicate the nature of the relationship between the Treasury and spending departments?

In order to balance the picture, we needed to talk to protagonists on both sides of the policy debate and we therefore asked to see the Principal Finance Officers of all the departments we had selected for study. The PFO is normally the first point of contact with the Treasury within the spending department concerned and has a general co-ordinating role within the department on expenditure issues. Most, though not all the negotiation with the Treasury will be conducted through them until issues reach ministerial level on both sides. As we anticipated, structural changes within the departments meant that the circle of those that we wished to see extended itself some way as we carried out the interviews.

Like other researchers (Heclo and Wildavsky, Thain and Wright, for example) who have also enjoyed access to the civil service, we were able to stipulate with very few restrictions the areas of policy that we wished to cover. And although we had no access to written advice (put in Samuel Brittan's terms, we were not admitted to the confessional), we were able to conduct our interviews on remarkably open terms. For example, we were allowed to tape record interviews and our experience (unlike our predecessors) was that the inhibiting effect was minimal and the advantage of generating a text agreed between subject and interviewers was very substantial. Interviews were conducted with officials at all levels in the hierarchy from Grade 7 upwards and we were also able to see two recent Chief Secretaries, one from each major party.

In all, we conducted 30 interviews and were able to tape record the great majority of them, the exceptions being at a senior level. The interviews were structured on the basis of a schedule constructed by the interviewers but discussion was allowed to develop without rigid constraints. The average length of the interview was an hour and a half; our strong impression was that those interviewed enjoyed the opportunity to discuss their work – in some cases to the point of giving respondents a welcome chance to unburden themselves of some current preoccupations. Respondents had the opportunity to comment on the use made of the material in the text and to correct their words if they wished. In a limited number of cases, we reinterviewed respondents to clarify issues and update ourselves on developments. This material has generally been anonymized in a manner that has obtained the consent of those concerned. Our main findings were reported back at a seminar with Treasury staff, which gave rise to vigorous comment and discussion. In general terms, we see this element in the research as being in the tradition of 'administrative anthropology' in this area – that is, the discussion on policy outcomes as a reflection of the personalities of those who work within the system as well as the process through which they operate.

Context, 'curse' and content

In our approach to setting down the material we have assembled, we have chosen to sketch in the background lightly, concentrating in the next chapter (Chapter 2) on the main developments in the period since the Second World War. This chapter also develops some of the reasons why we consider that the social policy perspective we have selected is relevant, reinforced with an account of developments at the point in the 1960s at which new techniques for public expenditure control came into play. This is based largely on research done by one of us (Richard Parry) in the PRO. We have also benefited from discussion on this period with a fellow grant holder in the Whitehall programme, Rodney Lowe. In Chapter 3, we go on to describe how the system of public expenditure control was changed and adapted to new circumstances during the long period of Conservative government that began in 1979.

One of the recurrent features of research on the Treasury, re-marked upon by our predecessors has been the way in which the publication of each successive study has been followed almost immediately by new structural reforms, incidentally invalidating most of the description contained in them. We were therefore strongly counselled not to devote time and space to giving detailed accounts of organizational arrangements which were bound to be outdated by the time our study saw the light of day (this phenomenon has become known as the 'curse' of the academic researcher on Treasury topics and we are no doubt falling victim to it in our turn, especially as a consequence of the new patterns of Treasury–departmental relations set by the Comprehensive Spending Reviews of 1997–8).

Nevertheless, our own study was heavily influenced by an import-ant internal reform within the Treasury that was introduced in 1995 as a result of the Fundamental Expenditure Reviews (FERs) taking place throughout Whitehall. For reasons we explain in Chapter 4, this led to a comprehensive reallocation of functions within the Treasury itself. The impact of the report on which these changes were based, known after its principal author as the Heywood report, was still very strongly felt at the time at which we began to undertake our interviews and we have therefore devoted a whole chapter to it. Chapter 5 is based largely on these interviews and deals with the implementation of the Heywood report and its implications for the team leaders in the Spending Directorate whose role was redefined by the report and their evolving relationships with spending departments elsewhere in Whitehall.

Interviews with key actors both in the Treasury and the selected spending departments (Social Security, Health, Education and Employment and the territorial departments) also form the main basis for the account given in the next three chapters (6, 7 and 8) of the developing relationship between the two sides in the period since the internal reforms that have affected all Whitehall departments. It is important to underline here how small the numbers of those directly involved in these exchanges are, in relation to the scale of their responsibilities, especially after the 1995 reforms. This has the incidental advantage for the researchers of enabling us to cover a large number of issues with relatively few interviews – the officials pay a price, of course, in terms of endemic heavy workloads.

At the same time, we have tried in our assessment of the material we have assembled, both from the interviews and the written record, to take a broader view of events and set the dialogue between the Treasury and spending departments in the broader context of political and economic change. In particular, the election of the Labour government in May 1997 (after the first round of our interviews had been completed) created a different dynamic in the relations between the Treasury and spending departments and the functions that the Treasury was expected to perform. We explore these issues further in Chapter 9.

Finally, there is another issue that arises directly from the research we have undertaken and on which we have things to say in our concluding Chapter 10. One of the concerns the Cabinet Office has had in supporting the Whitehall research programme has been to help identify ways in which government departments can function more effectively in the new environment in which they now have to operate. A particular question that has arisen in the early stages of the Labour government's period in office after 1997 has been the location of responsibility for dealing with 'cross-cutting issues'.

One of our own interests has been in the way in which changes in the overall structure of government has changed the nature of relationships at the centre of the core executive. The absence of a fully staffed and equipped capacity for policy evaluation at the centre and the clear linkages between economic and social policy make the Treasury at least a contender for a central co-ordinating role in policy development. But under the Blair government the Cabinet Office and the Prime Minister's Office have also been strengthened to take on this role. These alternative locations of the core power have substantial implications for relationships with the spending departments, and we explore some of the ramifications of this argument in Chapter 10.

2
The Evolution of the Treasury's Intervention in Social Policy

The Treasury's original line of interest in social policy derives from its wish to exercise tighter control over the operation of the government machine. In the words of Sir Thomas Heath (a former Permanent Secretary, writing in 1927), 'in essence it is the one permanent institution which stands between the country and national bankruptcy' (Heath, 1927: 1). Its position as an elite department was secured only slowly by the restriction of the rights of other departments to propose expenditure.

The history of the Treasury, as recounted by Roseveare (1969) and Chapman (1997), was for long a matter of low-level 'clerking' – the routine signing-off of accounts. This approach is typified by Gladstone's famous observation in 1877, when he wondered whether an aristocratic ministerial appointee could 'descend to the saving of candle-ends, which is very much the measure of a good Secretary to the Treasury' (Bridges, 1964: 29). This implied that an interest in high policy was a disqualification for the successful performance of this task; Heath suggests that romance or sentiment do not primarily attach to a financial department, which is what the Treasury was in essence until the Second World War.

In fact, it can be argued that the modern Treasury with its double function as both a Finance Department and a Ministry of Economics only dates from the period of the Attlee government (1945–51), when all the centres of advice and control on the economy, like the Economic Section of the Cabinet Office, were absorbed into the Treasury, through the semi-accident of Stafford Cripps becoming Chancellor in late 1947 after the resignation of Hugh Dalton. Cripps took over to the Treasury with him his responsibilities as Minister of Economic Affairs which had been in part given to him by Attlee as a counterweight to Herbert Morrison, the overlord of the Labour government's domestic programme. As Chancellor, Cripps became an archetypal figure of intellectual power and austerity, slamming the brakes on spending in the post-war welfare state for the first time. This began the sequence of developments by which the Treasury came to be seen as strong, perhaps unhealthily so, caught up in emergencies, security or economic, and also relatively detached from the reality of economic and social life.

Three images of the Treasury

We can summarize the influence of this perception in three adjectives:

(i) the Treasury seen as *concentrated* – bringing together the whole range of economic and financial functions;
(ii) the Treasury seen as dealing with *urgent* topics – at the heart of the action, especially international events; charged with making important government policies work. A series of memoirs by economic advisers captures this post-war atmosphere which perpetuated wartime themes of secrecy, alarm and crisis (Cairncross and Watts, 1989; Cairncross (ed.), 1989; Cairncross, 1997; Plowden, 1989;
(iii) the Treasury viewed as *rigorous* – running 'hard', impersonal models of the economy, going the extra mile in scrutiny of spending programmes, and setting an example in doing so. (Though this is a *selective* rigour, with the Treasury's small size precluding comprehensiveness).

The control of public expenditure

Among the range of tasks exemplified by these different aspects of the Treasury tradition, expenditure – or 'supply' – work has generally had relatively low status in the department. No Permanent Secretary of the Treasury emerged from it until Andrew Turnbull in 1998 and its relatively routine tasks, as prescribed by legislation or practice, stand in the same relation to the international and macroeconomic Treasury as does the rest of Whitehall to the Treasury. The slightly self-pitying flavour ('poor old Treasury') in the way in which these tasks are described resonates down the years:

> if it faithfully discharges the duties entrusted to it, [it] can never be popular; conversely, if at any time it should become popular,

that fact itself would be conclusive proof that it was not fulfilling the purpose for which it exists. In actual fact it is generally looked upon as a kind of bugbear or bogey.' (Heath, 1927: 1); and everyone knows that there must be some person, some organisation, charged with the duty of deciding how much public money can be made available to meet the almost insatiable demands for public expenditure. Nobody looks with envy at those who have the task of deciding this question, or the even more difficult one of how much money can be devoted to each particular purpose. And although there is always plenty of vocal dissatisfaction from the enthusiasts for particular causes, at the miserable amount accorded to them, most of the grumbles and dissatisfaction cancel each other out. Anyhow, nobody has ever produced a better system. But let no one underrate how difficult the job is. (Bridges, 1964: 41–2)

The creation of a less routinized role for the spending divisions has been a major theme of thinking in the Treasury. A function based on the reactive monitoring of policy decisions taken by others can never be fully satisfactory to a high-calibre department; the search has been to give the controllers of spending an enhanced role which does not just leave them more exposed and overburdened in terms of their responsibilities.

One way of discharging the expenditure control task more effectively is to look for allies. To understand the Treasury's search for a more effective way of carrying out its functions in this field, we need to make a distinction between *Treasury as an organization* and the *Treasury function*. By the latter we mean, not so much the repression of expenditure, which has always been contracted-out to the finance divisions of spending departments, as the imaginative consideration of the relation of specific projects to overall economic objectives. The Treasury knows that it cannot be everywhere, and so much of its task consists of the search for competent partners.

A further established theme in the range of techniques adopted by the Treasury is that of the 'porthole principle' – that it is only through the scrutiny of detail that understanding of the big picture emerges. Treasury authority over minor matters has been justified not just as a matter of propriety and accountability in the use of public funds, but as a quality check and a source of illustrative information. The weakness of this approach is that the spending

Treasury has been able to reassume those functions that it saw as germane to its task and on which it therefore had to maintain an interest.

A final long-term theme is the Treasury as a shaper and exporter of a civil service élite. Having resisted recruitment by merit longer than most, the Treasury embraced it fully in 1878 (Chapman, 1997: 23; Roseveare, 1969: 177) and started to take the best recruits to the civil service and if necessary export them to other departments. Treasury officials were seen to have financial ingenuity, but also to be the experts in reading and winning ministers' minds. So the Treasury mandarinate transformed itself from a supervisor of routine into a central force powerfully 'mixing it' with the rest of the government machine (Roseveare, 1969: 205). This became a self-reinforcing process, as the Treasury was in a position year after year to cream off the brightest young entrants to the civil service. These officials might not always be liked but the way in which they did their jobs – their credentials in terms of civil service values – could not be denied.

The Treasury and specific social policy issues

How has the Treasury reacted to more specifically social policy related issues? It has never been instinctively pro-welfare in the sense of wishing to extend the embrace of government to the needs of wide sections of the population and it has been particularly concerned to promote strict control of the funding of new schemes. It was sceptical at the outset about the Beveridge reforms (C. Barnett, 1986), doubtful about the cost of introducing them and nervous about the probability (as it saw it) of spending on the non-productive social programmes getting out of control. It was anxious wherever possible to promote reviews of welfare expenditure that would act as a much-needed brake upon growth, but these usually proved fruitless, since legitimate investigation presupposed expertise and this was likely to promote just as much as to restrain spending (for instance, the Guillebaud Committee on the National Health Service in 1953).

In the 1950s the Treasury started to face up to the pressures in financing the rising expectations generated by increasing national prosperity. It did not have the analytical apparatus to relate this to some overall conception of the political economy, nor did it enjoy the political resources to impose its view on the Prime Minister and Cabinet. Hence officials became prone to a kind of resentful resignation broken by occasional dire warnings about where the welfare state was leading. Rodney Lowe (1989) has recounted how in the mid-1950s a ministerial Social Services committee on the presumed unaffordability of the welfare state not only failed to impose the Treasury line but mobilized the spending departments into a making a coherent defence of its social and political necessity. This was the backdrop to the resignations of the Chancellor, Peter Thorneycroft and his entire Treasury ministerial team in January 1958 after failing to gain Cabinet consent to spending cuts.

This episode, and Harold Macmillan's politically adroit handling of the situation, made it clear that even under Conservative governments the political will to cut welfare was likely to be weak. It is worth examining this period more closely because of the importance of the decisions taken at this time, when welfare spending was settling into the pattern of incremental growth that it would follow over the next two decades. We can do so in some detail, because we can use the written files at the Public Record Office. Although in theory papers are released after 30 years the transfer and cataloguing of files is surprisingly slow. Not much was available beyond the early 1960s at the time of our research in 1995, although Rodney Lowe's research as part of the Whitehall project has been able to examine Treasury papers from later in the decade. Despite the passage of time, we felt that we were capturing attitudes and idioms that are likely to persist, and that typical 'Treasury-speak' on social policy in an era when the written word was a much more central means of communication than it is today was coming vividly to life. Tom Caulcott, one of the officials appearing in the files, confirms this in a recent published comment:

> The divisions of the Treasury dealing with public expenditure do not need to change their basic philosophy on a change of government. They know that the demands of the spending departments will always be more than the economy can bear. At least that will always be their starting point. The degree to which the Treasury is involved in spending decisions has varied enormously over the years. The latest moves to reduce such involvement have had their parallels in earlier times. But the approach, the philosophy of the department, has remained constant for many years. (Caulcott, 1996: 53)

The Treasury's approach to spending cuts: the archival record

After the loss of his Treasury ministers in January 1958, Harold Macmillan launched an 'economy drive' in which departments were asked to review which of their functions were necessary. The Treasury's Social Services Division were ready: an official minuted, 'what is needed . . . is a well-known list of Social Services horses for races of this kind' (Turnbull to Rossiter, 30.7.58, in T/227/1111). These included withdrawal of family allowances from the second child; restriction of the NHS dental service to under-15s and expectant mothers; abolition of the NHS ophthalmic service outside hospitals; a hospital boarding charge; and charges for school milk and welfare foods (Turnbull to Fraser, 1.8.58, ibid.).

The senior official to whom this laundry list was submitted, Sir Bruce Fraser, commented that:

> When one starts to think in a general way about the Health Service, one soon begins to think also about the structure of social services as a whole. I believe that sooner or later some Government will have to do this, because in some ways the structure really is rather a muddle, and the cost to the Exchequer imposes a growing inhibition on the Chancellor's freedom of manoeuvre. In the course of such thinking, one might find oneself trying to answer such fundamental questions as: Have we got a sensible level of social taxes contributions and charges? Is our present society not different in important respects from the society over which Beveridge cast his starry eye, and to which his thinking might have been more apt? Is our expenditure properly related to the real social value of what it achieves? (For instance, is it sensible to spend, as we do, roughly the same sum on universal family allowances as on National Assistance, which is a really fundamental social need?) (to Sir Roger Makins, 8.8.58, ibid.)

Despite the period flavour of these ramblings, the long-term conceptual structure of the 'Treasury approach' comes through strongly.

Inevitably, even the best runners were seen off after being put to the Cabinet (the Division's paper going all the way but more in hope than expectation). At a meeting with the Chancellor, the Minister of Health [Derek Walker-Smith] argued successfully that the ophthalmic proposals 'would bankrupt many opticians and would be contrary to the pledges which his predecessor had given to the optical profession' (ibid.: 2.9.58). A small increase in school meals charges was agreed. The impression from later files is of a Treasury regularly returning to the charge on social policy cuts, but usually knocked back by their own ministers, let alone others, and finding it hard to maintain a principle like the indexation of charges against inflation.

The Treasury's internal 'History of Prescription Charges' (1967, in T/267/16) reveals a more subtle approach by the Treasury over the years than a simple drive for revenue-raising from this source: there was a recognition that charging involved political problems, administrative complexity, risk of loading excessive quantities on the one prescription, and confusion of the more important task of encouraging more rational prescribing behaviour by doctors. As the author of this study notes, the Treasury was striving to be rational but lacked a secure information base and the analytical capability to raise its approach to a higher level of understanding:

> Administrators seem often to be obliged without enquiry to accept current generalisations (e.g. about 'abuse') because they have not the leisure or staff to examine the implications and get at the facts. The real costs of these inconveniences may be very high. In the particular case of the drug charges some progress has been made been made because the problem was given priority in the work of historical research, but even this has only helped to show what needs to be done and why. Thus the probability that larger research organisations generally are needed inside the Government Service seems to be an important conclusion emerging from this work. (ibid.: 13)

Files on social security at the time show a similar concentration on political realities coupled with an underlying approach, in this case to favour means-tested over universal benefits. Even allowing for the vast change in circumstances, we can detect the basic contours of the Treasury approach to social policy – politically aware, alive to economic analysis in a rudimentary way, not afraid to be opinionated, slightly defeatist, seeking a more precise targeting on need so that people do not gain from misfortune, and wary of the spending departments. These themes persist; it is the context of economic fortunes and assumptions that changes.

The Treasury's attitude to social spending departments

The pivotal event in post-war public expenditure planning was the work of the internal committee set up in 1959 under Sir Edwin Plowden to inquire into the control of public expenditure. The Plowden report, produced in 1961, set a new framework for addressing public expenditure issues within government, one the Treasury hoped would do fuller justice to their concerns and priorities. We consider below the work and outcome of the Committee and the question (still debated) of whether it represents a long-term victory or defeat for the Treasury.

The initial announcement of the Plowden exercise in July 1959 provided the occasion for the Social Services Division for taking stock of their relations with departments and so provides us with valuable evidence. A long memorandum submitted by Jack Robertson, Under-Secretary in charge of the division, to Sir Thomas Padmore on 13 October 1959, summarizes and sometimes modifies drafts submitted by his team and prepared during the relative calm of the General Election campaign. We can detect two major aspects of continuing value to the analysis of expenditure control in social policy: a notion of the underlying purpose behind Treasury 'interference' in social policy; and a sense of the relative level of esteem in which spending departments were held, which in turn constrains the amount of devolution of responsibility the Treasury will concede.

On the former, Robertson had cricketing metaphors at the ready to express what he saw as a detached system:

> nearly all our exchanges with the Health and Education Departments are on general principles, with individual cases serving, empirically, to give point to the determination of general principle and practice. This style of Treasury control – combination of 'control by policy decision' with the 'long-stop' function (which is discharged by being in the spot with an eye on the ball, but not necessarily *doing* anything) – fits in with the departmental pattern of control. (T/227/1224: 5–6)

So far, so strategic, but a later passage (most of which could plausibly be written today) suggests that this style is born out of necessity:

> we remain in relation to the vast moneys we help to dispose of, a small division. This limitation by numbers is a blessing and

keeps us sound on the primacy of not undertaking avoidable executive tasks. But I think that because the division is determinedly empirical, and rushed off its feet most of the time, we may still be party to the retention of systems of control that are 'phoney' or be pretending that control exists in certain areas where, by their nature or for lack of policy decisions to wield control, there is no effective control in fact. If so, this could be partly because our opposite numbers in spending and controlling Departments themselves see profit in the preventive or 'long-stop' aspect of financial control *vis-à-vis* other agencies spending public money, and like to keep it going, irrespective of its cost and occasional futility. (ibid.: 13)

On the second theme, relations with departments, distinctions and criticisms are a matter of nuance, as minuted by Robertson's staff to him (in T/227/1227): 'I think our relations with the Health Departments could be called good' (Boys to Robertson 8.10.59). 'We can fairly say that our relations [with housing departments] are good ... with one or two exceptions on grounds of personality' (Caulcott to Robertson, 9.10.59). 'In terms of effectiveness I would characterize our relations with the Ministry of Education as excellent, and with Scottish Education Department and with University Grants Committee as good' (Wright to Robertson, 8.10.59).

The reason why education received special praise at this time is to do with its compatibility with the 'Treasury function'. Expertise on the technical and financial aspects of educational building has been built up in the 1950s to allow all capital control to be delegated, whereas the Ministry of Health did not have the conceptual apparatus to allow its delegation on hospital building to be raised above £60 000. MoH was also disliked for trying naively to obtain a loosening of capital controls while having the Treasury prop them up on pay negotiations by being present at meetings – again, a long-standing Treasury complaint.

On social security, the problem lay in the Treasury's weakness on the policy side, rather than in interdepartmental relations. They would be conscious that in 1959 the Ministry of Pensions 'was able – if not to obtain its optimum policy – at least to defeat the seemingly invincible alliance of Macmillan, Butler, the Treasury and the insurance industry on the principle of contracting out from occupational state pension' (Lowe, 1997b: 603). In a minute which seemed to guide Robertson's general thinking, Andrew Collier (then a Principal on pensions and benefit matters, later a Deputy Secretary in DHSS) set out the problem and one solution then being floated in the Treasury:

The main difficulty in the recent period has been the energy and ability of the Minister concerned [John Boyd-Carpenter]. If a Minister has the time and inclination to delve into every aspect of administration Treasury control is bound to suffer; Treasury ministers just do not have the time to argue the Treasury case on these relatively unimportant matters. This is not entirely a question of personalities. There is a case – though it is beyond our present terms of reference to argue it – that 'executive' Departments ought not to have a Minister in direct charge of them. The conclusion of this would no doubt be to set up a policy-making Social Services Ministry, with subordinate Departments administering insurance, health and employment. This has been much considered elsewhere in the Treasury, and I only mention it to suggest that it may be that the present difficulties for Treasury control are inevitable under present arrangements. (Collier to Robertson, 7.10.59 in T/227/1227: para. 11)

What was the real issue here? It might be argued that the Treasury interest was served either by consolidation – of health and social security in 1968, education and employment in 1995 – or by hiving-off (Manpower Services Commission in 1974, Benefits and Contribution Agencies in 1991). But this does not seem to be quite the point. What Collier and Robertson seemed to find most worrying was the dynamic of politically fuelled pressures for expenditure in 'deserving' human fields that were both required by and made possible by an expanding modern economy. A 'strong' Treasury was no answer, because at the political level a coalition of spending ministers could call the shots, unless restrained by a state of manifest crisis (not achieved in 1958, when Treasury ministers' bluff was called and they resigned, but successful in 1976). Therefore the Treasury was left with institutional devices (their 'Social Services Ministry' that would internalize spending choices and force economies in service delivery – the Treasury function replicated at one remove) coupled with Canute-like 'ploys' (where, as in the same [1959] manifesto, 'the Minister got away with an unqualified promise to raise the earnings limit, our next ploy was to point out that the pledge was undated, and to work for postponement of its enactment' (Robertson to Padmore, 13.10.59 in T/227/1224: 12). At the same time, a wish to relate better to departments in a psychologically more sophisticated way can be detected. This was evidenced in two approaches advocated in the files: informal personal relations with the department at an early stage, and direct dealing with policy divisions. The first is a familiar theme – if only they would trust us and not hoard information, we could be so much more helpful. Miss Boys saw as a main factor in the relationship

> the extent to which the occupant of my post can maintain informal, as well as formal, official contact with about a dozen of the people on whom we rely. By informal contact I mean visits to see their services, meeting their contacts in the field and unscripted discussion over lunch and in the corridors. I have found in recent months that, compared with a day in the Treasury, ten times as much work can be done and ten times as much money can be saved, by a day spent in the department. (ibid.: Boys to Robertson, 8.10.59)

The second embodies tactical awareness in negotiation well expressed by Caulcott:

> from the Treasury's point of view there is much to be said for dealing direct with the administrative divisions. It gives the Treasury division the opportunity to negotiate direct with the people who know precisely what their objective is and how far short of it they are prepared to fall. If the contact is with the Accountant General [Finance] Division only, the Accountant General Division is itself advocating the particular piece of expenditure and it may be far less flexible in negotiation than the administrative, because it fears that to accept anything less from the Treasury than what it asked for is to imply that they ought not to have put the case to the Treasury. (ibid.: Caulcott to Robertson, 9.10.59, 1227)

Forty years on the Treasury was still exploring these two themes.
When, as part of the Treasury's preparations for the Plowden exercise, Sir Thomas Padmore launched an exercise on delegated powers, he seemed to be conscious that the Treasury was on the defensive on the issue of relations with departments, and might be

unfairly criticized for the failure of departments to seek to assume greater devolved authority. On 4 February 1960 he wrote to his Heads of Divisions:

> The evidence given to the Plowden committee suggests that much of the criticism directed at Treasury control, as now practised, springs from what is felt to be over-meticulous scrutiny of Departmental activities, with a negligible return in terms of finance. The Committee is likely to recommend that such control should be further relaxed, so as to give Departments a greater measure of managerial freedom and corresponding responsibility.
>
> It would be helpful, I think, to be able to demonstrate to the Committee that the Treasury is not averse from reviewing delegated authorities and has in fact increased these powers substantially in certain directions; and that the process of review is continuing. (in T/227/1228)

The Social Services Division response was to point out that further delegation was always open to request, and that departments themselves were sometimes averse to losing the shelter of Treasury responsibility. However, there is difference of view evident between the *radical strategic decentralizers* prepared to contemplate substantial withdrawal of Treasury oversight, and *cautious sceptics* concerned that departments lacked the capability to safeguard the taxpayer interest, leaving the Treasury with a prudential as well as economic need to be present.

Typical of the former was Mrs Rossiter:

> there is no doubt in my mind that we ought to raise the cash limits of delegated authorities. And if this is coupled with
> a) suitable unit cost standards in appropriate cases (e.g. the hospitals)
> b) long-term programme planning, where appropriate (e.g. the universities and hospitals)
> c) an annual estimates scrutiny of the cash expenditure in the year, there should be sufficient control to satisfy the Treasury. (ibid.: to Robertson, 29.3.60)

On the latter was her Under Secretary Jack Robertson, who cooled down his team's drafts to report to Padmore that in the biggest programmes there is no room for the Treasury to extend any further existing delegated authorities over works programmes, including projects; but that on hospitals (once broad policy and organisation is agreed with the Treasury) we envisage increasing the responsibility of the Health departments subject to the conditions outlined being satisfied. (ibid.: 21.4.60)

These conditions sought broadly to bring Health up to the standard of Education in giving a sufficiently strong lead to the delivery agencies on the financial and technical standards of projects.

Treasury attitudes to the Plowden report

The Plowden report put in place the expenditure control system run by the Public Expenditure Survey Committee and known as 'PESC' or 'the Survey'. This system represented a radical departure from previous practice, in setting in motion a multi-year process that provided a framework for planning that would match expenditure over the longer term to government objectives.

The Plowden system has earned an increasingly bad press over the years, its reputation moving, in David Heald's words, 'from model child to delinquent monster' (1981: 175); but the lines of criticism tend to be somewhat contradictory. Rodney Lowe's detailed study using official documents argues that the Treasury was able to use Plowden to its own ends, and impose its own views on the political economic impact of the welfare state:

> the Plowden report, with its covert agenda to restrict both public expenditure and public discussion, reflected the resistance of the British political elite to radical change. It also reflected a traditional scepticism towards collective provision which – because the quality of management was essential to its ultimate success – unsurprisingly became self-fulfilling. Consequently the Plowden Committee was not a milestone and, if not a millstone, was at least a buoy marking an undercurrent of hostility to state welfare which linked the 1930s to the 1980s. (Lowe, 1997a: 491)

But the dominant interpretation in the public expenditure literature is not that the Plowden system was reactionary but that the Treasury got it wrong by promoting a multi-year, volume-based system that was too ambitious and in the end accelerated expenditure rather than contained it:

The Public Expenditure Survey was built upon the assumption that collegiate decision-making by Cabinet ministers on public expenditure plans would lead to a willingness to forswear departmental loyalties and take a broader view. In practice, however, the tendency to how effectively he advances his department's interests, or protects it in hard times, is deeply ingrained in British political culture. Furthermore, ministers proved reluctant to join the Treasury in an attack on other ministers' programmes. . . . (Heald, 1981: 187)

Our own archive research on the Treasury Social Services Division throws some light on these contentions. The Committee was a closed one which took no public evidence and did not publish its reports. It consisted of civil servants and a few co-opted industrialists and worked through a main committee and eight sub-committees, only one of which examined a social service (the hospitals aspect of health). In Lowe's view, Plowden, overburdened with other commitments, 'deliberately gave the Treasury its head once he had assured himself that the committee was 'on the right lines' and the modernizers within the Treasury were in command' (1997a: 476). Was the outcome therefore a fully achieved statement of the Treasury view of expenditure control?

It is clear that Plowden offered a rare opportunity for the authoritative endorsement of Treasury positions, an opportunity that had to be seized. As Jim Macpherson, the Committee's secretary, minuted to Bruce Fraser in the context of discussions about consolidated non-specific local authority grants (in sub-committee 6), 'without something more positive from the Plowden Committee than that there should be a regular review the advantage of the Plowden Committee will be lost because there is not, I imagine, any greater likelihood that the Treasury will succeed in widening the scope of the general grant system now than they were able to do in the 1957 review'. Also part of the context was the existence of an oppositional view, personified by the Permanent Secretary of the Ministry of Housing and Local Government, a member of the committee:

we must not lose sight of what Dame Evelyn Sharp's attitude is likely to be. She may well take the line (as she has done in Sub-Committee 3) that the course of action I suggest is a long way from the task of the Plowden Committee as she sees it, i.e. iniquities of Treasury control' (there is a manuscript correction

of 'inequities' on the typescript; either is apposite). (18.12.59, in
T/227/1226)

The Treasury mandarins well understood those considerations. In
local government finance the final report of the sub-committee was
bland: 'the primacy of putting the whole responsibility on the spender
seems to us to be right, and we hope that any new grant to local
government will be brought within the general grant unless it is
impracticable to do so' (ibid.: report para. 6). In this important
area of potential disengagement, the Treasury continued to lose out
to the controlling instincts of major spending departments. In response, Robertson was sceptical about giving more delegated powers
and swallowing the Sharp line that the Treasury's heavy hand was
the problem. Treasury perceptions of the very variable calibre and
economic awareness of social spending departments were a further
cause for reluctance about any general relaxation.

At the level of macro-control, the PRO papers can throw some
light on the contention that Richard ('Otto') Clarke, Treasury Deputy
Secretary on public expenditure from early in 1960, imposed his
own views on the exercise. To analyse this proposition, we must
separate the general spirit of proactivity that Clarke undoubtedly
injected into Treasury thinking from his particular vision of the
content of policy. Clarke's own writings (1971, 1978) tend not to
reveal the evolution of his thinking at this stage, but Theakston
(1999) has fleshed out our knowledge of this remarkable and dis-
concerting personality.

On the former, Clarke seemed quickly to realize that the
Committee's initial discussions were going in radical directions
potentially unwelcome to the Treasury. In an important note of 29
January 1960 (in T/227/1224), he commented that at the Committee's
meeting on 25 January, 'opinion seemed to crystallize on the proposition that expenditure should be looked at as a whole, alongside
prospective revenue in the short term and in the long'. Clarke noted
that 'we can write our own ticket, I think, provided that it gives
effect to the essential principle – and provided that we produce a
plan quickly'. Seeing the importance of fleshing-out this approach
in a Treasury-friendly way, he drafted out a pattern of four linked
exercises: a Forecast Government Balance Sheet; a Five-year Resources
Review; Public Sector Investment Review, and '"Forward Looks" in
particular areas of public expenditure, e.g. i) defence, economic aid
ii) social services'.

This might be taken as proto-PESC, but in fact in paragraph 12 of his draft Clarke sets out what might be taken as the authentic Treasury position of 1960:

> It would not be practicable, in our view, to try to bring all expenditure decisions together to be taken in one allocation process. The size and complexity of the allocation process would be too great. Only very bad and rule-of-thumb decisions (e.g. cut everyone by 5 per cent) would be possible. It is natural and feasible for expenditure decisions to come in a steady stream throughout the year – provided there is the right background of opinion on which to judge them.

Jack Robertson, supporting Clarke's approach, elaborated Treasury concerns from his practical experience of Social Services divisions: 'by extending the set-up for presenting the problem as a whole to Ministers for sensible decisions, do we in fact advance the chances of such decisions, or do we provide Ministers (not their officials) with ammunition, with which they can attack or frustrate the Chancellor better than before?' (ibid.: to Clarke, 2.2.60: 1). Robertson was bruised by 'the 1960/61 Estimates, when I suppose all the unquantified Election half-pledges came home to roost in the messiest possible fashion' (ibid.: 3); '. . . I suppose that what we shall usually want in the short run is to present, on factual basis, a stuffy enough atmosphere or background to prevent all the spending ministers going to town simultaneously . . .' (ibid.: 2). He saw a likelihood of 'rigging the controlling assumptions too much on the side of prudence as e.g. to be out of line with the Government's election manifesto on things like the level of unemployment', leading to 'Ministers supporting their spending proposals at the more optimistic point of the range (ibid.: 2).

The thought had not been formulated with total precision, but it resonates down the decades – the Treasury nightmare of uncontrolled public expenditure promoted by spending ministers on the back of optimistic future economic projections. The educative aspects of forward planning were regarded with scepticism: 'how long will it take converted departmental officials to train their Ministers? Nothing can prevent issues like better pay for the Services or for the Police busting up the balance sheet' (ibid.: 3).

Therefore from the social policy perspective the outcome in Plowden was not necessarily what the Treasury wanted. Clarke had been right to suggest in his first memorandum that there might well be 'some snags', the malign process being that spending departments, and especially their ministers, would pick up manifesto commitments and positive economic forecasts and stoke up long-term growth. Plowden provided opportunities for a step-level improvement in the techniques of managing public expenditure, but it was not wholly a Treasury-friendly approach, and its encouragement of the forward commitment of spending was more to the liking of the spending departments. Clarke inserted in the exercise various anti-welfare noises, like a survey of 'waste', but this may be better seen as a going against rather than for a tide that even the Treasury recognized. With a Prime Minister in Harold Macmillan who had been a consistent critic of the Treasury the potential for turning the new control system into the institutionalization of expansion rather than contraction was present from the start (Lowe, 1997b: 610–11).

Social policy in the early PESC reports

We can now study the early PESC reports and trace how the recommendations of officials on the committee were handled by ministers. Of particular interest is the first report of all in 1961 (presented by the Treasury but 'fully worked over by a committee representing 24 departments') and the first of the Labour government in 1965.

What is evident is the association of social policy with the optimistic general economic forecasts about the availability of resources; and some evidence that the Treasury could use PESC to control incremental creep and use macro-economic evidence (especially in 1965) to rein in the more ambitious manifesto undertakings.

Sometimes the contemporary echo of these early reports is startling. The Chancellor noted that in the first PESC report 'increasing weight has been placed upon the role of public expenditure both as an obstacle and as an instrument for bringing about competitiveness, growth and solvency' (C(61) 88 28.6.61 in CAB 129/105, para. 3); and went on to write that

I would hope, therefore, that my colleagues would certainly authorise me to announce at once our intention of keeping the growth of public expenditure in step with that of GNP. But I must make it quite clear that I could not properly make a statement of this kind or indeed any other that was designed to give the impression that we were going to take effective action to moderate the growth of public expenditure unless my colleagues were prepared to agree that this should be associated with action on the scale and general direction of that proposed in the report. (ibid.: para. 15)

The 1961 report set the tone by being Treasury-driven ('the report can in no sense be regarded as being agreed between the Departments or as committing them in any respect, but it has been prepared with their full knowledge and co-operation' (ibid.: 2)); and by incorporating social policy in an economic analysis ('. . . the basic principle is that the more the resources of labour and capital go where they will yield the best return, the better for national solvency and growth. The 'plan' for development of the public sector should follow this principle. A primary aim should be to stimulate the most economic deployment of resources in the private sector. It is not to be expected that this aim can be directly applied in every field of public expenditure, but it should remain a guiding principle. Of course political and social considerations have to be taken into account, but if these are allowed to prevail over economic considerations in the widest sense, this is at the expense of the competitiveness of the economy' (ibid.: 16).

This approach did not in practice predominate in 1961, where the report sought to predict the effect of government policies rather than change them, but it was taking effect in 1965 when Douglas Houghton, as the social policy overlord in the Cabinet and chairman of a sub-committee set up to arbitrate between bids for additional expenditure, found himself stranded: 'the chairman dissented both from the premise on which the Committee's recommendation was reached (that graduated short-term benefits were an essential part of the programme) and from the recommendation itself. He considers that the income guarantee is an essential constituent of the programme both because of the unqualified pledges given and because it would concentrate the available resources where they are most needed' (C(65)108 p. 5 23.7.65 in CAB/129/122 Part I). Houghton had suggested that the promise of an income guarantee for 1966–7 would provide a basis for postponing the next general uprating, but his colleagues though that this course 'would in the event be likely to lead to both a general uprating and the income guarantee' and that even if the income guarantee (a manifesto pledge exempted from qualification about resources) was deferred to 1969–70

Monetary Fund, has been interpreted as a cathartic moment in expenditure planning. The IMF cuts were a second emergency instalment of a process that had started earlier in the year. Simon Jenkins sets it as the starting-point of his critical account of the Treasury's recent behaviour: 'to the Treasury the crisis had two consequences. The first was organizational: the urgent search for new tools to limit public spending. The second was psychological: a determination never to see the Chancellor suffer such humiliation again' (Jenkins, 1995: 222). For the Labour Party in government, the crisis marked the termination of attempts to regard the development of public services as a primary call on national economic resources; this applied particularly to housing. The haplessness of public spending ministers when faced by the apparently remorseless logic of international capitalism, and checked by the Treasury's monopoly of information, was striking.

Two consequences of the 1976 crisis were important for the subsequent development of the Treasury. The first was the assertion of the joint authority of Prime Minister and Chancellor in the working out of the crisis. Once James Callaghan was convinced that Denis Healey's perception of the crisis was correct and not just Treasury scaremongering, he stood by Healey in the Cabinet and did not allow detailed discussion of alternative strategies. Nor did he allow Anthony Crosland, the most articulate defender of public investment in the Cabinet, to destabilize the process by a series of well-leaked arguments challenging the economic basis for the cuts (Dell, 1996: 433). When put to the test, Crosland conceded the impossibility of successfully challenging Healey and Callaghan's united approach and did not press the issue.

This episode marked the decisive break with the approach of Macmillan, Wilson and Heath which sought to balance the influence of the Treasury and the spending departments and more often than not came down on the side of the latter in the interests of political credibility. From 1976 onwards, the image of the Prime Minister–Chancellor axis as a symbol of toughness and necessary hard choices came to dominate.

The second consequence was the opportunity that the crisis provided for the Treasury to introduce new techniques for controlling expenditure. Control in cash terms was partially reintroduced to aid the achievement of a target denominated in cash – the Public Sector Borrowing Requirement. The approach tapped into an inherent tendency to underspend ('shortfall') in many public services through managerial caution when times are tight and penalties for non-compliance are feared. The result was a fall in aggregate expenditure in real terms in 1976–7 and 1977–8, and some sense that the crisis had been a Treasury 'con', abusing deliberately pessimistic economic forecasts. This generated a further strand of anti-Treasury resentment, though a more analytical approach would see it as another failure of economic stabilization in which booms and busts were more extreme than they should have been.

The imposition of cash limits in 1976 marked the end of the classic PESC regime. Inflation was brought back in as a restraining variable for the roughly half of public expenditure deemed to be controllable – wage-related costs and capital expenditure. 'Demand-led' expenditure was not included – above all social security, but also expenditure based on entitlement or contractual independence, like general practitioner services. New distortions were introduced: central government expenditure and employment (including the health service) could be controlled directly, but local government services required exhortation or manipulation of grant; capital expenditure, especially housing, was hit savagely; and the system was biased towards caution and the over-achievement of targets.

The 1976 reform was not complete. Volume term plans were still issued, and the approach of planning expenditure changes as a matter of real terms changes adjusted for inflation was normal. It was not until 1982 that cash planning, the denomination of spending plans in cash terms, was introduced. In retrospect, the intellectual victory of 'money as cash' has been surprising. Its effect has been to reinforce caution upon programme managers and encourage hoarding of money. As contingency reinforcement of spending has remained necessary, the Treasury has gained extra authority, and more precise political manipulation of spending enhancements has proved possible. Heclo and Wildavsky's second edition backtracks from the first by suggesting that 'all of these problems – the pitfalls of planning, the dangers of unreality in annual re-costing, the enshrining of incrementalism and loss of revenue restraint – were pointed out in our first edition ... what we did not see clearly enough were the cumulative implications in a period of explosive inflation' (Heclo and Wildavsky, 1981: edn: p. xxvii). Their suggestion, reinforced by Thain and Wright, is that the atmosphere of continuing crisis enabled the Treasury to correct the deficiencies of control in its original PESC formula, and so win an even more complete victory.

The Treasury under the Tories again

After the Conservatives returned to office, the Treasury under Geoffrey Howe, Chancellor from 1979 to 1983, gained organizational weight from the absorption of most of the Civil Service Department in 1981, although some of these tasks were unwelcome accretions like civil service catering. But the title of Head of the Civil Service went to the Cabinet Secretary in 1981 and not back to the Treasury. Many of the managerial initiatives that marked the first stage of the Conservatives' reforms of government were launched from outside the Treasury, especially by Michael Heseltine at the Department of the Environment and the Prime Minister's Efficiency Unit under Derek Rayner.

During the early 1980s, there was an ambivalence between hands-on and hands-off approaches by the Treasury. At the beginning of their period in office, the Conservatives had proclaimed that public expenditure was at the heart of the nation's economic problems: achieving substantial reductions either in absolute levels of spending or (later) in public spending as a proportion of GDP accordingly became a prime objective of policy. The means by which this goal was to achieved were less clear-cut. The background was of rather generalized approaches such as the Medium-Term Financial Strategy (premised on tight control of money supply) and the Financial Management Initiative (premised on closer ministerial control of departmental activities) which sought to be self-regulating but promised more than they eventually delivered (Thain and Wright, 1995: chs 3 and 4). In the foreground was the most controversial budget of the past-war period, in 1981, in which Geoffrey Howe, fortified by what he subsequently called Margaret Thatcher's 'powerful, if sometimes erratic Treasury instinct' imposed on reluctant Cabinet colleagues a £4 billion increase in taxation in mid-recession (Howe, 1994: 207, 213).

The view from outside was of a Treasury eagerly complying with ministerial remit to practice what they had always preached regardless of the consequences. But a fascinating series of documentary programmes on BBC radio provides a rather more complex account of what was taking place internally. These were based on interviews carried out in the Treasury and with former ministers in 1982 and 1983. Among officials involved in the debates on public expenditure there were certainly those, notably the Second Permanent Secretary in charge of the control mechanism, Sir Anthony Rawlinson, who told the interviewers that the Treasury was merely concerned with the aggregate of public expenditure (Young and Sloman, 1984: 44) and those who argued that their role went beyond totals to a concern with the content of programmes.

There were the familiar arguments from the 1960s debate that control was essentially a form of principled opportunism. Rawlinson's (eventual) successor, Nicholas Monck, told the interviewers that:

> you don't actually have the power to get to a desirable total by a combination of expanding some things which clearly have a good economic case and knocking out this other rubbish: you have in practice to take a cut wherever you can get it. (ibid.: 56)

Some of Monck's colleagues went further and were prepared to accept that they held views about the cost as well as the content – and potential dispensability – of programmes, though not so far as to accept that the Treasury had policies of its own. As one interviewee put it, there is no 'Treasury housing policy' as such, rather there is a 'housing aspect of a general public expenditure policy' (ibid.: 44).

In an exquisitely tactful summary of the debate, the programme's organizers quoted an (anonymous) third party in the Treasury as concluding that

> within our present (Conservative) administration, the Chief Secretary and the Chancellor are much more concerned with keeping money down to tight levels and don't care very much on what it delivers. They say that's for the spending minister. I don't think that's quite the view of Treasury officials. They're brought up to take a longer view and say it isn't only what goes in but what comes out. (ibid.: 132)

The end of PESC

Finally, the formal apparatus of PESC unravelled: the committee itself ceased to meet, and disputes were resolved by bilateral discussions between the Chief Secretary to the Treasury, and if necessary by reference to the so-called 'Star Chamber', a committee of senior ministers avoiding the main spenders and initially chaired by William Whitelaw, which met six times between 1981 and 1987 (Thain and Wright, 1995: 277–9). Unsystematic bargaining during the autumn became the norm. The fourth year of survey projections was removed in 1982, and the White Paper was arranged by departments rather than programmes in 1986 and disappeared altogether in 1991 in favour of departmental annual reports.

The general impression was of a rather unsystematic and politically contingent approach: Thain and Wright suggested that 'the elasticity of the upper limit varied with both the political and electoral cycles. It is impossible to say authoritatively what the upper limit was in most years of the period 1976–92, and hence whether the final Planning Total came close to it, or fell comfortably below it' (ibid.: 237).

Thain and Wright's generally sceptical conclusion is that 'the survey is methodologically almost unrecognizable from that eulogized by Heclo and Wildavsky in the 1970s' but 'the process by which these decisions are made, legitimated and made public has changed much less' (ibid.: 288–9). Not surprisingly, they find a trend towards formalization and codification of many practices over the years. Their detailed research is a catalogue of failure against objectives, but as presented by the authors these objectives centre on conformity to spending control targets. In this perspective it is easy to be critical of the Treasury rather than recognize that the outcomes represent the balance of bureaucratic politics in which the Treasury was rightly thrown back into a weaker position than it would have liked. As it evolved, the public expenditure survey system became a conceptualization of the issues and choices rather than necessarily a solution to what the Treasury had regarded as the problem of insufficient control. As we trace in Chapter 3, it was only during and after the Lawson chancellorship (1983–9) that the Treasury began to obtain effective purchase on the making and implementation of social policy.

3
Treasury Politics in the Post-PESC Era

From 1983 the Treasury comes into sharper relief because of the personality of a Chancellor – Nigel Lawson – who was keenly interested in policy matters. However, he had no substantial base of support in the Conservative Party and so was not a likely candidate for the top job. But as a former financial journalist he had the perspective, the skills and the energy to write the most detailed and revealing memoirs of any post-war Chancellor. Lawson's tenure coincided with 'late Thatcherism', the period of bold reappraisal of many aspects of the welfare state, including pensions, the education system, the National Health Service and local government finance. Lawson's position on these changes was threefold: he was determined not to let the Treasury's grip on spending control or prerogatives within Whitehall slip; he doubted the intellectual capacity of other departments to carry through a rigorous review of what they were doing and felt that the Treasury could do it better; and he subscribed to a general view in the climate of that time that the welfare state was not serving the economy well and that it carried a significant share of responsibility for the country's longer-term economic and social weaknesses (C. Barnett, 1986).

This did not mean that Lawson himself was able to control the reviews of policy that took place during this period himself, much though he might have ideally wished to do so. Here, his relationship with the Prime Minister was crucial. He could suggest new courses of action at their 'post-prandial' gatherings; but it was Number 10 that was normally in charge of these operations, in consultation with the department responsible. In the notorious case of the poll tax, when his relationship with Margaret Thatcher was already deteriorating, Lawson took a position of detached disdain. But his interventions in social policy matters (pensions, education, health) reflected his view of ministers and officials in social spending departments as not understanding the economic system and in the grip of producer interests, a view that came to strongly influence the Treasury approach. In one particularly notorious case, his attitude to education reform was determined by his sense that this was a topic too important for the economy to be left to the educationalists.

The context of the political economy

In the early 1980s there was a much more explicit Treasury philosophy on 'political economy' matters and the Treasury itself was staffed at political level as 'the training college for future Cabinet ministers' (Ridley, 1991: 162). Most of the Treasury's attention during these years was on macro-economic policy, focusing especially on efficiency, targeting and incentives. Sometimes this conflicted with Conservative ideology of choice and privatization, which resulted in the slow pace of rationalizing access to school places and the high takeup of fiscal incentives for personal pensions (admitted by Lawson to have been 'quite unnecessarily costly' (Lawson, 1992: 594)).

The most explicit statement of the relationship between economic and social policy under the Conservatives came in the Green Paper 'The Next Ten Years' (HM Treasury, 1984). This is perhaps the grimmest statement of the scenario with which the Conservatives entered office, with its warning that 'as public spending takes a larger and larger share of GDP, so the public sector steadily encroaches on the rest of the economy' (ibid.: 20) and 'finance must determine expenditure, not expenditure finance' (ibid.: 21) – though in fact, given the lead times involved this is not quite compatible with the suggestion that the total of public expenditure must be determined first and then adhered to. The paper is deeply pessimistic in tone, asserting the impossibility of securing sustained economic recovery unless the demands for expenditure in social programmes are rigorously restrained. In his memoirs, Chancellor Lawson notes with satisfaction the 'absence of political own goals', in the form of identification of spending deficiencies (1992: 305).

Three years later, after the Conservatives' third election victory, the approach was entirely different. Yet Lawson sees nothing strange in the contrast in his tone between 1984 (when there was no hint of the glittering prospects of increased revenue to come), and the optimism of 1987, when he was able briefly to reduce the PSBR to zero and prompt some feverish speculation about the possibility of paying off the National Debt.

In fact, there was a surplus from 1987–8 to 1990–1, but in the first and last years only because of privatization receipts. Expenditure seemed to pursue a fairly stable trajectory of its own, leaving the overall balance to be determined by the fluctuations of tax receipts (again at largely stable tax rates) according to economic activity. After the bubble burst, with the end of the 'Lawson boom', the sharpness of the recession led in 1992 to a plunge into a deficit (£37 billion in 1992–3) of a size unimaginable three years earlier.

Nigel Lawson's social policy

We set out in an earlier contribution upon which we draw here (Deakin and Parry, 1993: 33) our interpretation of how Lawson became interested in social policy reform through a combination of hunches from his constituency knowledge, perceptions of the calibre of the Whitehall departments, and a framework of understanding about Britain's economic problems coupled with a degree of naivete about the implementation of social policy, apart from the crudest market-based assumptions. This is typical of the way that Treasury ministers engage with social problems, and is dominated by the sense that policy must be determined by the economic constraint, not from any social imperative. But unlike their officials, Treasury ministers have an awareness of wider political considerations from their collegial dealings in the government, and of personal issues through their constituency surgeries.

Like Richard Crossman's diaries, Lawson's memoirs have an egotistical swagger which is not necessarily a guarantee of their absolute truth. What comes through clearly is his defence of what he calls the 'official' Treasury as the custodian of good sense and clear thinking against complacent, lower-calibre spending departments which have usually been captured by interest groups. Coupled with this is a possibility of intervention based on the Chancellor's political weight. We have already quoted his assertion that 'the Chancellor, if he proceeds with care and caution, can affect the content and not merely the cost of other Ministers' policies' (1992: 273). However, as he recognizes, the implementation of these ideas remains subject to the ultimate sanction of their next-door neighbour in 10 Downing Street.

One sign of the Treasury's caution in this period is their attitude to the budgetary frameworks for the new executive agencies, which embodied some new freedoms (e.g. the right to use income to finance higher running costs). Lawson describes how after the Next Steps report of 1988 on the creation of these agencies 'a long battle ensued, resulting in a lengthy written concordat' (ibid.: 392); he also admits to an often-surmised hidden agenda of his own, saying that 'the main practical advantage I see is that by creating accounts, boards of directors and saleable assets, future privatization may prove less difficult' (ibid.: 393).

This 'slipway' notion of agencies as being simply a stage in a smoothly inevitable process of privatization has not proved to be a very accurate description of the purpose and character of most of them. The earliest ones (such as the Vehicle Inspectorate and HMSO) tended to be potentially self-financing; the more interesting questions arose when some income is at hand but a degree of permanent Treasury subvention is required. 'Pure' social policy agencies, like the Benefits Agency in DSS, raise different control problems which may only become evident over time should the efficiency objectives of the agency not be realizable within the resources made available to them. Leo Pliatzky, a former senior Treasury public expenditure official in the 1970s, is probably right when he says that 'I doubt whether the Treasury saw this as primarily a matter of Whitehall power politics or whether they had any hostility to the concept of agencies. They would, I think, have been greatly concerned with the problem of reconciling this concept with the Treasury's responsibilities for public service pay and manpower and public expenditure generally' (1989: 104). In the event, what started off as clear Treasury objections were overcome by the political impetus of the project and the adroit placing of Treasury official Peter Kemp in charge of its implementation. By the time of our research, there was little interest in direct constraint of the agencies, and the principles of delegation they embodied had been extended throughout the civil service.

On social policy, Lawson was able to combine his intermittent personal interest with the assertion of the old Treasury right to intervene when cost implications arise (the turf as well as substance being important); this includes reserving the right to keep coming back at an issue. Norman Fowler is eloquent on this as he recalls how the Treasury put round a minute trying to reopen the abolition of SERPS two days before the Cabinet was to approve the Green Paper (Fowler, 1991: 219) and then (though Fowler is more coy about detail) forced him into 'the worst decision that I had ever to take in government' (ibid.: 221) when the opposition of the employers and the pensions industry allied itself to the continuing objections of the Treasury to allow SERPS to be preserved after all.

This was a particularly interesting case because the Treasury promoted the less ideologically ambitious course of action (in Conservative terms), but for the 'wrong' cost-control reasons. As Nigel Lawson explains it, the Treasury had no objection to the abolition of SERPS as long as there would not be any compulsory private scheme (1992: 591). He (unusually) blames the incompetence of officials for not alerting him until the last minute to the cost implications of Norman Fowler's original proposals. For the Treasury, this seemed to be a slide-rule issue, and Lawson himself was happy with the freedom not to make provision for old age. The operational principles were a safeguarding of tax revenue and the avoidance of burdens on business, without any sense of a duty to promote social protection across the life-cycle.

The Treasury also reserved its sole proprietorship of 'budget' matters such as tax expenditures and national insurance contributions. This was a source of much frustration to Norman Fowler during the social security reviews, where he quotes Nigel Lawson as saying 'you have no authority to make proposals on National Insurance' (1991: 214), a stance later modified but always available to the Treasury if it wanted to be awkward; as Lawson puts it, 'holding fast to the hallowed doctrine that taxation is a matter for the Chancellor and must not be put into commission' (1992: 596).

Lawson took a particular interest in education reform as the nexus between social and economic policy. He had read Correlli Barnett's *The Audit of War* (1986) with its debatable thesis about the role of the education system as one of the causes of Britain's post-war economic weakness, and launched a Treasury paper on educational reform with 'not a word to DES' (Lawson, 1992: 607–8). Eventually (in his account, though not that of his Prime Minister) this leads directly to the Education Reform Act 1988. His election campaigning in 1987 convinces him that the electorate want social security benefits to favour the elderly rather than families (ibid.: 726), a thought he picked up from Richard Crossman (ibid.: 595), and he is happy to record the 'long-standing ambition of the official Treasury' to freeze child benefit (ibid.: 720).

Here, as elsewhere, Lawson uses the term 'official Treasury' to characterize an institutional view. As he puts it, the ethos of the official Treasury – and for all its qualities, I retain both respect and affection for the Department – is unremittingly austere. They disapprove of tax cuts as much as they dislike increases in expenditure. They cannot imagine what the public have done to deserve tax cuts, which will inevitably be put to frivolous use. (ibid.: 686)

In terms of policy as well as the management of government, this austerity produced a cautious attitude to many of the wilder schemes of late 1980s Thatcherism. Lawson's close colleague Jock Bruce-Gardyne, the author of a stimulating study of ministers and civil servants, noted that there is the 'philosophical bias of the villagers [civil servants] against the concept of the student loan' (Bruce-Gardyne, 1986: 122) and on raising mortgage relief thresholds 'the Treasury was ineradicably opposed. This was an issue on which mandarins and ministers stood shoulder to shoulder' (ibid.: 200). Even a Chancellor like Lawson with his strong personal imprint on politics was happy to line up in defence of the traditional Treasury role as the sceptical critics of social policy innovation.

Lawson resigned in 1989 because of conflict with the Prime Minister over the responsibility for managing economic policy and his stock has subsequently declined because of his perceived misjudgments. Unable to secure British entry into the European exchange rate mechanism, he presided over an economic boom which temporarily reduced the public sector share of GDP but rested on weak foundations. The current verdict on Lawson is of ultimate failure on the expenditure side, perhaps because he was more concerned with other issues, like the reform of taxation. Edmund Dell, who is sympathetic to some of Lawson's wider objectives, is none the less severe in his overall verdict:

Through self-deception and inadvertence, he allowed the development of a boom which his successors had to cool at great political cost. An exaggerated air of prosperity was induced, not just by an unsustainable boom but by a significant increase in the share of national product going to consumption . . . Lawson did not appear to understand that such transformation as was claimed in party propaganda was an unlikely outcome of the few years of economic management under Howe and himself. (Dell, 1996: 538–9)

Lawson's reputation in the Treasury is not especially high, despite his long tenure; his style was seen as having a certain air of capriciousness about it and – like Crossman – he has tended to be admired more from the outside than on the inside. Structural changes in the relations with spending departments had to await his departure.

The evolution of the EDX system

Almost without expecting to, the Treasury cracked many aspects of the control problem after 1992 and got the rest of Whitehall to focus on the Treasury's themes more effectively than it had under PESC. This was partly the result of orientating the whole public expenditure exercise around a single aggregate, in cash; and partly the result of the creation of a new structure for decision taking, the Cabinet committee known as EDX and the way in which it has functioned. In place of the ambitious variables of the PESC exercise, everything was now based on a single measure – an overall control total laid down from above, within which all departmental demands have to be fitted.

But there was an ambivalence about what needed to be included in this aggregate and what might be deemed not to need control. In 1990, local authority self-financed expenditure (from the community charge (poll tax), since non-domestic rates were at this point put under central government control) was excluded from the planning total in an ill-fated attempt to have total local accountability for poll tax levels. The next aggregate to be tried – the new control total – made more analytical sense. All local authority expenditure was reinstated but the unemployment-related cyclical element of social security expenditure was excluded (along with debt interest). This control total proved robust to the point of becoming a talisman for a Labour government committed to maintain Conservative plans.

This occurred because of the way in which the Cabinet's public expenditure committee (EDX under the Conservatives and PX under Labour) operated since its establishment in 1993. It differed from the Star Chamber of the 1980s by being chaired by the Chancellor and serviced by Treasury officials, from the General Expenditure Division. Ministers appeared before it (without their own officials) and the discussion focused on conformity to the control total rather than the merits of departmental bids. Scrutiny of departments was meant to become a regular part of the process in contrast to the 'court of appeal' nature of the Star Chamber. The membership of

EDX was wider than that of the Star Chamber, but still weighted towards senior non-spending ministers.

Our research threw some light on the operation of the EDX system (which Labour's approach from 1997 of comprehensive review and long-term plans largely superseded). Our departmental respondents felt that it had worked to the Treasury's advantage by effectively requiring the members of the Committee to provide a body of support within the Cabinet for the Treasury approach. Some ministers might still insist upon a ritual argument in Cabinet but the risks of Treasury defeats were moderated. The formal bilateral meetings with the Chief Secretary became less important in themselves, and the end-games with departments take different forms; 'quick deals' seemed to have occurred more frequently, sometimes representing unwise concessions by departments.

EDX also made it easier for the Treasury to demand information in the name of the Cabinet rather than on its own authority. Generally, the system demanded clear instructions and a strategy sustained throughout the whole spending round. Our respondents noted the problems that had arisen in 1995 when the government reshuffle and the appointment of Michael Heseltine as Deputy Prime Minister had resulted in a recasting of the EDX's 'line' during July.

Questions arise about the quality of argument at the Committee. The members were briefed by the Treasury to probe departmental bids, but they were not always up to the task. The accident of the past departmental careers of members may produce a sympathetic or ignorant appraisal of business. As one departmental respondent put it about the Major government:

> once ministers get talking anything can happen . . . although the Secretary of State is invited to attend EDX they will have discussions about his programme without him being there, he will not be there for the discussions, and so there are real risks. I think running costs is another area where political instincts could override judgment. Saving graces are the fact that Tony Newton is on EDX and he knows our business. We've had other Chief Secretaries who've known our business which is a saving grace, and particularly as it comes back maybe to the particular problems in our programme because the decision isn't that we receive 'x' money, the decision is that we will or won't proceed with cuts 'a', 'b' and 'c', therefore if they don't understand what these measures really mean, we can't substitute something else there, so it is a slightly high risk process.

EDX was part of the package that introduced the long-mooted 'unified budget' – the fusion of decisions on expenditure for the upcoming financial year (which need to be announced in the autumn) and on taxes (previously held back until the spring). The concept was introduced by Norman Lamont, the only direct promotee from Chief Secretary to Chancellor, but he lost his job before the first one, which was carried out by Kenneth Clarke in November 1993. The threat to the Treasury from the unified budget was that the taxation side would be brought into play for ministerial discussion and that trade-offs between spending cuts and tax increases would be laid open for inspection. In the event the primacy of the control total dominated during the remainder of the Conservative period in office, with the tax-cutting habits of most senior ministers (especially the biggest spender, Peter Lilley at social security) restraining them. Any fears about rip-roaring Cabinet debates about how ministers could spend a penny more on income tax proved fanciful.

The Fundamental Expenditure Reviews (FERs)

The Fundamental Economic Reviews (FERs) were launched by the then Chief Secretary, Michael Portillo in 1993 in order to re-examine the objectives of public expenditure in the medium term. The review had come about largely as a result of the loosening of expenditure control that had taken place in the period running up to the 1992 Election, which the Conservatives had not been expected to win. It was conducted with the full authority of the Prime Minister, John Major, himself a former Chief Secretary and briefly a Chancellor before his windfall from Margaret Thatcher's enforced departure. As an exercise, it had something in common with earlier attempts at a comprehensive survey of public expenditure, like that undertaken by the Conservatives under Harold Macmillan, in that it sought to find a basis to arrest what appeared to be a developing process of unsustainable growth in certain demand-led programmes.

But although the exercise was launched with much rhetoric about the fundamental character of the review, with no options being ruled out, it gradually subsided into a looser process, with its main impact on the spending departments being eclipsed by the senior management reviews launched in the mid-1990s with the aim of cutting down on senior staff numbers across Whitehall.

Perhaps ironically, the FER that had the most impact was the one conducted within the Treasury itself, which was linked with a rigorous assessment of senior staff functions and numbers. But this is of such significance for the theme of this book that we have given it the next chapter to itself.

Better engineering of the 'nuts and bolts'

Thain and Wright's comprehensive study sets out well the 'nuts-and-bolts' matters like end-year flexibility, in-year control, and modifications in cash limits and running costs control. They see a general trend for the Treasury to become more reasonable, not withdrawing but rebalancing effort, but they are sure that 'the Treasury is prepared to subordinate other policy objectives to the paramount aim of containing public expenditure in times of acute fiscal crisis' (Thain and Wright, 1995: 400). This was the experience of our research. The general loosening of control was a reward for good behaviour and a convenience for the Treasury. When aggregate expenditure was being managed within the stated margin, the Treasury could be helpful in facilitating the adjustments within the aggregate that circumstances are bound to require. Where it was not, a range of bargaining strategies was used to restore good behaviour in the Treasury's eyes in which the status of 'nuts-and-bolts' items as concessions rather than rights became evident. This was particularly evident in the 'bureau-shaping' area of the core budget, running costs control.

Running costs control

A central Treasury tradition is of restraint on what departments might do on the pay and gradings not just of their own officials but of the public bodies they funded. Fear of mismanagement and precedent-setting was rife. As we trace in Chapter 4, the launching of Next Steps agencies implied a devolution of these functions within an agreed budget and strategy, and the decision to abandon compulsory market-testing in the civil service required a substitute constraint. A first step was the abandonment of uniform central pay factors for the public service (Thain and Wright, 1995: 297), though this was reimposed in 1992 (ibid.: 400). From 1993 departments had rolling three-year budgets for their running costs. Negotiations on fixing these limits were tough, and usually caused more pain than the fixing of programme expenditure. But eventually the Treasury did accept that the detailed control could be

Market-testing

A further irritant in Treasury–department relations has been the introduction of a competitive environment for the provision of services. In the 1980s, when this approach was imposed upon local authorities and the health service, it was not a Treasury-led activity; but by the 1990s it came closer to home in the form of market-testing, as set out in the 1991 White Paper 'Competing for Quality' (HM Treasury, 1991). This called for 15 per cent of work to be put out to tender, with the in-house workforce able to compete. The principle was mandatory but the implementation was flexible, leaving departments free to decide which services to expose to competition. The chosen candidates were usually peripheral services like information technology or training, and there were varying degrees of enthusiasm and tactical skill in the way the process was handled by departments.

The policy has been researched extensively by Richards, Newman and Smith as part of the Whitehall Programme (1996). The Treasury's role is best seen as part of their ongoing sceptical battle with departments. The personal role of Francis Maude, then Economic Secretary to the Treasury, was important. One senior expenditure official at the time, noting that Maude 'really pushed that through' claimed Treasury authorship of the White Paper and noted that 'benchmarking is all important': tendering 'completely changes the motivation of people: before it 'everyone has a mission for saying that their costs are astronomic'. In this official's view, 'you need in government . . . a lot of people who are very good at letting, writing and managing contracts'. The decision to let departments off compulsion was interpreted as 'someone persuaded the Prime Minister that 'departments are getting too much coaching' and could reach their own decisions. In the event the recalcitrants in the departments won a victory: the targets for the amount of market-testing in the first year were not met (even when the 'year' was extended to 15 months). The Efficiency Unit evaluation of the policy in 1996 provided an equivocal verdict and suggested that the search for net savings had often been compromised by unimaginative packaging into small units of work whose market-testing was costly to process (Cabinet Office, 1996). In the Treasury's eyes, departments were still up to their old tricks, more concerned with the protection of their institutional position than with the saving of money.

The Private Finance Initiative

Financial mechanisms that hide or defer costs are a commonplace of private business. Assembling a package for a major investment that does not impose an insupportable burden in the short term is a main technique in allowing the private sector to move forward and grow. The Treasury's position in the public sector context is different, and somewhat ambivalent. They have always had a liking for 'clever wheezes' in the presentation of public expenditure (notably through the use of tax expenditures, capital receipts and the moving of some items off-budget) in order to produce a helpful headline total. But they have been suspicious of the use of private financing to get projects under way and conceal the long-term public cost. As the most creditworthy borrower, government itself has been seen as the most economical way of raising finance once it has taken the policy decision to do so, and also the most broad-shouldered bearer of risk. Paying a premium to private financiers in order to offload this risk has been seen as a bad bargain. The 'Ryrie rules' of the 1970s embodied these principles by setting restrictive limits on the circumstances in which private finance could be used.

In time, the Treasury position changed enough to allow the 'Private Finance Initiative' of 1992, and its Labour successor of 'public–private partnership', and to cast the Treasury as the chief promoter of the policy in the course of several relaunches. This may be attributed to four factors:

(i) most important, the clear ideological preference of Conservative ministers, especially Norman Lamont, making this an initiative which had to succeed;
(ii) the evidence that the preoccupation with the aggregate control total of public expenditure was creating a systematic bias against capital investment and damaging the public sector infrastructure – in contrast to the fast pace of private sector investment in the 1980s;
(iii) a more sanguine estimation of the bad record of government in planning and carrying through capital projects, often as reported by the National Audit Office, in which the presumed virtues of planning and economy too often became vices of poor advance thought and poor project control;
(iv) an optimistic reassessment of the practicalities of transferring risk to the private sector, protecting the public interest, and gener-

ally not being the victim of smart negotiating by profit-seeking private financiers.

Increasingly, the policy became of importance to social policy as it became the preferred way of financing first hospitals and then educational investment and maintenance. One Treasury official on the health side told us that 'we're great enthusiasts for the PFI . . . if you want to persuade yourself that this is not just creative accounting you only need go and see one or two of them' and insisted that 'we won't agree if schemes are just ways of borrowing more expensively'. Departments gave the impression of being dragged along reluctantly with the latest fashion. As one Principal Finance Officer put it to us:

> I think we've taken it progressively more seriously. We would say we had always taken it seriously, but as the resources are built, as the calibre of people put on the work has got better steadily, you couldn't argue that all our efforts in this area were generated by our own commitment to it, and I think there is doubt in the Treasury as to whether anybody is wholeheartedly in support of this policy, as they ought to be, and they conduct themselves on that basis with lots of communications that clearly are intended to capture balls, if not hearts and minds.

The Ryrie rules were abolished in 1989 and the PFI was launched in November 1992, but the operationalization of the policy proved very difficult. The decision in 1994 that private finance had to be explored first for public sector capital projects was actually unhelpful to the policy is it overloaded the market and obscured those few projects with real potential. Typically, private-sector consortia of banks and builders were formed, but problems arose about the specification of the projects and the precise legal status of the public bodies involved. Private bidders objected to incurring costs on projects with long shortlists or even withdrawn at a late stage from the programme. Where projects were social organisms like hospitals rather than physical artefacts like roads, there was a particular need for specification in advance of all aspects of the service, in the knowledge that later amendments might be very expensive (and a source of profit to the contractor).

Fitting in the desired specification to the cost limit was a problem in the later stages of negotiation. The private-sector teams had cautious (and fee-earning) legal advisers who were determined to chase down the precise risk of a public agency's ever defaulting. Uncertainty over NHS trusts required two pieces of legislation involving ultimate climbdowns by the government (one in 1995 to require the government to pick up liabilities of any NHS trust that might be dissolved, one in the end left to the Labour government in 1997 to remove any possibility that PFI deals might be *ultra vires* for trusts and so repudiable). There was also an arcane debate with accounting standards bodies about just how 'off-budget' PFI schemes could be in the government accounts, again resolved (in September 1998) by something of a government climbdown.

Within the Treasury, the main impression is of successive relaunches of the PFI support team (the Private Finance Panel, an independent body set up by the Treasury) as the implementation of the policy slowed but the rhetoric was talked up. In 1995, Michael Queen was transferred from the Treasury to the Department of Health, reportedly to give a boost to the hospitals initiative in which not a single contract had actually been signed. Treasury respondents were upbeat about the policy:

> If the Health Department ever had any doubts, and I'm not sure that many parts of it did from the outset, they've all disappeared. If you talk to [the NHS Executive finance chief], he's just as enthused about progress as we are, and putting a lot of effort into pushing it forward, and the interesting thing is that they can see the advantages.

In fact, the transformation of supposed deals into signed contracts was excruciatingly slow, as the parties haggled over who should bear the risk of construction problems, especially those caused by any future changes in building regulations. Despite periodic announcements from 1995 that various projects had agreed terms, the first actual contracts (for projects in Dartford and Carlisle) were not signed until after the 1997 election.

The conversion of the Treasury to the PFI was mirrored by that of the Labour Party. Under Labour, public–private partnership became the brand name (integrating the long-standing use of private money in housing), but the essence of the policy remained the same under Labour's businessman-fixer at the Treasury, Geoffrey Robinson, Paymaster-General until his enforced departure in late 1998. It became the main vehicle for hospital building and an increasingly preferred option for maintenance and management tasks. The preparedness of the Treasury to embrace a policy in such apparent tension with their traditional approach to expenditure control is a testament to their new enthusiasm for driving through bold initiatives which relieved current-year pressures on the control total.

Resource accounting and budgeting

The final initiative of the early 1990s was the decade-long plan to change the basis of public-sector accounting from the flow of income and expenditure during a financial year to the 'accruals' basis normal in the private sector. This basis is more transparent about the position of creditors and debtors across financial years, and, most importantly, by charging depreciation apportioned the cost of capital expenditure across the life of the asset rather than to the year in which it was incurred.

The initiative was planned from 1992–3, launched in a Green Paper in July 1994 and a White Paper in July 1995 (HM Treasury, 1995); the White Paper took the potentially undermining decision to have a cash 'Total Financing Requirement' for each department alongside the accruals 'Resource Control Total' rather than the single control figure previously suggested. The policy is associated primarily with a civil servant – Andrew Likierman, a former academic who became 'HOTGAS' (head of the Government Accountancy Service) in 1993 (Likierman, 1995 and 1998). In 1986, Likierman had written a textbook on *Public Expenditure* because he found nothing existing for his students to use, and these proposals also fill a vacuum of thinking about the measurement of the public sector in the economy. For it to be advanced at all required political support from the Conservative government, and also an endorsement from the House of Commons Public Accounts Committee (sometimes with reservations). But for all its businesslike overtones, this is not an ideological proposal, and it is best regarded a new conceptualization of public expenditure that fits in well with the other new approaches of the early 1990s. It proved compatible with the pro-investment orientation of the 1997 Labour government, since the rules, golden or otherwise, of the government's Economic and Fiscal Strategy embodied an unusually strong distinction between current and capital expenditure. The publication of the National Asset Register in 1997 was a further boost to the search for an accurate public sector balance sheet.

The two sides of the policy are *resource accounting* – a means of presentation which is unlikely to excite non-experts – and *resource budgeting* – an expression of budgets on the new concepts which will favour some departments at the expense of others. In broad terms, capital-intensive budgets will do better under the new system. Departments which have traditionally mixed capital and current expenditure in their budgeting (notably the Ministry of Defence) will have problems making it work. Social policy departments are less exposed, but have responded well to the challenge of implementing the system. As put by one Treasury proponent, 'we can't force it to happen in departments' but they have been told 'this is not an obnoxious Treasury initiative . . . you might find it jolly useful'. Planning has broadly remained on course for the first Resource Accounts to be prepared for 1999–2000 and the first Resource Budgeting year to be 2001–2 (as set out in the HM Treasury Guide of January 1998 and Resource Accounting Manual of May 1997).

As with the original PESC system, what matters is whether governments can be persuaded to think in resource terms rather than in terms of costs in and out. They will at least have the two totals – resource and financing – to resonate with each other, and there will be a schedule of the accounts (Schedule 5) giving a 'Statement of Resources by Departmental Aim and Objective' with, outside the accounts, an 'Output and Performance Analysis'. But as with a private business, the cash flow within a time-frame has a powerful influence on performance and can sometimes displace more rational indicators. It is easy to imagine that the same reductionist process that made cash displace volume in public expenditure planning after 1976 – and eventually undermine the entire conceptual structure of PESC – might start to operate again.

Conclusion

The new technical repertoire of the early 1990s gave the Treasury, sometimes by accident, a more secure basis for controlling the public sector. The 1992 pre-election spending spree was probably the last of the line of departmentally driven incremental relaxations for which a price had to be paid afterwards. This was achieved through the unified budget, which related expenditure to receipts more pointedly than the Medium Term Financial Strategy had ever done. The EDX system was an expression of Treasury dominance within the Cabinet system, which hitherto had set out to balance the spenders and the controllers. After 1993, with Lamont's replacement by Clarke there was again a comfortable Prime Minister–Chancellor relationship but one in which John Major's diminishing political authority left him in too weak a position to challenge the Treasury.

In their major study, Thain and Wright are critical of the Treasury's record between 1976 and 1993, seeing it as ineffectual in comparison with its objectives and lacking ingenuity in the means employed. While noting some progress in removing the causes of irritation in relationships, their picture was of a weak system whose malfunctions tend to help the Treasury. They conclude that 'Conservative Governments were unable to achieve either the heroic objectives set in 1980 or the less ambitious ones which replaced them in the mid-1980s' (ibid.: 439–40); that the Survey lacks effectiveness for ministers and is biased towards the Treasury in matters like systematic underspending (ch. 22); and that the pressures for control threatened a change from the historical paradigm of 'negotiated discretion' between the Treasury and departments to one of central prescription (ibid.: 543).

For social policy departments, the EDX system intensified longstanding concerns about the Treasury. They felt that the system had become even more biased against them, and that they would be punished on their running costs if they failed to meet spending targets through reasons not under their control. Allied to this was a suspicion that Lawson-type arrogance was still abroad in the Treasury. But in fact, the Treasury itself was starting to think about these issues and face up to the risks attached to these suspicions. In the next chapter we show how the fundamental review of both expenditure trends and organization in the Treasury became the vehicle for a reform which brought about drastic changes both the internal structure of that department and the basis on which it relates to the rest of Whitehall.

4
The Treasury Reinvents Itself

By the early 1990s the Treasury was doing well in the balance of control and influence over social spending. As we have traced, it had repulsed moves towards countervailing forces in the Cabinet; had won an intellectual influence over reforms in pensions, health and education; and forced departments to conform with the Treasury's aggregate thinking in the EDX committee. But, rather than consolidate its position, the Treasury thrust itself into its biggest organizational change since the 1960s, which it coupled with a thorough re-examination of its working style and culture.

The Treasury's *Fundamental Review of Running Costs* of October 1994, generally referred to as the 'FER' (Fundamental Expenditure Review) or the 'Heywood report', from its main author, the (then) Treasury grade 5 Jeremy Heywood (with Sir Colin Southgate, the chairman of EMI who steered the review, sometimes also lending his name to it), was a radical and controversial document. As in the case of so many other reforms under the Conservative government, doubters were swept aside and the report was implemented without major amendment. And although the strategy in the report attracted much scepticism at first, it has paved the way for generally more fruitful working relationships with the social spending departments. Understanding how and why this happened has been central to our research.

The theoretical background

Lying behind our approach are rival explanations of the reasons that organizations feel compelled to reappraise themselves, and their motives when they do. In the 1970s, political and economic explanations of this process tended to change. Once a naive interpretation of the purity of organizational motivations had been abandoned – as in the end it was bound to be – theories of rational choice and budget maximization came to dominate, popularized by William Niskanen and Anthony Downs. These explanations, based on the notion that bureaucrats will inevitably seek first to maximize their own self-interest, were themselves then undermined by manifest evidence that bureaucrats satisficed rather than maximized, and at least connived in the taxing and spending cuts which took hold in the 1970s. In the 1980s, the most influential explanation was Patrick Dunleavy's bureau-shaping. This had two important insights: that budgets had several components, with oversight of a large but decentralized budget of little attraction in itself; and that bureaucrats would calculatedly 'shape' their task to obtain the optimal mixture of rewarding and achievable work. It introduced an implicit theme of bureaucratic unselfishness, or at least of a more subtle kind of selfishness – that size and aggrandisement were not ends in themselves (Dunleavy, 1991).

The Treasury is a good subject for an analysis based on bureau-shaping. It has the ability to shape the structure of the government machine. Its intellectual style is of a subtle but rational kind. It exudes a personal austerity which sets no store on symbols or trappings. It routinely handles very large sums of money but through indirect channels. It has a keen appetite for power and real rather than apparent influence, often exercised indirectly. It would be likely to embrace managerial change that would refine its tasks and focus its energies; but why would it embrace a path which, like the FER's, seem self-abnegatory, with severe staff cuts? As we will see, the FER has a major bureau-shaping element – the focus on effective rather than symbolic control. But it also has a slightly perverse element – a lack of confidence in previous ways of working, a wish to please the people and organizations with whom it deals, a desire to adopt management styles developed in very different organizations. As we saw in Chapter 3, several cross-government initiatives like market-testing and next steps agencies were not initially congenial to the Treasury but eventually facilitated a greater spirit of delegation to, and confidence in, the Treasury's clients. For personal and organizational reasons, this motif of trust and stability became the Treasury's main strategy in the 1990s.

Contingent Treasury events: the role of Terry Burns

The personality of the Permanent Secretary was a key factor in the developing situation. The importance of the appointment of Terry Burns in May 1991 is a factor which we have sought to assess. Burns, who retired in 1998, represents a further progression – partly foreshadowed by Peter Middleton, with whom he worked closely – away from the 'Treasury toff' towards someone with different expertise and a 'modern' personality. The son of a Durham miner, he had an academic background at London Business School and continued while in office to give speeches to academic audiences. He was accessible and friendly to observers of the Treasury, retaining the winning smile displayed in the masthead of the *Sunday Times* economic forecasts he did with Jim Ball when at the LBS in the 1970s. His love of football and golf is well-known. Geoffrey Howe, the Chancellor at the time of Burns's appointment as Chief Economic Adviser at the age of only 36, has described in his memoirs why it was opportune to promote – in effect overpromote – a young academic, with a flexible but not ideologically rigid monetarist perspective (Howe, 1994: 156). By the time he became Permanent Secretary at the age of 48 Burns had been assimilated into the career civil service, but his route to the top post had been an unusual one and associated with the long tenure of the Conservative government.

Burns has greatly benefited researchers by putting on record his thoughts about his job and the way in which he approached it. He did this initially in a chapter in a Festschrift for Jim Ball (Holly, 1994) and then in the speeches he posted on the Treasury's internet site – Durham (April 1994), Manchester (March 1995), South Bank University (December 1995) and Civil Service College (September 1997). These can be read alongside the evidence that Burns, Paul Grey and Jeremy Heywood gave to the House of Commons Treasury and Civil Service Committee on 16 May 1995. From these we can trace his interest in modern management and concern with organizational success and reputation.

Burns' approach emphasizes the weakness rather than the strength of the Treasury. This is a theme which (we found) has had much influence even among the most ambitious Treasury officials. As he wrote in the first, rather tentative article in 1994, 'the Treasury's relationships reflect its position at the centre of government but with few executive responsibilities. Since it does not have the power, it must rely on influence' (Burns, 1994: 48). Burns argues that 'in the end the Chancellor decides – just like it says in the textbooks. In practice much of the debate on policy is the battle for the Chancellor's mind' (ibid.: 56). He speaks of the 'fascinating dialogue' between the Treasury and the spenders and says that 'the image of the Treasury a the taxpayers' agent is useful one' (ibid.: 54).

What were Burns's concerns about social policy? His appointment reinforced the pattern that Treasury permanent secretaries are not drawn from officials familiar with the details of public spending (in contrast to the frequent progression to the top job in other departments). Burns's background is strongly macroeconomic and his only previous civil service job was the specialized one of Chief Economic Adviser. His speeches reveal an interest in business and in market-based allocation mechanisms. In so far as Burns' personal input is concerned we might expect an interest in systems but not in detail. As Permanent Secretary he became immersed in organizational and personnel matters, but his critical approach did not extend to the public policy aspects of the Treasury's role. He took for granted the Treasury's mastery over expenditure control and was more interested in the integration of the Treasury's systems with those of the spending departments.

He cites as an influence on his approach process management:

the principles of modern quality driven process management puts the emphasis on good design, including testing of all stages in the process as well as the final product itself. The intention is that failure rates should be very low with the emphasis on getting it right first time. This contrasts with 'old style' process management where products were launched with insufficient attention to design, reliability and robustness and little testing. Instead testing was done on the road in response to failure rates and warranty work. (1994b: 14)

This analogy is drawn from the specific circumstances of the automobile industry (and elsewhere Burns mentions the influence of the boss of Unipart) but it cannot be transposed into a distinction in public policy between 'initial design and testing' and 'rectifying faults or trying to figure out whether individual cases do or do not fit into the policy' (ibid.). In the civil service, it is an unusual stroke of luck to encounter a policy that can be 'got right' first time and then left to run automatically. Apart from anything else, the inconsistency of much political support for policies makes such a mechanical model unrealistic.

Burns's other theme (developed in his Manchester lecture) is 'the dramatic fall in the cost of acquiring, processing, manipulating and disseminating information' (1995a: 3), leading him to conclude that

> to exercise effective control in today's fast-moving information-intensive world one should not seek to hoard power and information at the centre or at the top of a carefully structured hierarchy. Instead one should make clear what the bottom line objectives are and then delegate more responsibility for the detailed day to day decisions down the line. This applies in the case of senior Treasury managers giving more responsibility to younger staff who are closer to the action. And it applies to the Treasury . . . giving more freedom to individual departments to manage themselves each tear within tight budgetary limits. (1995a: 20)

The gap in this thesis is between the general mass information-handling point and the use of information within government. In the latter sense, information is far less subject to technological change. Most of the information in which the Treasury is interested is valuable because of its political deployment, its relation to other pieces of information, the completeness of its release, the presentational form in which it is made available, and considerations of timing. A main problem is the centre's lack of power and information, not their hoarding (which is the opposite variable from fast-moving). The real issue here is the taking out of back-up circuits (personnel and procedures) that provide a qualitative resource in the case of complex cases which cannot be resolved by the application of 'bottom-line objectives'. The growing sophistication of political communication, the weakening of ideological commitments by the main political parties, and the ever-clearer interdependence of areas of public policy are all good reasons for maintaining this capability. Burns's vision of a cybernetic Treasury navigating a sea of accessible information on automatic pilot is a long way from the nature of the actual business that it has to transact.

Another business-derived theme is that of relationships management: as Burns put it in 1995, this is

> the move we are seeing in other successful organisations throughout the world away from the old adversarial, 'cat and mouse' approach in which mutual distrust is the guiding principle, towards a more open, co-operative and consistent approach which

accepts that both parties to a negotiation can benefit if they share information, discuss objectives and respect each others' differences. (1995a: 20)

This may be achievable in some purchasing relationships but the simple and stable basis it requires is not often available in government. Ironically in the light of the delegation theme, in business relationships management often takes the form of amassing information on consumers in order to manipulate their preferences and elicit new demands. In government, it is about psychologically more mature relationships (a theme we return to in Chapter 5). The Treasury faces no problem about 'customer retention' or of being 'defeated each year in the annual re-negotiation of contracts and prices', the disciplines Burns notes as the important ones in commercial relationships (1995a: 6–7). Instead, it has a captive market in which it needs to produce outcomes by some combination of warm and cool behavioural traits.

A final related matter is the lasting effects of 'Black Wednesday', the UK's enforced withdrawal from the exchange rate mechanism in September 1992, on the Treasury's confidence and its standing elsewhere in Whitehall. This event had been preceded by a period of increasingly frenetic financial diplomacy with tensions often intensified by the personality of the Chancellor, Norman Lamont. The actual withdrawal was a traumatic event, as several of the Ministers involved have testified. But it did leave the Chancellor 'singing in the bath' and the exchange rate floating away from government responsibility. Public expenditure, once freed from the profligacy that had been part of the price for winning the 1992 election and the expenditure demands of the recession, passed under effective top-down control under the EDX system described in Chapter 3: as one senior official told us, 'with EDX we've made much more progress than we ever had before in getting a collective view on priorities'. The technical tool for restraining expenditure that the Treasury had been seeking since 1976 fell into place almost by accident and there was spare capacity to attend to the more qualitative aspect of the relation of the Treasury to spending departments. But this might not have happened had the Treasury not had the inclination and the necessity to put itself under some sort of review at this time.

The approach to the Heywood review

Before the FER came the Treasury's own 'change programme'. Burns
told MPs in May 1995 that 'we have been engaged for some time
at looking at the organisation of the Treasury and the way that we
do things. We started the process really in the Spring of 1992 and
we had a number of exercises going on' (House of Commons Treasury
and Civil Service Committee, 1995: Q5). He seems in 1991, his
first year as Permanent Secretary, to have been developing an approach that would reconcile traditional Treasury priorities and a
hands-off approach by positioning the Treasury as the 'taxpayer's
agent' when it comes to the pursuit of value for money. But this
could also be said to be true of the centres of departments, Agencies or indeed any business unit in the public sector though many
would concede that the ultimate guardian of the taxpayer's interest had to be the Treasury. In January 1992 Howard Davies (then
Director-General of the CBI) was brought in as a facilitator and did
a survey of outside clients. In spring 1992 Burns took his senior
managers to Chevening for a day, but in the event the pressure of
business through 1992 and into 1993 put a brake on the process.
The impetus then resumed, with the engagement of 'change consultant' Wendy Pritchard, who had previously done well-received
work in the Department of Social Security, and the decision to
commission a morale survey. Burns's 'something had to be done'
spirit fused with the knowledge that the Treasury would have to
undertake a Fundamental Expenditure Review to put in place the
approach to change.

The results of the (unpublished, but widely circulated) morale
survey, undertaken in February–March 1994 by International Survey Research, were sobering. Only 23 per cent claimed to have a
clear understanding of the Treasury's programme of change and
only 13 per cent though it sufficiently clear and focused. There
was an extraordinary divergence in perception of the immediate
work team and of the Treasury as a whole. Seventy-two per cent
thought their own branch was well-managed but only 16 per cent
the Treasury as a whole; 41 per cent reported high morale in their
branch against 7 per cent in the Treasury as a whole (pp. 6–9). Top
management scored particularly poorly on visibility, promptness of
decisions and communication with staff. Only 26 per cent thought
that the Treasury would act on the major issues identified in the
survey (p. 41). The results showed a classic 'love the job, hate the

organisation' profile. In April 1994 Burns interpreted this as exter-
nally-induced: 'not entirely surprisingly our recent attitude survey
of staff shows some bruising from the adverse criticism the Treasury has received combined with the amount and extent of the reform
of the civil service' (1994a: 9). It would be more plausible to see it
as a negative evaluation of the particular top management the Treasury had at the time.

The motif of 'fundamental review' entered the scene in the 1993
spring Budget (the last pre-unified budget), which provided for the
fundamental review of the driving forces of government expenditure, to which we have referred in Chapter 3. The Portillo reviews,
as they became known from the Chief Secretary of the time, did
not supersede nor interlock with the normal public expenditure
round. They provided information and a focus for looking at issues
in a different way, but they did not overtake the incremental basis
of expenditure determination and the slow search for savings. Reviews were phased by department and the Treasury itself was placed
in the second (1994) cohort.

As we suggested in Chapter 3, in some ways more significant
were the Senior Management reviews taking place in Whitehall at
the same time. These were of more direct salience to the civil service because they affected the 'core budget' (salary and running costs)
and also promotion prospects, a main currency in a grade- and
age-sensitive organization. Through the 1980s attempts had been
made to take out senior positions but the notion of a hierarchy
prorating upward had been preserved. The SMRs sought deeper savings
in running costs and the shifting of responsibility to lower levels.
This related to market-testing and the decision in 1993 to move to
a rolling system of three-year budgets.

As the Treasury has no significant programme expenditure, it did
not fit into the concept of the Portillo reviews – which were an
additional burden on its running costs. Why, then, did the Treasury not behave rationally and seek an exemption from the full
review? In April 1994 Burns was coy: 'this year, in common with
some other departments, we are carrying out a fundamental expenditure review of both the Treasury's programme expenditure and
its running costs. Here we have a conjunction of motives. The Treasury
has an ingrained wish to set an example and gain leverage by doing thing better itself. The change programme was underway and
this was a good opportunity to take it forward.' In 1995 he said
that 'when the Fundamental Expenditure Review programme was

appeals is possible. As we have seen, the Treasury is notably non-hierarchical in its approach (surely the best way to deal with ministers) and comes closer than its spending department partners to operating in a flexible, project-based manner. As Burns has recognized, it is at its best when conducting a team effort requiring imagination and urgency (Burns, 1994a: 10). The FER's philosophy was designed to provide a structure in which the credit and responsibility in such exercises should be given to those doing them rather than the seniors who sign them off.

The main themes of the FER as they eventually emerged were:

(i) the team leader as the centre of gravity;
(ii) the potential redundancy of senior levels by taking them out of the line;
(iii) the written codification of priorities and procedures;
(iv) the primacy of objectives rather than pre-existing organization.

These were implicit in the conduct of the review. Team leaders were at Heywood's own level (Grade 5) and corresponded to the generation being given responsibility in successful private organizations. Senior officials were faced with a corresponding reduction in responsibility which in turn would allow visible staff cuts at the top of the office. Improved working relationships could not be secured by exhortation but required specific mechanisms whose implementation could be checklisted. Above all, the FER was allowed to design an organization chart that fitted in with the Treasury's objectives.

But before we examine some of these proposals in detail there was a bottom line to the review, expressed cogently to us by one official:

There was a *huge* amount of opposition to it ... I remember one member of the Management Board saying he felt physically sick when reading the first draft of it ... it wasn't the organizational structure that worried him, it was the implicit reduction in jobs, and that was the bit that really sort of hit people in the face ... if the management changes being made on the public expenditure side had gone through, and the same number of jobs came out at the bottom ... I think it wouldn't have caused a fuss ... for someone to be coming along saying 'Well, actually, 25 per cent of the jobs can go' was actually a real shock to people.

Even though it seems likely that the review started with no predetermined cuts level, the proposed staff numbers proceeded inexorably from the concept put to directors 'well, if you've got these team leaders and you've got yourself, do you need any help in managing these people?'; even though there were no compulsory redundancies (indeed three offers to take voluntary redundancy were refused (Treasury and Civil Service Committee, 1995: Q68)), and even though a few jobs were put back after consultation – it was the '25 per cent off' motif of the review that grabbed attention. It set the tone for other Senior Management Reviews (on which the Treasury were represented), diminishing not just the position of those in the decimated grades but also the prospects of those lower down (unless the civil service abandons grades altogether). However much working styles may or may not change, the space above the grade 5 will remain as a monument to, according to taste, Treasury austerity or Treasury arrogance about the capability of their middle-ranking staff. A senior Treasury official described it as a 'deeply painful process', especially taking away from staff the ability to 'move at the time of their own choosing'; but it was necessary because 'we had failed to do the continuous adjustment that organizations should do ... we had too much to do in one go'.

The main features of the new structure

1 Delayering and more power to team leaders

The FER built on work done by the Management Levels Project Team (MLPT – one of three teams set up to provide detailed information on organizational issues) to conceptualize the tasks of staff at Senior Civil Service grades in the Treasury into three levels: *strategic management* (determining overall strategy and resource allocation); *sector management* (setting up and monitoring teams to take forward a coherent block of work); and *team leader* (delivering identified objectives by managing a team within a budget) (ibid.: 6.2). Moving even further away from civil service 'gradism', the team suggested that the sector management role might be carried out by a board rather than an individual; that management levels should not be confused with civil service grades; that individuals might participate in several teams and be prepared to be led by someone of a lower grade; and that there should be many fewer sub-hierarchies within teams (ibid.: 6.3).

The new approach had the effect of substituting 'changeism' for 'gradism'. The advantages of the FER's proposed structure, which carried through the MLPT principles, were seen as including that 'to the extent that this model does *not* in general reflect current reality, it will force senior managers to push more responsibility down the line, closer to where the day to day expertise is, thus reducing the overlaps and second-guessing that slow Treasury business down'; and 'it marks a symbolic break with the past, and one which should help to reinforce a key message of the FER – that the Treasury of the future must be more managerial, less gradist, less hierarchical and more flexible' (ibid.: 6.30).

There was a line of thought in the Treasury deeply sceptical about the pathologies of redundant grades: in the words of a senior respondent, 'nothing is more frustrating than finding all your work is being second-guessed by someone who is not the final person in the chain of command ... by having more people in the line you can actually produce less' – 'do they want their English correcting?'

The key decision was that the 'assistant director' role below the 'sector managers' (to be known as directors and usually grade 2s) would not equate to the old grade 3 (ibid.: 6.20). Instead they were to have a flexible role as an occasional 'substitute' for Director, as a team leader (on a project) or as a team member (ibid.: 6.18). The numbers of Deputy Directors 'reflects the 'bids' we have received from the directors concerned', as the Review says (ibid.: 6.20) (as put to us by one of the latter, 'I'd be saying four or five and he'd [Heywood] be wanting two or three').

Everyone recognized that the role of Deputy Director was a difficult one. The Director quoted above recognized that 'one looking after three (was) seen as ludicrous by private sector standards', but 'it's all cerebral stuff ... negotiating and fighting – that's what it's all about. An official closely in line with the thinking of the FER put the position of young Grade 5s more trenchantly:

> you started off as being one of the best in your year group in the country. You've then got ten to fifteen years' experience, so (if) we really are saying that such people in the Treasury can't be trusted to only have one layer of management between them and ministers in the UK civil service, then I think there's something seriously wrong with our recruitment or training systems, because these people, people in their thirties, forties, in private industry have *huge* responsibilities.

With the ratio of more senior staff to team leaders remaining at something like one to three, there were to be many people available to perform the function of coaching and advising the team leaders, but this required a new kind of almost inverted relationship, difficult to combine with the role of a senior as writing an annual report. In the spending field, the additional complication arose that the other departments could not be required to configure their senior posts in the same way as the Treasury. Since their Principal Finance Officers were Grade 3 or even Grade 2, they would not necessarily authorize their own Grade 5s to settle direct with the Treasury team leader. So what we had was the prospect that Treasury Grade 5s would 'trade up' in Whitehall dealings even more explicitly than before, or that Treasury Grade 3s would seek through dealings with other departments the status now lost to them in the Treasury. We will see in Chapter 5 how this worked out.

2 The separation of spending and budget functions

The Heywood report addressed the ability of the spending divisions to deliver the government's objectives. It noted that

> although the first unified Budget delivered last November [1993] was in many ways an organisational success, it was not fundamentally a *unified* Budget. By and large, the 'tax' and 'public expenditure' sides of the Treasury carried on pretty much as if nothing had changed; and the final Red Book was largely just a conflation of the old FSBR and Autumn Statement documents. In our view, if we are to get all the benefits of having a unified Budget, we need to bring the tax and public expenditure sides of the Treasury much closer together. Our proposals should help to achieve that. (ibid.: 9.11)

Elsewhere, it noted the 'strong and differing views that exist in the department about how the Treasury's public expenditure work should be organized in future' (ibid.: 10.2), including some who 'pressed very hard' that expenditure divisions should be dispersed according to the objective of the sending (ibid.: 10.25). How then did the Heywood proposals and the new structure as implemented alter the Treasury's way of dealing with these matters?

Heywood's proposals are set in the context of a rather critical appraisal of the expenditure divisions – short-term, reactive, and reluctant to let go of casework and second-guessing (ibid.: 10.18).

Hence he loads the major strategic work on to the proposed new Public Finances Directorate, who were to take responsibility for managing a Survey and formulating a Budget to carry through the Treasury's objectives (ibid.: 9.5). They were to take over the rather ill-defined 'general' or 'central' work on public expenditure from the public expenditure Second Permanent Secretary (9.12) who was, however, to chair the Survey Management Committee (10.34). The new Spending Directorate kept its independence (10.30) and took over most, but not all, of the spending divisions (10.36 (the exclusions served to maintain the independence of 'ginger groups' like the FMI unit)) but as presented by Heywood takes on a rather 'poor relation' quality, potentially deficient in strategic perspective. Colin Southgate's single most critical comment on the present Treasury is that 'much of the department's policy analysis and public expenditure work is excellent. But not all divisions have been able consistently to sustain the same high standards' (ibid.: 20).

In line with the Heywood approach, the recommendations in the spending field are influenced by the thought that organization should mirror priorities – that divisions between functions are bound to institutionalize tensions, and that the important thing is to ensure that they are constructive rather than debilitating ones. In Heywood's (implicit) view, the constructive tension would be between a supply-side led promotion of public policies that would benefit the economy, and the delivery of a structure of public finances compatible with macroeconomic management. The debilitating tension would be between a PSBR monitor struggling to fit spending aggregates into a budget framework, and a spending division competing for some of the same responsibilities by pursuing unconstructive battles with the spending agencies.

The implementation of this proposal was recognized to be the most difficult of all. The official argument, in the words of one respondent, was a behavioural one that 'unless you force Treasury divisions to actually deliver some economic analysis rather than spending cuts, you'll never change the culture'. The decisive argument in practice was that a joint Budget and Spending Directorate would become a 'department within a department', setting up an imbalance in the Treasury and possibly being ripe for a demerger into an Office of Management and the Budget. It appears that Chancellor Kenneth Clarke, here drawing on his spending department experience, was attracted by the idea of breathing more air into the Survey process by some institutional separation. The opposing view centred on the separation of the General Expenditure Division, the engine of the Survey, from the functional teams; the same official recognized that 'there were some people who felt that if the spending divisions were separated out from GEP they would lose their inborn Treasury instinct, and it would be impossible to deliver the aggregate totals'. Another official, now retired, was blunter about the idea that 'the Budget Directorate would be saying no and the Spending Directorate are the people who would be admiring the programme' – 'I thought it was mad'. But how would this 'admiring' role take shape?

3 The proactive role of spending divisions

The idea of the proactive spending division emerges in Heywood out of its interest in the notion of a Treasury mission to strengthen the economy by a broadly supply-side, long-term approach. This implies the positive use of public expenditure, rather different from the welfare state promotion of the 1960s and 1970s, but still with an upward pressure' as in objective 5 (despite its defensive mention of affordability): 'promoting policies and public expenditure priorities which improve the use of resources and the efficiency of markets throughout the economy, within an affordable level of public expenditure' (ibid.: table 1). This prompts the suggestion (again hedged) 'that, without losing sight of their crucial public expenditure control responsibilities, the Treasury's expenditure divisions should be more prepared to think pro-actively about how their departments' spending or policies might be adapted or developed to strengthen the economy, the efficiency of markets, the competitiveness of industry and the outlook for jobs' (ibid.: p. 14). This in turn implies 'a significant *increase* in the Treasury's resources devoted to education policy and spending, reflecting the major impact we believe the country's stock of 'human capital' has on the long-term supply performance of the economy' (ibid.: 10.14). It is not stated, but such a 'human capital' approach might support other areas of social policy spending as well; Southgate mentions that the Treasury should pick up 'the potential interactions between spending on social security, employment and education' (ibid.: p. 20). The final step in the argument is that 'the Treasury should be more prepared on occasion to advocate or support policies which deliver useful savings, improved value for money or a stronger economic performance over the longer-term even if they might increase public expenditure in the year immediately ahead' (ibid.: 10.18). Such an internalized formalization of public spending debates would be something new for the Treasury and much harder to secure than the straightforward organization changes that have already taken place. Treasury reaction to this proposal was to see it as unnatural and hence not worth elevating to a operational principle.

4   The production of strategy papers

One new instrument for proactive thinking on expenditure is the idea of a 'strategy paper' setting out for each Treasury team how the Treasury's objectives (or is it the Government's? Both are used on successive pages) are best to be achieved during the Survey round. The papers are intended to take a wide view of the trade-offs and options available, including private finance and tax expenditures, and 'the scope for changing the allocation of departments' budgets or increasing departments' budgets in favour of programmes more likely to improve the supply performance of the economy' (ibid.: table 10.3).

Such papers may help to counter short-termism and resolve cross-directorate conflicts within the Treasury (ibid.: 10.45 (e)) but they do appear to confine to the Treasury debates which would have been exposed in the whole PESC system when it was operating in its original multilateral way. Rather than the Treasury's reacting to the spending department's service-led priorities, departments would be expected to play their part in Treasury-defined national economic objectives.

As for the contents of the papers, and the Treasury agenda they would represent, Heywood is reticent and the ones actually written since 1995 have not been published. We may speculate that they have related to aspects of the old Treasury agenda – work incentives, discouragement of dependency, encouragement of industrially relevant skills, maximum use of charging or private funding, promotion of labour mobility. Strategy papers were an opportunity to reinforce the repeated scrutiny of programmes that were purely 'soft' social spending and did not appear to meet any of the approved objectives. We are (nearly) all supply-siders now, and all the talk about strengthening the economy might be a cloak for whatever prejudices and hobby-horses Treasury officials and ministers chose to ride at a particular time.

5   The role of contracts

Central to the FER's argument on spending was that the Treasury had to learn to behave differently in relation to spending departments. As we will trace in Chapter 5, these relationships are subtle and complex and depend ultimately on the psychological skill of the parties involved. The FER's approach was a search for tools, and it recommended all the teams 'to agree a "contract" with the department(s) with which they deal, setting out he rights, duties and obligations of each party in the relationship' (ibid.: 10.55). The content of these contracts seems straightforward – the information the Treasury needs, the issues on which expects to be consulted or which it is content to delegate – but the item on 'the deadlines by which each party agrees to reply to the others' requests' is the giveaway; this is an attempt to systematize behavioural patterns which in fact proceed from the dynamic of each situation. There is naiveté in the suggestion that 'the "negotiation" of such an agreement . . . should help to enhance each party's understanding of the other's responsibilities and requirements thus helping to improve their working relationship more generally' (ibid.: 10.56), reinforcing the feeling that the FER team did not have first-hand acquaintance with a spending division. The contracts idea has proceeded slowly and came in for much criticism, as we report in Chapter 5.

6 The directing role and cross-cutting issues

The FER led to the definition of cross-cutting issues on the Spending Directorate organization chart. These issues are not listed in the FER but emerged during the setting-up of the directorate (during which its name was simplified from the 'Expenditure Policy and Analysis' mentioned in the FER) and reflect the personalities and expertise of its senior management. The Director, Robert Culpin, remains a Second Permanent Secretary (and as such attends Permanent Secretary meetings) but the review outcome doubly changed his position because he became one of seven Directors alongside Grade 2s and lost the General Expenditure division to the new Director of Budget and Public Finances. Culpin, a tall and bearded figure with a slightly more unconventional appearance than some senior mandarins, has taken the lead in the management tasks necessary to making the new approach work, especially the choice of personnel and the setting of explicit and consistent objectives for his teams. He has also built up policy monitoring capacity and links with academic research.

The Deputy Directors were assembled to form a team (partly on the lines suggested in the FER (ibid.: 10.13)) and survived as such until early 1998. The three dealing with social policy were all economists by training. Gill Noble had spent the bulk of her career in the Treasury, several years of it dealing with social security policy during key periods of reform where she showed an engagement with detail valued by her spending partners but potentially less so by the FER concept. Peter Sedgwick was a Treasury economist with a thoughtful interest in the economics of social problems and in employment-related issues; in 1998–9 he worked on the review of the deficiencies in average earnings data in official statistics. Norman Glass was also an economist with a wide experience as economic adviser in several government departments (Social Security, Health, Environment); an extrovert Irishman, he had a particularly strong external profile as a member of the Economic and Social Research Council and chair of the steering group of the Social Exclusion Centre at the London School of Economics. In 1997–8 he took the official lead of an inter-departmental team that conducted a comprehensive spending review of policy towards young children, to which we will return later. Both Sedgwick and Glass have taken on responsibilities chairing European and international expert committees. Alice Perkins, the fourth Deputy, came from the Department of Social Security at Grade 3 level. Her speciality was personnel management; in February 1998 she moved on promotion to the chief resource allocation job at the Department of Health and was not directly replaced, although Nicholas Macpherson, who had been working on the Chancellor's work incentives policy, was made a Deputy Director.

A main purpose of the Deputy Director role was to enable cross-cutting issues, which have become increasingly a matter of concern within government, to be addressed. The FER stressed the complementarity of standing and issue-based teams. The Management Levels Project Team said 'we suspect that a substantial minority (25–50 per cent) of our work could be organized on a project or issue basis reflecting our mix of work' (ibid.: 4A.13). But a distinction needs to be made between 'team effort' initiatives (like joining or leaving exchange rate mechanisms, or devising new budgetary systems) and issues which are permanent ones but cut across functional specialisms and are often generally intractable or hard to resolve. This latter type are found frequently in social policy. As the FER noted (ibid.: 4.10), 'at present even when ad hoc groups are set up to consider specific "cross-cutting issues" there is a tendency for these groups to be regarded essentially as committees –

with participants representing the interests of the divisions for which they normally work – rather than as *teams* whose members are working towards a common objective or addressing a shared problem'.

The FER is weak on taking forward the issue-based idea in the spending field, speaking only of 'ad hoc projects concerned with the interface between, for example, social security and employment spending and policies or between employment and education' (para. 10.13). But once the organization chart of the spending directorate was elaborated, some interesting issues were listed: social exclusion and the co-ordination of housing policy and housing benefit under Peter Sedgwick, and 'links between social security and (a) tax, (b) employment' and 'supply side agenda' under Norman Glass. The three Deputy Directors with concerns for social policy fields (Alice Perkins had foreign, defence and agriculture policy) were given slightly overlapping responsibilities which did not facilitate as coherently as they might have done the Treasury's approach to emergent issues.

Interpreting the FER

The public expenditure aspects of the FER have attracted some cogent critiques. The most powerful come from within the Treasury. Burns himself (in April 1995) put very fairly two concerns:

> first, the worry that the sheer scale of the job reductions we are implementing will leave the Treasury under-resourced and simply unable to cope with the tasks it has to undertake; and second the concern that if we seek to spend less time on the detail of how other departments are spending their money and to adopt instead a more strategic approach we will risk losing our flow of information about other departments, and ultimately our ability to control public expenditure itself. (1995a: 18)

Burns's remedy, basically to be more strategic, is less convincing than his diagnosis. He does not address the process of removing the statutory basis for in-year controls (which required scarce legislative time) or for preventing spending departments from making preventive referrals on points of detail. The 'fact-holders' at team leader level are not being reduced in number, and in principle they should be able to rebalance their concerns between detail and strategy; it is less clear that whether they will wish to do so and be given the right incentives to do so (given that avoidance of embarrassing

mistakes remains an important career motivator). A greater problem arises in the 'engine-room' at below team leader level, where
casework is important and the job does not escape from detail.
And, as Burns recognizes in his second point, we know very little
about just how far the 'porthole principle' operates and detail informs strategic understanding. The review has based major changes
in working style on a rather thin basis of understanding of the
process of the work. Sensitivity to objections, which Burns has shown,
does not weaken their force.

The main source of criticism within the Treasury has been associated with an 'old guard'. It does seem clear that there were some
senior officials who were more vigorous in defence of the old Treasury
style, and in particular were resistant to the importation of models
from private industry – such as 'decimating headquarter staff in a
recession' and doing better as a result, as one respondent put it to
us. Burns had some 'modernising' allies but could not have secured the changes without more than passive acquiescence from
senior colleagues steeped in the old Treasury. What seems to have
happened is that Burns used private sector insights to reinforce a
feeling that the Treasury had become too bloated on the government management side and should concentrate on becoming a more
focused ministry of economics and finance, second to none in efficiency and intellectual power. Burns formed a consensus around
this vision – using the authority of his office and the support of
the Chancellor – and the democratic nature of the exercise caused
the impetus for change to take off.

However, the FER reinforced the feeling of the 'spending side'
that they were not properly understood at the top of the Treasury;
that the detailed statutory obligations laid upon them by Parliament were undervalued; that if the Treasury were not an active
force for rigour throughout the public sector no-one else would be;
and that mechanical devices like concordats were not a simple way
of locating Treasury interventions at the right level.

A related line of internal criticism is from the young Turks who
did not dispute the need for change but were sceptical of Heywood's
enthusiasm and simplistic solutions. We encountered robust criticism, especially of the role now expected of Deputy Directors, the
ability to address cross-cutting issues, and the quality of concordats
and strategy papers. The main objection was that the FER did not
display an intellectual quality worthy of the Treasury; that its proponents had got carried away; that they exaggerated the actual or

potential expertise the Treasury possessed to carry out its pretensions. Given that the intellectual buy-in to the FER declines with grade (for those lower down work is just work, or they are clever enough to be cynical) this is criticism that has to be taken seriously.

Naturally enough, there was also a line of criticism from the spending departments, taking two variants: either that it was a Treasury plot to extend their control, or that it was a technically deficient exercise that would undermine the Treasury's ability to play its role in the spending process. The speed of implementation of the changes and their embodiment in staff cuts also attracted criticism.

Critical appraisals in the academic literature have been few but take the form that the review was an oversimplified management consultancy type of exercise which might seem to be 'successful' but embodies fallacies of control which unravel even as the organization remains committed to the proposals. In an early contribution (*Financial Times*, 24 October 1994) Samuel Brittan attacked the review as excessively managerialist and setting in organizational stone cautious economic assumptions which are inherently contestable. He was also worried about the lack of policy examples, particularly on the spending side. Under the headline 'Management can't replace thought' Brittan condemned the review as being in the grip of woolly management thinking.

Subsequently academic writers have been respectful and descriptive (Wright, 1995 and Chapman, 1997). Parry, Hood and James (1997) take a line similar to Brittan's: that such exercises induce a belief system and so claim too much. They note the fact that many of the FER's proposed innovations, especially on the public expenditure side, did not seem to be proving very useful. Noting how difficult it can be to 'distinguish minor delays in implementing reforms from quasi-biological 'rejection', their conclusion is still that 'inherited processes and roles in the Treasury's business may constitute a clock that cannot be readily stopped to allow the culture to be changed' (ibid.: 413 and 414). The history of the Treasury shows the persistence of approaches and practices promoting detailed expenditure control even as the orthodoxy at the top of the office is to 'go strategic'.

Taking forward the FER approach

After 1995 a strategy team under Nicholas Holgate was left in place and it carried forward the FER work and respond to the wish to develop a longer-term strategy after a analysis of what one senior official described to us as 'the boring bits' like demographic analysis. The fruits of this were a report on *Strategic Considerations for the Treasury 2000–2005*, written in early 1996, not published, but then leaked to the press (most extensively to *The Times* of 17 July 1996) to the embarrassment of the Treasury who were forced to dismiss it as being the product of a 'bunch of kids' (including one who was linked with aspirations to become a Labour MP). In fact, the report was part of the central strategic work of the Treasury and contained sentiments very much in line with its thinking on social issues when its officials are in uninhibited conversational mode. The report runs too far ahead than might be proper and prudent, but it builds upon the crucial step in 1994 that the Treasury would have its *own* objectives (including one to improve the efficiency of markets) and not just the aim of assisting Treasury ministers to achieve *theirs*. The paper's formulation that 'Treasury officials have a high level of commitment to the efficiency of the market mechanism; to neo-classical welfare economics and to the utilitarian ethics on which they are based' lacks the usual civil service caution but is a fair formulation of the direction in which the Treasury was heading.

The 'Kids' Paper' continued the theme of organizational review based upon an analysis of what the needs and objectives of the organization are. It recommended a new directorate on the long-term performance of the economy: 'responsibility for promoting policies which improve the performance of the real economy, especially the private sector, is spread too thinly across directorates'. This may have been a reasonable approach, but the report got into trouble by taking as its backdrop two scenarios; no radical change in the role of the state, or a so-called 'Contract with Britain', a smaller state in which the state would concentrate on financing individuals rather than institutions. This backed the wrong modernizing horse (Newt Gingrich rather than Gordon Brown), but was the basis of reporting a trend of thinking in the Treasury; in a characteristic phrase, the authors say that 'consideration is currently being given to reducing state support for post-16 education on the grounds that rising demand is "unaffordable" and private returns to individuals and their employers exceed social returns'. While many commentators saw the 'Kid's Paper' as an outrageous bid for hegemony (especially Anatole Kaletsky in 'Why the Treasury must now be brought to heel', *The Times*, 18 July 1996), we would regard it as a summary of the underlying modes of thought of Treasury officials. They want departments to do more (the paper speaks of 'flexibility of deployment away from the best self-regulating departments, towards the worst'), but believe that only the Treasury has the rigour and disinterest to enforce correct economic thinking on public policy.

Has the FER worked as it was meant to do? Or, to put it in Dunleavy's terms, did the reshaping of the bureau promote the outcomes that the main begetter of the exercise intended? Terry Burns, reflecting in September 1997, could offer only limited conclusions:

> the changes had as their first step rewriting the department's objectives and spending time making them known and appreciated by as many people in the department as possible. It is clear from our latest attitude survey that we have been successful in this respect ... none of these changes has been easy. And we have made much more progress in some areas than others. But across the range of initiatives we have important gains to show. (1997: 4–5)

Our research suggests that there remains a problem of exporting the sanguine perspective of senior officials to all levels of the office; and that there has been a gradual shift from proclaiming success to suggesting that achievements are reasonable given the difficulty of the exercise. Above all, the definition of 'strategic' as the word defining what the Treasury wants rather than does not want to do has proved hard to operationalize. It is hard to seize the high ground while renouncing interest in the low ground. We develop this point further in Chapter 10.

On the simplest test of organizational stability, the FER structure of spending teams lasted less than four years. In late 1998 General Expenditure Policy was reunited with most of the spending teams in a 'Public Services' directorate under John Gieve, while Robert Culpin took on Budget and Public Finance which incorporated social security and work incentives. The concept of the proactive spending teams at one remove from those monitoring the expenditure aggregate was lost, but another innovative one was put in its place – that the big numbers of social security and the policy issues at the tax/benefit interface raise different issues from those of policy development in the non-cash services, a distinction we discuss in Chapters 6 and 7.

5
The Treasury Forms New Relationships

As we saw in the previous chapter, one central theme of the FER is that the team leaders should be the main focus of action in each of the Treasury's areas of business; they should have the responsibility for taking forward the Treasury's activities, and the means to do so. Most of these team leaders are, in civil service parlance, Grade 5s, formerly Assistant Secretaries. With the delegation of gradings in 1996, these titles are now strictly obsolete: in the Treasury, team leaders are now band F, their deputy directors G, and their Principals E. But, like many civil servants, we have tended to use the old titles.

The team leader focus

Heywood's approach affects his view that the private sector has clearer job descriptions which allocate responsibilities more logically. His analysis is also sceptical of the worth of a system that demands that highly intelligent and motivated people serve a lengthy apprenticeship before moving slowly up a hierarchy. The new concept is of a much shallower hierarchy in which the job specification rather than personal status becomes the defining factor.

The team leader focus is of particular significance in the Spending Directorate, where the external relationships are largely contained within the civil service. The Spending Directorate is also the main focus for our own study, since it operates at the interface between the Treasury and the main social policy departments and consequently deals with the issues that are our main concern. The FER also had equally sweeping implications for other parts of the Treasury, but most of that part of the story is of only indirect relevance for our specific themes.

understanding and leading to cooperation rather than conflict are held out as the ultimate objectives. As one official put it, the goal is 'to be more overt with each other about what our objectives are so we can work together to find solutions which actually satisfy our wishes and theirs'.

Internally, the Treasury, too, is asked to accept behavioural changes in the form of a new set of values with the acronym RESPECT. Some of this is soft human relations idiom which has attracted a certain amount of derision, but we should not overlook the pace of generational change in the Treasury and the civil service generally. Civil servants in their thirties have different personal styles from their predecessors and have a greater sense that personally agreeable and overtly friendly behaviour should be part of the conduct of business. Such behavioural matters can be an important part of an attempt to create a new and more balanced relationship between the team leaders and their departmental partners.

The background and styles of team leaders

An important focus of our research has been on the spending team leaders and the way they have dealt with their responsibilities and external relationships. In the 1970s Heclo and Wildavsky commented whimsically that: 'we certainly know less about the customs and mores of finance officers and Treasury principals than about witch doctors and faith healers, though each shares a bit of the others' functions' (1981 edn: p. lxix). Their successors, Thain and Wright, have a rather primmer general commentary on the 'expenditure controllers' who dealt with departments, the approach they should ideally adopt ('not through inquisitorial means to establish an objective "truth" but adversarially through argument, critical examination and counter argument to oblige departments to justify their bids' (1995: 534) and delineating the attributes they needed. This is useful, but in our view suggests a homogeneous personality type which does not do justice to the range of personalities we encountered.

During the period of our research (1995–8) there were some changes of personnel. Joseph Halligan (social security) had a stable brief throughout the period, finally moving in January 1999. Joe Grice (health) was promoted to a macro-economic forecasting post in 1996 and succeeded by Andrew Hudson (formerly in the Treasury press office). Ruth Thompson (education) took charge after some delay in a joint Education and Employment team after those departments had merged; later her post was re-denominated as head of 'welfare-to-work' spending and she held it until March 1999. Suma Chakrabarti was brought in from the Overseas Development Administration on secondment after the 1995 Survey to succeed Richard Bent as head of the Environment team; he won notable and rapid promotion in 1998 to become head of the General Expenditure Division, a key post in the Treasury and a particularly sensitive one to be put in the hands of an 'outsider'; later in 1998 he was moved to another sensitive post as Director of the Performance and Innovation Unit in the Cabinet Office. The territorial departments team leadership (recommended for downgrading to part-time status in the FER) was vacant for a while after Moira Wallace moved to the private office at No. 10 in 1995, and was then filled by Mark Neale. Ian Taylor (local government) also had an interest in some aspects of social policy.

The responsibilities and backgrounds of these officials can be traced in the *Civil Service Yearbook* and the Treasury's *Office Directory* (accessible on the internet) and we got to know many of them by acquaintance or repute. They have some things in common: age (usually thirties and forties); enthusiasm; political awareness; a certain relish for the fight (the 'knife to the gullet' approach, as one Deputy Director expressed it); and an independent and forthright attitude to recent changes in the Treasury. There are three cross-cutting variables of difference: gender; whether a long-time Treasury official or brought in from another department; and whether or not with an academic training in economics. As one team leader put it: 'we are economics-dominated, which is fine by me because I'm an economist by training, but you can't really have rounded views on policy unless you have access to non-economists like sociologists, criminologists, and so on. . .'.

In our observation all of these variables had an effect on the way the job was done. We can observe a range of types from the 'male/long-time Treasury/economist' to a 'female/formerly other department/non-economist' through various intermediate combinations (an equivalent range of characteristics also apply at Deputy Director level). Two subsidiary variables we also noted were whether the team leader was comfortable that they had proper access to sufficient sources of information necessary to do the job; and whether there was a stable management structure in the team in the sense of the mix of expertise and ability to accept or even promote delegation. Both these issues have been flagged up by Terry Burns as being of particular significance for the efficient functioning of the new structure.

The role of being the leader of a team as well as the Treasury's point person in the functional area is one that it is easy to neglect. Getting the best out of the 10 to 15 people in the team, setting the right balance between delegation and supervision, and choosing new staff is a challenging task and is not always approached as a matter of textbook personnel management.

The job of a spending team leader is an attractive one and recruitment poses no difficulty for senior management. Team leader appointments are the responsibility of the Director, with a process of interview of several candidates. One respondent told us how leaderships of two teams were on offer: but the apparently more interesting area was not the one they took, because the senior official 'did not want major change in the way that that job was done, because that job was being done rather well in terms of relationships with the department, what he was looking for was a change of the tone in business' in the other one (which the candidate obediently took). A recent problem is that delayering, with the drastic loss of Grade 3 posts, has at times led to a virtual block on change at team leader level. In the Spending Directorate the cyclical nature of the job is a further constraint, since there are only certain times of the year when it is opportune to fill them. The civil service tradition of a rapid making of mark in a post followed by promotion out of it is being superseded by blocked progress in the context of a contracting bureaucracy.

The relationship between experience and 'capture' in a job like this is a long-standing one. There is a sense that every team leader is brought in as a contrast to a predecessor for whom relationships with the spending department have become less fruitful. Many team leaders will eventually exhaust the possibilities of their position. With several types of team leader on offer, as we discuss above, such an oscillation is possible and makes a lot of sense. The change can be accompanied by notes of regret about failures of communication in previous spending rounds, a new set of introductions to policy divisions in the spending department, new orientation visits and a general sense of clearing the air. Although, logically, the opposite progression was also possible, to be justified internally as 'taking a grip' in an area which has 'gone slack', in most of the changes we observed during our mid-1990s research – health, education, environment – there was an attempt by the Treasury at added-value in terms of improved tone at the point of personnel change.

The team leaders' job

Turning to the nature of the job done by spending team leaders, we would emphasize a certain sense of isolation in their position, particularly after the FER changes. There is a separation of office environments, a little reminiscent of a university, in which individuals get on with their work and the system does not build in opportunities for exchange and support. As one with outside experience told us:

> it's one of the features of the Treasury that nobody knows what other people are doing, and opportunities to learn from one another's best practice are random. One of the things I noticed about the department coming from a spending department is that you try to share your knowledge and expertise with people and they tend to look at you and wonder what you're on about. So I gave up. It's a good thing that happens when we get new blood, people say, hang on, how do they do it over there and I think to give credit to directorate management they are trying very hard to do more of this.

As the FER structure has stabilized, the sense of informal exchange and spontaneous co-ordination between the team leaders and their superiors seems if anything to have diminished. In order to reinforce the team leaders' positions the Deputy Directors have usually stayed out of both formal and informal discussions of spending issues – distanced from the 'hurly-burly', one said to us. Replacing a grade-based by an issue-based working pattern takes time and in the interim the Deputy Directors seem to have chosen their own agenda of items in which to become involved.

Which activities make up the working life of a team leader? Their work environment is that of a paper office – weary-looking files stacked-up, a sense of continuous engagement with the in-tray and a lack of much evident new technology. The traditional secretary still types memoranda, guards the outer office, manages the diary and brings in the tea. A meeting table and a computer terminal are basic items in the inner room. The terminal is used for exchanging short messages around the Treasury building, but a main activity is the production of carefully drafted letters and submissions, which can now be speeded on their way by fax. The other important instrument is the telephone. Spending team members are on the telephone a lot of the time, not just for speed but because of its ephemeral status: ideas can be tried out, hypotheses suggested, facts evaluated, and warnings given inside and outside the Treasury. As one team leader put it to us, 'on the whole there is quite a lot of "having a word" – I imagine much more is "having a word" than is in the letters now. And the PRO won't get that stuff'.

Team leaders have had a combination of cyclical, issue-specific and speculative tasks. The idea of a budgetary cycle has long dominated the Treasury's working life, and Terry Burns has noted the almost military precision with which Budgets are prepared and (in the old days) changes in interest and exchange rates presented. The assembly of documentation on Budget day is impressive, and even more so is the skill with which a consistent and positive gloss is put on whatever the Chancellor is saying. The material may not be read by that many trained and expert eyes, but the possibility that it might be is taken very seriously. Within the teams, there have been the departmental annual reports to approve, and statements and reports about major Government policies like the Private Finance Initiative. Exercises about management issues in spending departments, like the Senior Management Reviews of 1995–6 tend to have a particularly pointed flavour. It is here that the team leaders take on the role of guardian of the 'Treasury as a function' and probably attract the maximum irritation from those that they seek to keep on the straight and narrow track.

Negotiating public expenditure is at the heart of the cyclical task, and divides the year into the part when information is being used as part of a negotiating process, and the part when a more detached appraisal of the issues is possible and, increasingly, systematic reviews of specific problem areas can be undertaken. The suspension of spending rounds from mid 1997 to late 1998 created the apparent luxury of a long break from spending negotiation, but in fact there were even more severe pressures from the Labour government's Comprehensive Spending Reviews and the high political cost of authorizing even minor amendments of the Conservative 1997–9 plans. The risk of jeopardy from defective negotiation is an ever-present part of this work.

That said, the issue-based aspect of a team leader's work has been largely a reactive one. The issues may be pursued by the spending department at ministerial level, or be the object of scrutiny by MPs, the media, parliamentary committees or the National Audit Office. They will often involve a matter of long-term intractability, the setting of precedents or the suggestion of malpractice. If the spending department is doing its job the issues will be trailed in advance, but sometimes they will emerge suddenly. Resolving them will often require the reading of thick files and the obtaining of more information from the responsible department. It is this kind of work that team leaders post-FER want to be able to delegate to their team or back to the department.

Delegation is fine in principle, but it can run counter to the 'nose' that is an indispensable part of the team leader's equipment. This includes a sensitive political 'nose' which is present in all able civil servants – and expressed most characteristically in an appetite for political gossip – but also requires a sense of what is the potential for small issues to cause trouble and open up cans of worms. Departmental motives for bringing in the Treasury can vary – often to give themselves protection, or to associate the Treasury with an unwelcome decision, or as part of manoeuvring within the department. Good team leaders understand the sub-texts of their interchanges: as one put it, expressing the hope that the FER would improve departments' willingness to accept ownership of decisions:

> there's no doubt that this happens at times, where because of the internal politics within the department, a proposal may well come to the Treasury, swiftly followed by a phone call which says 'If you let this through, you're off your rocker'. There are all sorts of games that people play, and if one just sets the ground a bit differently for how those games are played out, then people will react to that . . .

It is the speculative part of a team leader's workload that is the most interesting, and it is the part related to their sources of information and for 'getting out of the office'. We asked team leaders about this and got a sense of a relatively unsystematic task that had been undervalued in the past but would not automatically come to the fore post-FER. Team leaders read the press and the specialist media in their field. The question of visits is difficult, because of lack of time and the 'state visit' syndrome in which the spending department or its clients presents an impression designed to promote their case. As it was put to us by one team leader:

yes, I would say you always learn something going out of the building, even if it's something that seems trivial. You learn culture, you learn intuitive things and you sometimes learn hard facts. It's a combination of 'touchy feely' stuff and confirmation or otherwise of generalizations that you are served up with. It makes you suspicious of generalization and deeply suspicious of anecdote. We sometimes have anecdote overkill because we don't go out enough. I think that we should be penalized if we don't do that once a month or more, and we try to operate on that basis here, with limited success.

A question for all levels of the Treasury is how far they generalize, not just from the cases to which they are exposed, but also from anecdotes emerging from their own lives or those of their families and friends. One departmental respondent acidly noted 'an awful tendency for the Treasury's brilliant ideas to come from cocktail parties with their neighbours, you know, "I was talking to a consultant only last Friday evening, and what he said about the National Health Service was . . ."'.

It is asking a lot of the team leaders to expect them to take account of their observations while remaining detached in their appraisal of them. What might be expected is a collegial atmosphere in the consideration of issues, and here the individualistic basis of the team leaders' current style may not be the best one. The choice of what to read, whom to speak to, where to go and what to see is part of the repertoire of the job, not just something to be fitted in by individuals on the margins of what time is available.

Another issue concerns the extent to which outside expertise is drawn upon, especially in subjects and in disciplines where the Treasury has not traditionally been strong and if so in what form – advisory panels, seminars or informal discussions. One or two outside observers have been tart about the extent to which Treasury teams have relied on superficial reading of the professional press to acquire a gloss of instant expertise on complex social policy issues.

Inside the spending teams

As with the FER, our research concentrated on the axial role of the team leaders, but the internal organization of the teams is very important. What we have are the former Grade 7s who are often highly qualified and can in some cases be put in charge of wide areas of policy; and an 'engine room' of HEOs and below who hold the facts, approve the minor items, and keep track of the figures. The distribution of economists is significant – one team leader said to us:

> I've got four [grade 7s]. There are two who are economists and two who are administrators, but it doesn't work like that, and in fact one of the administrators has got a PhD in economics. So this distinction is more apparent than real. He is our most highly qualified economist but he is isn't one! I'm not one, which is pretty unusual round here. There is a division of labour which is partly to do with specialisms – if there is a large economic content in the work then the economists would work on those.

Another team leader told us that the Grade 7s were virtually doing team leader level work, 'because they're having to cut deals . . . maybe with a quick chat with me, but they're having to do that and that would have been done at Grade 5'. Grade 7s put their submissions direct to ministers, except in some difficult cases 'where the extra cover of someone a bit more senior is just useful for Ministers, because they will ask that question, has the team leader looked at this problem . . .' Below this level, though, in the team leader's opinion HEOs were 'doing rather traditional work still'; one of this HEOs was dealing direct with the Principal Finance Officer of a regulatory body because there were big issues here that no one else had time to deal with. We found some evidence that the 'engine-rooms' were buying into the FER approach less fully than their seniors, and that there might be problems if the pushing-down and reduction of staffing continued. As the team leader quoted above noted, 'the strain shows, actually, they feel under enormous pressure to deliver things which they're not delivering, and to make decisions on their own, and at the same time their promotion prospects are zilch, so this is not a pleasant environment . . .'.

Yet, as with the Grade 5s themselves, the calibre of those recruited to these posts remains high. One leader comments of his team that:

> I've no trouble in attracting the highest calibre of staff here because . . . it's an attractive place to work, because the issues are important, they're interesting, they're on the front page of newspapers, you see a lot of senior ministers, you're involved in a lot of highly controversial issues.

The leader added that:

> I do like people who have got ideas and views, not necessarily
> my own. In fact, I think it's a positive advantage if we have
> differences of views, and I will sometimes go deliberately for
> somebody who indicates a different perspective on something so
> that we get a good debate and a good discussion going ... We're
> involved in serious issues here and we owe it to the organiza-
> tion and to ourselves to give it our best and to work to the best
> of our abilities, but it should be fun ... and when I'm inter-
> viewing people I just like to make a judgment on whether they're
> going to be interesting to have around.

This gives a good sense of the degree of freedom of action that an
experienced team leader can expect to have in managing his team
in the new structure. At the same time, as we showed in Chapter
4, the position of their immediate superiors in grade terms, the
Deputy Directors, has become more problematic. They are now almost freelance bureaucrats, internal consultants in the Treasury and
sometimes wider Whitehall, carving out whatever role interests them.
As we have seen, this was a boost to the team leaders because it
stopped the 'court of appeal' role of their seniors. Coupled with
the increasing delegation within the team, this gave the team leaders what virtually amounted to an 'Under Secretary' role (in old
parlance). As time as gone on, certain less positive features have
become evident. Team leaders do not need to communicate much
with the Deputy Directors and so may not see them frequently;
team leaders will have one of the Deputies as their superior (not,
one team leader insisted to us, 'line manager') making assessments
for promotion purposes but will often deal with several of them
on one issue or another. And then, as one team leader put it:

> the person above you doesn't know the details, and therefore
> there's a problem when you go to ask for advice – on specific
> issues you've got to go through all the explanations of what's
> going on before the person can offer you any help.

Another was even more pointed:

> I thought the place was very heavily managed in terms of policy
> management and it was always justified to me that the sensitivity

of issues was such that we had to have lots of checks and end-less hierarchy – I think it was a load of cods actually. You either have a dog or you don't have a dog, but you don't have a dog and bark yourself!

Nor was there any evidence that, within the Directorate, the Direc-tor (*alias* Second Permanent Secretary)'s role – which derives much of its force from his long experience in the field and his perma-nent secretary status – is being extended downwards to fill any gaps that may have developed.

But in many ways the most important consequences of the recalibration of the role of team leaders and the 'shaking loose' of the Deputy Directors from the structure have been felt outside the Treasury, in the spending departments with which they have to deal. It is to these that we now turn.

The view from outside: Departmental Principal Finance Officers

PFOs occupy a key position in the hierarchy of spending depart-ments. They are invariably of senior status, and there is a tendency in departments to have a resource chief (sometimes linking finance and personnel) at grade 2 level rather than the traditional grade 3; they work closely with their Department's Permanent Secretary, who carries the ultimate responsibility for expenditure as Accounting Officer, and who in that capacity will be subject to scrutiny by Parliament. They are intimately involved with their departmental ministers in preparing cases for each spending round and defend-ing the department's case against the Chief Secretary and the Chancellor. The importance of their post means that they are them-selves likely future permanent secretaries. They both carry the internal departmental responsibility for maintaining financial good order and also deal with the Treasury on financial issues. To discharge this responsibility they usually act as primary point of contact with the Treasury, standing between the department's policy and implemen-tation sections and the Treasury and usually acting as the main channel of communication. On occasion, this may lead to tensions, with the Treasury wishing to make contact direct with executive branches or agencies and the finance division seeking to maintain the principle that they are the gatekeepers to the departmental system.

This situation has been complicated in many departments in recent years by the appearance of executive agencies, many of whom have developed their own lines of communication with the Treasury, though ultimately they do not have a fully independent financial identity. As we saw in Chapter 3, the creation of these agencies in the course of implementing the 'Next Steps' programme was initially seen as potentially threatening to Treasury interests, as being likely to extend and complicate lines of financial control. However, after taking a close interest in the 'framework documents' which govern the agencies' financial and managerial regime the Treasury has been generally content to take a pragmatic view of their activities. In this sense, they have been treated very much like long-established intermediary bodies with financial responsibilities falling within individual departments' sphere, like the Housing Corporation.

Apart from being senior figures in their own departments, PFOs are also likely to have wide experience of Whitehall and to have served in a variety of postings. They will have close connections both with their fellow PFOs in other spending departments and in the 'Whitehall village' generally (Heclo and Wildavsky, 1974: ch. 3). All this will mean that they are well equipped to deal with pressure generated in the relationship with Treasury spending teams – they are not wanting for allies among other Whitehall villagers. They are also uniquely well placed to observe the effects of the internal changes in the Treasury.

In the past, the preparation and argument of a departmental case has been an 'iterative process' (as management jargon used to describe it), a regular cycle of discussion and fining down of detail. At one point, the last stages could degenerate into a frantic scramble, with deals being made between Chief Secretaries and departmental Ministers in hotel bedrooms at party conferences. Much of this frenetic flavour disappeared, as we saw in Chapter 3, with the evolution of the EDX system; but even so, obfuscation and ambushes could still play a disproportionate part in the settlement process. One team leader spoke eloquently to us of their feelings about one particular episode when the Treasury 'pulled something out of the hat' at the last minute. 'It came out in the middle of August and everyone had gone off on holiday and it was really bloody awful. And very difficult for us as well.'

As we have seen (Chapter 4), the Treasury restructuring after the FER was explicitly designed to improve customer relations – at least in part because the reaction of spending department customers when

consulted about existing relationships had been distinctly unflat-
tering. But the form the restructuring took posed a number of
important issues for PFOs. The first, already discussed above, is the
issues of the relationships between grading structures in the Treasury and the spending departments. As we describe, it was already
well-established practice for comparatively junior Treasury officials
to deal directly with their seniors by rank in other departments.
The key difference that the FER made was that the departments
had effectively no alternative option but to deal with them. The
disengagement of the Deputy Directors in the Spending Directorate from the detailed content of survey work and the effective
withdrawal of the Director from acting as an ultimate court of appeal marked a substantial change in the working environment.

Not all the PFOs liked this. They looked back wistfully to times
when a telephone call could fend off trouble generated by over-
zealous young Treasury officials. It does remain possible for a
discontented PFO to involve his or her permanent secretary through
the weekly meetings of permanent secretaries, at which the second
permanent secretary/spending director is also customarily present.
Or the issue might be raised separately at permanent secretary-to-
permanent secretary level. But to do this would be an admission
that relations had broken down: and this in turn would be 'a dis-
aster', one PFO told us.

One thing that departments were gaining from the Treasury was
an increase in the level of delegations, allowing departments greater
freedom to take decisions on capital projects without Treasury approval. But there was a price for this in terms of understandings
about basic principles to which both parties would adhere, which
tended to yield more strategic control to the Treasury than might
have been the case in the old system.

Another significant feature of the changed environment identified by some PFOs we interviewed was the division within the Treasury
between General Expenditure Policy division and the spending directorate. Some PFOs felt that this substantially diminished the
importance of the spending teams and hence of their relationship
with them. More broadly, it was suggested that what the Treasury
has gained through delayering may have been lost through the more
centralized way in which the control of public expenditure is dealt
with through collective Ministerial decision-taking in EDX. The old
days of eyeball-to-eyeball between departmental ministers and Chief
Secretaries are over; in the less tense atmosphere of EDX a good

departmental case stands a better chance ('a better day in court', as one former Chief Secretary put it).

The role of personalities

But almost certainly the significant of the issues around relationship after the FER is the question of personalities. This was always present, of course – in the past, there was absolutely nothing unusual about a Treasury Assistant Secretary acquiring a reputation as an unclubbable opponent prone to employing the whole range of familiar Treasury dodges to win last minute tricks. But the stripped-down hierarchy exposes the issue of personalities more clearly than ever before.

It seemed to us that many department–Treasury relationships characterized in personal terms were in fact products of the nature of the business and the spending department's previous history. To take one example, a Principal Finance Officer in a spending department said of the corresponding team leader:

> he is very able, if you want an analytical dissection of some proposals that they're making he would do a damn good job of it; if you're looking for a creative contribution on something he might well make a damn good job of it, but he's not a hearts and minds person, that's for sure.

But the same official drew a contrast with one of the leader's predecessors, who (they said):

> was notorious in the way that ( ) tends to be, notorious. They were demonized, but in fact I was able to work with them, get them into a sense of give and take, you know 'why don't you help us in these small things and the important things, the big things, you're going to win that anyway, aren't you', a give and take, a personal relationship dimension that adds something to the theoretical relationship. You don't have that with ( ). He is quite clinical about focusing on today's issue, and is it whether he can carve a million off us or can he not carve a million off us. He comes across and I believe I think politically he is hostile to expenditure and so he actually approaches the subject with a passion that goes beyond the cause . . .

In this case the lack of an interventionist Deputy Director only added to the frustration with the team leader. Speaking of the former, the PFO said:

> it's partly that he is mentally more delayered than his predecessor was, but actually we have difficulty using him; he isn't sufficiently plugged in to work as court of appeal when we're driven to it, which is actually quite a problem for us, given the nature of ( ) ... Even if we've always had all the steps in the hierarchy, rarely here or certainly rarely there would everyone in the hierarchy be actively engaged but I do actually feel a loss in no- one visibly showing much active interest above ( ), except the Chief Secretary, and it seems to me to have dangers. There's a quality control issue, there's a knock-on to my role – I find it hard to operate as the person brought in if things are getting difficult if my counterpart isn't performing that role, and with a different Grade 5 there for ( ) the fact that I picked up the phone and said 'This is really troubling us' might have an impact. With ( ) there he would say 'What are the three arguments again?' and address the arguments and not put any weight on the fact that we attached such importance to it that I'd got involved'.

Nor was this a unique case. In some departments, the issues seemed to matter less, the personal style more. Another PFO volunteered the following description of their working relationship:

> I think an oddity that affects our relationships with the Treasury is a kind of *ad hominem* consideration, which is that for the last five years or more the Grade 5 in the Treasury who is the head of the expenditure division with particular responsibility for ( ), happens to have been a very, very strong, very active and capable personality, cordially detested on all sides in the Department of ( ) but cordially respected as well by wiser people ... he's a very energetic person, I think with an agenda of his own, probably, but not to the point of being unprofessional in pursuing an agenda which Treasury Ministers wouldn't agree with.

A colleague of our departmental respondent suggested a reason why a team leader might harden rather than soften with experience:

people go native and [the Treasury] have to move them around because they get soft on the programmes. Some people respond in that way. I think there are others who respond by getting more and more committed to certain strands of thought and objectives in relation to the programmes they cover. I suspect ( ) was more in the second camp than the first. He'd have been moved before if they thought he had gone native.

In a third case, a former team leader was described as 'a traditional Treasury thug . . . whose people skills were not particularly evident'. It seemed to us that the worst cases of bad relationships arose from some combination of uncollegial personal style (being rude, going outside the hierarchy, undermining previously agreed positions) and the relentless pursuit of a 'line' that did not seem to be quite the government's. It is the combination of the two that is potent, because it has resonances with themes of the Treasury as arrogant and in a sense 'above the law'. We should emphasize that the three cases mentioned above are drawn from incumbent team leaders at various points in the 1990s, all of whom subsequently moved on. What seemed to change after the FER is that 'niceness' joined as a countervailing virtue and was recognized as such in appointments to these key posts.

Uncollegial behaviour can be the worst problem, because it can involve feelings that may linger on, presenting successors with a severe problem of rebuilding confidence. One PFO put it like this about a former team leader:

I'm afraid that my view of the relationship is one which is just a bit personal . . . I think he was told that he wouldn't win further Brownie points in the Treasury by being at total daggers drawn the whole time with the department. I think signals were given to him that it was possible to have a robust and challenging relationship without it involving visible demonstration of personal contempt for the people you were dealing with, and he sort of pulled back a bit. He has written some of the most appalling letters that I've ever seen written between civil service colleagues in the past thirty years to people at very senior levels in this department.

This respondent told us that 'I think things have got better, but in my view it is overwhelmed by personalities, which is almost useless

more closely together in a sequence of tasks undertaken during the dying days of the Conservative government. In January 1997 the grading exercise was repeated and the average score rose from 6 to 7.5 (from satisfactory to good). More significantly, no PFOs now saw their relationship with the Treasury as unsatisfactory and 65 per cent said that they thought relations had improved over the past year. Similar views were expressed by Treasury teams, though in one or two cases there were reservations about the openness in departments in discussing policy development.

However, it would be idle to claim that these developments had swept away all doubts about the FER and its consequences. Apart from the issue of personalities and the persistence of stereotypes on both sides, there continues to be a less than perfect match between objectives. The Treasury's eagerness to claim the title of 'taxpayer's friend' and guardian of the public interest against the importunate pressure groups can still be a source of irritation. Wild notions from over-enthusiastic juniors going straight up to Ministerial level on the Treasury side without prior consultation is another. On the other side, Treasury officials still expressed frustration about the slow pace with which certain departments took on board the importance of such policy developments as the Private Finance Initiative.

There was also an argument, at least from the spending department side, that by admitting the Treasury more directly into the policy development process under the rubric of the strategic role and abandoning the old and well understood adversarial relationship, the spending departments were giving hostages to fortune. For example, the semi-detached roving role of the Deputy Directors now enabled them to intervene in cross-cutting policy areas under the guise of impartial arbitrators and facilitators in a manner that would have been inconceivable in the old regime.

Thus Treasury 'trespass' into matters of policy substance could become legitimated; a development that at least one gamekeeper turned poacher (the former Second Permanent Secretary, Alan Bailey) found very alarming, at least when viewed from the spending department perspective:

Treasury officials are accountable to the Chief Secretary and Chancellor, but in no real sense (in their public expenditure role) to Parliament, the Public Accounts Committee or the public. At ministerial level, the conventions of collective Cabinet responsibility mean that departmental ministers have to defend their own projects and programmes, including 'cuts' and failures to spend, without blaming these on Treasury colleagues . . . it is difficult for people working in the Treasury to realize how sheltered they are from the constant pressures of public accountability to which those in spending departments are exposed. The danger is that [the Treasury's] powers and privileges are carried across into policy issues which are not (or not mainly) about public expenditure, but about all kinds of microeconomic issues. This gives Treasury officials too much power to block other departments' proposals, without they or their ministers having any need to defend the consequences. (Bailey, in Corry (ed.) 1997: 297)

Against this background of alleged Treasury sheltering, we examine how the changing role of the Treasury affected relationships and policy content in a number of key areas of social policy in the second half of this book.

6
The Calibration of Cash: Social Security

Social security is central to any study of the Treasury's social policy, if only because it has by far the largest budget of any department, now amounting to around 40 per cent of public expenditure as a whole. The problem – as set out in a speech in 1995 by a former Education department permanent secretary, Geoffrey Holland – is that the magnitudes of spending are so great that even the margins of error in estimating in social security eclipse the more important substantive issues in other departments. He said:

> some time after I was appointed a Permanent Secretary came the realisation that in the public expenditure round the whole public façade of rational argument about priorities and merits was in part a nonsense. One Department and only one really concerned the Treasury – the Social Security Department. There might be a pretence that other Departments were bidding for funds, were discussing their bids seriously with Treasury officials and Treasury ministers, but the fact was otherwise. Unless and until the Treasury had tied down the Social Security budget, they simply did not know how much money was left over for the other over the scraps that fell from the Social Security table. (Holland, 1995: 44)

Similar points were put to us in the course of our interviews. One DSS official said:

> Social Security is just so large that virtually anything that we're on is going, if not immediately, to eventually build up into substantial savings. Quite often one thing that is a Survey issue

between the DSS and the Treasury will be bigger than the total disagreement between a medium size department.

Another, recalling time in the Treasury, said that:

> you would be arguing about £10 or £15 million on the overseas aid budget or on the galleries or the slaughter houses or something, and spilling a lot of blood about them, and then the DSS would come in and there'd been a new round of forecasting and they'd say 'oh and by the way our estimate has gone up by £600 million' – or down, but it's usually up.

The long-term position of social security

It would seem logical to expect that this weight of expenditure would be matched by high political salience of the issues. This certainly became the case towards the end of the Conservatives' period in government, after 1993 and in the Labour government's welfare reviews of 1997–8, and yet in a longer historical perspective it is the absence of visibility that is the more prominent theme.

One reason for this past lack of prominence of social security in political debate is the nature of the expenditure, which overwhelmingly takes the form of transfer payments. This means that spending does not produce tangible outcomes in buildings or equipment owned by the state but is expressed as cash benefits or grants paid to individuals. Rodney Lowe argues that this has limited the economic impact of expenditure in this field, at least as viewed from the centre (1993: 122). True, social security was always a substantial employer, running vast clerical 'factories' devoted to the calculation and issuing of benefits: but until the 1990s these activities was organized according to general civil service rules on recruitment, training pay, and relations with the public, and were not a variable in departmental budget discussions.

A second historical reason was to do with the general perception that the key policy issues were settled by 1948. Administering such large sums was an important technical responsibility but the question of the role the state had assumed for eliminating 'want' (as Beveridge had defined it) and the means by which this was to be done was now closed. Political parties and public expected the Ministry of Pensions and National Insurance, and the National Assistance Board, bodies of low political status, to get on with the job. The subject failed to attract the attention or closer involvement of ambitious politicians, though the volume of personal cases raised by MPs provided an early opportunity for Margaret Thatcher, John Major and Michael Portillo to make an impact as junior ministers.

As far as Treasury perceptions of the area are concerned, we can trace a consistent theme of latent anxiety about social security which initially was submerged in reluctant resignation, but later became more boldly expressed – especially once social security replaced defence as the largest single item of public expenditure in the 1960s. Although the Treasury had reasserted their control over the general direction of economic policy after the crisis of 1947, they became concerned in the 1950s that a minister – as we saw in Chapter 2 in the case of John Boyd-Carpenter, later the Treasury's own Chief Secretary – could accumulate sufficient technical expertise on narrow issues to see them off. Hence their hankering for a department with a wider remit with whom they could engage more effectively.

The Labour government provided this new configuration in 1966, initially by establishing the Ministry of Social Security – reviving Beveridge's original concept – with a subordinate Supplementary Benefits Commission as an umpire of the system, partly insulated from operational interference. Under a later chairman, David Donnison, the Commission won the symbolic concession of freedom to publish their annual report without prior approval. This appalled the Treasury, as evidenced in the hilarious letter from an official which Donnison later published (1982: 149), citing as justification for the attempt to suppress publication a need to economize in the use of paper.

However, there was no direct Cabinet presence for social security until 1968 when the newly titled 'Secretary of State for Social Services' entered the Cabinet, in the person of Richard Crossman, at the head of the merged Departments of Health and Social Security. Crossman was an authentic political heavyweight who loathed the Treasury and all its works, as is evident at many points in his diaries, with especially sulphurous references to the workings of PESC. He was a veteran of disputes over pensions reforms, which he had attempted to promote in the late 1950s with the aid of a small group of academic advisers drawn from the London School of Economics – the first of many attempts at a 'New Beveridge'. Crossman's arrival at the head of the new department greatly reinforced its status. As he jauntily put it in his dairies, 'I have now got ... on to the back of a huge department in the Elephant and Castle where

I rule my own roost. It is as big as Defence and in a way much nearer to public opinion' (Crossman, 1977: 590).

Crossman more or less convinced himself that he had laid the bogey of social policy as a peripheral activity. Personally, he remained at the centre of events in the final years of the 1964–70 Wilson government. In policy terms, he used his position to press the case for the reforms with which he had failed in opposition. His (joint) permanent secretary, Sir Arthur Atkinson, summarized his achievement as having been to 'change the climate. He brought social policy to the forefront of politics and made it possible for people to do more. Before Crossman it was seen as something too boring for intellectuals, and too difficult for everyone else. He made it a live subject for discussion' (quoted in Timmins, 1995: 216).

Crossman's Conservative successor, Keith Joseph, was equally notable in helping to transform involvement in social security from a mass-production executive task to one demanding the highest level of policy analysis. One illustration of the strength of Joseph's own position and the increased effectiveness of his own department was his approach to unification of the tax and benefits system, in which the Treasury were apparently willing partners (in sharp contrast to their subsequent position). Yet Joseph's proposed pensions reform suffered the same fate as his predecessor, both being lost through early dissolution of Parliament. Nevertheless, he left behind him a reputation in departmental folklore both for boldness in the initiation of significant new policies and, in the words of his official Robin Wendt, 'his great ability to secure resources from the Treasury' (quoted in Timmins, 1995: 291).

The next Secretary of State, Barbara Castle, was another formidable political operator, well able to stand up to Treasury pressure, at least according to her own account of jousting with the then Chief Secretary, Joel Barnett (Castle, 1980: 709). Her status – and a certain war-weariness among all concerned – enabled her to establish the State Earnings-Related Pensions Scheme (SERPS). She also legislated for Child Benefit, a significant new universal benefit that incorporated tax relief for children previously dispensed by the Treasury and so raised tricky problems of presentation (as it appeared to add to public expenditure) and implementation (in the end, it was phased-in).

In retrospect, Castle's replacement by David Ennals, the first in a line of worthy middle-weight ministers to occupy the post, was a turning-point. Under the pressure of economic difficulty, the focus of debate shifted: the cost and incentive effects of social security started to become more prominent than the needs that programmes were intended to address. Soon, the economic crisis of 1976 brought the IMF to Britain and provided the Treasury with the opportunity to make the largest cuts in public expenditure, year on year, in the whole postwar period.

But economic stringency did not bring an end to all reform in social security (Timmins, 1995: 313). The SBC under Donnison launched an exercise ('Social Assistance') to simplify an intolerably complex system, recognize the rights of claimants (now strongly pressed by a variety of pressure groups) and promote a more open style of administration. The review was intended to serve as the vehicle for wider reforms (Donnison, 1982: ch. 6). But the change of government in 1979 sank most though not all of these reforms – the new system of Housing Benefit, later the Treasury's great bugbear, was the conspicuous exception – and put an end to the Commission itself.

Donnison was not the only commentator to see the measures in the new government's Social Security Bill (especially the cutting of the 'dual link' which had meant that benefits rose in line with prices or wages, whichever was the higher) as marking the point at which social security became an ideologically contested area. The Treasury was now emboldened to move decisively away from the role of a resigned price-taker of a demand-led, 'uncontrollable' body of expenditure (and as such exempted from the cash limits of 1976) and became the chief critic of the biggest 'demandeur' among the spending departments, driven by the belief that there were substantial economies to be made. The new Secretary of State, Patrick Jenkin, was at first content to treat social security 'like a loss leader to keep health going' (Timmins, 1995: 377); but pressure from the Treasury intensified and Jenkin's successor after the 1983 Election, Norman Fowler, resorted to a different tactic. Confronted with a new Chancellor, Nigel Lawson, who was determined to assert his authority, he resorted to the device of a review, the next in the sequence of 'New Beveridge' exercises.

As we have already seen, Lawson was a Chancellor with very clear ideas both about the importance of reducing public expenditure and the ways it should be brought under control. He had a wide reaching concept of the role of the Chancellor and executive functions of the Treasury in government, partly formed during an earlier period at the Treasury as Financial Secretary (Lawson, 1992:

105–6). He had a poor opinion of the calibre of the DHSS and was sceptical about the capacity of its ministers and officials to deliver reforms of the kind that he wanted.

Lawson's main objective was to use the Fowler reviews to deliver substantial savings; Fowler's response was to broaden the remit of the reviews and to conduct the exercise as a semi-public operation. But despite massive public evidence-taking there was still a scramble to finalize policy, as we saw in Chapter 3. Changes were not radical, but even the limited involvement of the pensions industry secured through facilitating opting out from occupational pensions was a boomerang which in the short-term increased public costs through lost revenues (Lowe, 1993: 315) and in the longer term helped to cast doubt over 'pure' market-based solutions to welfare policy issues – as well as leaving a scandal of 'mis-selling' which it eventually became the job of the Treasury to resolve.

The conflicts between Fowler and Lawson dramatize the different perspectives brought to the issue of social security spending. Lawson used the No. 10–No. 11 axis (while it still worked for him) and his own perception of the Chancellor's licence to roam across all policy areas to try to impose his own approach. At the same time, he refused all attempts to set up joint working parties with the DHSS on issues like the tax–benefits link – unlike Tony Barber a decade earlier he was determined that there were to be no intruders on his own turf. On the exercise as a whole, he comments in his memoirs: 'I failed in my bid to secure significant immediate savings out of the reform of this massive programme but the changes Norman made with my full support undoubtedly checked the escalation that would undoubtedly have occurred' (Lawson, 1992: 593).

On his side, Fowler had stood his ground – becoming seen in the process as departmental champion – and was able to prevent the review developing into a simple cuts exercise. The mutual suspicion arising from this episode was still an important feature of the landscape we explored in our interviews, a decade later.

For the time being, the stand-off meant that location of responsibility for the direction of strategic policy in this field remained an open question. The small 'social security intelligentsia' became increasingly alienated from government in the 1980s, as did the existing pressure groups, many of which had come into being as campaigning organizations around benefit issues. But at the same time, 'New Right' think-tanks had their own access to ministers and used it to emphasize the link between social security and broader questions about economic and social behaviour. Seen from their perspective, the term 'welfare' came to imply not support for those in need but a subsidy to dependency. Yet however influential their ideas became, the policy mechanisms for relating the two barely existed. Social security ministers thought in terms of rules and entitlements of 'their' clients, Treasury officials of aggregate expenditures – and their reduction. Both had developed stereotypes which were often unsystematic and in the Treasury case not founded on evidence, observation or even reading. Donnison has a telling anecdote about the Treasury official who thanked God that he didn't have to read *New Society* – a magazine now defunct but then an indispensable source of assimilable information about welfare (Donnison, 1982: 58).

We can trace an accelerating pace of concern from 1987 about social security as the axis of the public expenditure debate, in terms of both magnitude and policy significance. The Conservatives' third term in office after their re-election in that year is now seen as the point at which the Conservative government cast aside inhibitions about the reform of the welfare system and embarked on a break-neck process of change marked by deliberate defiance of interest and pressure groups.

But in social security the more significant immediate variable was the personal failure of Fowler's successor, John Moore, who became embroiled in a series of difficulties around the future of child benefit, acidly portrayed by Lawson (1992: 720). Moore's lack of mastery of his wide brief was the precipitating factor in the split of the department in 1988 by separating health and social security. Kenneth Clarke took on health, while Moore limped on for a year at the new Department of Social Security before being replaced by the more emollient Tony Newton. Newton was subsequently seen as having been responsible for an over-generous response to the pressures brought to bear by the disability lobby and (less fairly) for the tribulations brought about by Margaret Thatcher's last contribution to social policy-making, the creation of the Child Support Agency (1990). This Agency was also part of the application to the DSS of 'Next Steps' policies under which agencies were to take over executive responsibility for the delivery of government programmes. Social security was an especially appropriate area for such changes, since it already had a history of subordinate bodies with defined responsibilities for the distribution of specific benefits.

The 1990s: an evolving relationship

In general, a less than harmonious relationship with the Treasury prevailed at the end of the 1980s. As one senior DSS official put it to us:

> it tended to be a sort of stand-off. We kept our counsel, we volunteered nothing, or very little. The Treasury pressed for enormous things and it always ended with an enormous amount of work and discussion between ministers . . . fighting off the Treasury from their budget.

Put crudely, the Treasury now became fed up with social security. With most of the budget not cash-limited, the Treasury had to accept demand-led increases which were hard to predict with reliability. The unpredictable element of forecasts (inflation, unemployment and trends in fitness for and participation in work) seemed to displace demographic changes that should be straightforward to assess. Where substantive benefit changes were agreed, the Treasury usually had to wait for legislation which needed prolonged preparation and parliamentary scrutiny. To cope with these problems and force a sense of rigour on DSS, there was an increasing tendency to resort to ambushes at a late stage of public spending rounds. Furthermore, with the new system after 1992 of the EDX committee and a fixed control total (see Chapter 3), other ministers developed a sense that social security could be an easy pushover: either a source of cuts that would protect their own budget or a dumping-ground on which to deposit costly or unpopular provision – an echo of the notion at the time of the Fowler review that the social security budget could be the 'new North Sea Oil' (Timmins, 1995: 405).

After the Conservative's unexpected fourth election victory in 1992, the new Chief Secretary, Michael Portillo, introduced the fundamental expenditure reviews for all departments whose impact on the Treasury we traced in Chapter 4. Perhaps unexpectedly, in the light of recent history, the DSS's FER became the basis for shifting the character of relations between the Treasury and the Department. The sense of mutual irritation remained for a while, but gradually an accommodation was reached, under which the Treasury and DSS came together around common objectives, in terms of grappling realistically with the problems of spending control in the area, with the Treasury eventually sending over several key senior staff to accept managerial responsibility.

An important stage in this process was the appointment of Peter Lilley as Secretary of State in 1992. A cerebral right-winger with statistical training, Lilley's strengths as a policy developer suited the Treasury very well. Lilley had a twin-track approach of mastering the technical detail in order to lay down a phased programme of change, while safeguarding his populist appeal through much-honed conference speeches on fraud. The compatibility of his basic agenda with the Treasury's was helpful in negotiations even though it did not permit an instant convergence of objectives and approach. A Treasury official confirmed to us in 1996 that by this time:

> At the level of overall strategic objectives there is a fairly good degree of agreement between Treasury and DSS Ministers as to what should be done, which is largely because of Peter Lilley's particular attitudes. He is not somebody who favours maximisation of the Welfare State, as some of his predecessors have done, or certainly have done to a degree anyway. His attitude to Social Security is completely different to Tony Newton's attitude, for example, and that has obviously made it easier for us to have worked out where we want to get to. But often that isn't the most difficult thing, to agree strategic objectives in general terms. The most difficult thing is usually to actually agree some measures to implement them, and I would say that the tension between the Treasury and the DSS has largely been about the speed at which things should be done.

Lilley had a clear notion of what he was attempting to achieve; and the Portillo review had given him a good opportunity for doing so. This time, there would be no 'big bang' or 'New Beveridge' but a phased programme, concentrating on the areas of maximum pressure. As he subsequently told the House of Commons Select Committee on Social Security:

> my approach to the reform of the social security system is to try, where possible, to do it on an incremental basis and not to go for some wonderfully logical elegant theoretical framework replacing some existing system which perhaps does not work as adequately as one likes; but invariably, if one does try to do that, you will find that the realities of a complex world work

out less satisfactorily than one would hope (House of Commons Social Security Committee, 1995: 186).

This approach was codified in his Mais lecture in June 1993. This had nine basic propositions, which he had naturally had to agree with the Treasury:

1. there are no easy solutions (e.g. merging tax and benefit systems);
2. any effective structural reform must involve either better targeting, or more self-provision, or both;
3. disincentives are inherent in statutory benefits ('usually the choice will be between a small extra disincentive on a very large number of taxpayers or a larger disincentive on a smaller number of claimants');
4. means testing is not the only way of targeting benefits more closely on need (other ways include more precise categorization by age or circumstance, more conditionality, tighter contributions tests);
5. the existing array of benefits – contributory, universal and income related – are rather more targeted than some comment suggests;
6. no-one has the right to opt out of contributing to help those who cannot provide for their own needs; but there is no reason in principle why people should not (in addition to others) opt to make provision for themselves privately rather than through the state system;
7. contracting-out inevitably involves a switch from pay as you go to fully funded provision (which is good for the economy);
8. the more the provision for needs and risks is monopolized by the state the less incentive to work and save to provide for them;
9. the reform of something as vast as the social security system is best carried out sector by sector rather than by the 'big bang' approach.

Sitting rather oddly alongside his crude use of 'sponger' stereotypes in Conservative party conference speeches, Lilley then also attempted to educate the Treasury and everyone else through the publication of a discussion paper, *The Growth of Social Security*. This had two objectives: to show the scale of likely expansion; and to identify the crucial areas in which this expansion is being generated. The paper projected that benefit expenditure would rise by 26 per cent between 1992–3 and 1999–2000 if unemployment remained constant and suggested that '. . . it is not possible for the system to continue indefinitely to grow more rapidly than the economy as a whole'

Table 6.1   Peter Lilley's 1993 estimates of social security benefit expenditure as a percentage of GDP

Year		%
1992–3		12.3
1999–2000	Case 1 (2% real GDP growth, stable 3m unemployed)	13.5
	Case 2 (2.5% real growth, unemployment a quarter less)	12.4
	Case 3 (3% real growth, unemployment half less)	11.3

Source: Department of Social Security, *The Growth of Social Security* (London: HMSO, 1993), table 6.

(Department of Social Security, 1993: 3). This ominous conclusion was encapsulated in tabular form:

On this footing, a phased action programme was constructed. Lilley's consistent emphasis on 'affordability' was calculated to win the approval of the Treasury. In fact the 1998 estimate is for benefit expenditure to be 11.5 per cent of GDP in 1999–2000 (calculated from HM Treasury, 1998g: tables 2 and A6). Economic growth and particularly unemployment turned out to confound Peter Lilley's worst fears.

In this process of public education and the attempt to define the policy agenda, Lilley also had an important ally in the Labour MP Frank Field, who was then the Chair of the House of Commons Select Committee on Social Security. Field had a cross-party reputation as someone with independent views, promoted by a stream of books and pamphlets on welfare reform which stressed his opposition to means-testing. Field was recognized by the Treasury as a valuable source of influence on a new approach to social security. One official told us in 1996 that:

Frank Field is an enormously influential player in the public debate, and he is also influential in some of the government's thinking. For example, the changes to Child Support policy which were made at the beginning of 1994 and then at the beginning of 1995 were certainly discussed with Frank Field before the government finally unveiled its proposals. There was a deliberate attempt there to build some consensus with the Social Security Committee and particularly with Frank Field, and there was a feeling that was a committee where it was actually possible to do some business, and that the Select Committee's function wasn't just to sort of produce reports and try and make fools of Ministers and DSS officials appearing before them, but they were actually engaged in an enterprise to try and get one or two of these things right, rather than scoring debating points, and Field personally, as I say, is enormously influential.

Meanwhile, in common with other departments, the DSS was obliged to respond to the new managerial agenda. By the time the internal reforms were completed the DSS had become a conglomerate, with 98 per cent of staff in agencies, the biggest of which was the Benefits Agency. By this time the Treasury's once strong objections to the Next Steps concept had subsided: the status and responsibilities of agency chief executives were settled and, after initial opposition, the Treasury conceded that they could be accounting officers. One DSS official described the Treasury as 'schizophrenic on this. They would like to break departments into accountable units but on the other hand don't want to lose something as big as DSS ... they normally don't see Chief Executives direct. They certainly don't see them to discuss resources. That's done through the Permanent Secretary. It's a departmental bid'

The Senior Management Review was a great source of pain to DSS, and debates about running costs (see Chapter 3) tried even Peter Lilley's Treasury-inclined patience. But in the end the managerial consciousness won out in the form of DSS's 'Change Programme' which was inspired by theories of the efficient management of large organizations. The long march back towards securing Treasury trust in the DSS operation as a whole was now well under way.

Towards Staged Change

The approach laid down by Lilley in the Mais lecture did not preclude fundamental change, within the context of an approach intended to confine benefits to those in genuine need and 'make the whole system sustainable and affordable' (House of Commons Social Security Committee, 1995: 28). This led to the review of a sequence of individual programmes, in the selection and examination of which the Treasury played a significant part. On this basis of our evidence, we can point to ways in which the Treasury's input influenced outcomes, both generally and in the case of individual programmes:

1   Child Support Agency

This was one of the most notorious cases, because of the widely held assumption that a potentially progressive policy had been undermined by an unrealistic Treasury insistence that it had to deliver savings. The title of one study of the Agency, 'Putting the Treasury First' (Garnham and Knights, 1994) has entered folklore as a shorthand for what happens when social reform gets caught up with cost savings. In fact, our research suggested a more complex process in which there was more of a shared agenda between the Treasury and the DSS than many have suggested.

The creation of this agency sprang from an awkward mix of a moral agenda – the perceived need to establish the principle of parental responsibility – combined with an attempt to contain the cost of providing for the rapidly increasing numbers of single parents. It owed its orgins to Margaret Thatcher; yet was paradoxically the product of consensus, passing through Parliament unopposed by either opposition party. It was another approach to DSS's long-standing concern to enforce obligations on 'liable relatives'. No one in government expected that the new administrative apparatus of the Agency could be justified in any other way than fairly rapid savings on the social security bill for lone parents. This dictated two key issues of principle, the Treasury's first call on the money raised from absent parents and the retrospective reopening of agreements reached as 'clean breaks'. These were raised at the time only by individual politicians; Tony Newton's caution about the Treasury's position failed to convince the Cabinet, and DSS associated itself with over-ambitious targets to gain leverage for other policies. One DSS official explained to us that:

> We were pushed by the Treasury on two things. One was to not phase it in. Well we did this, but not phasing even longer. We said it was done in Australia and America and they are now starting to hit the hard core, but they have taken four or five years to get there. If we had phased it in there wouldn't have been any real fuss. And the other was clean breaks, where we wanted to start like Australia did from current date and, of course, you don't take in very much money so the Treasury were fussed, and we've had to adjust that, but to give the Treasury their due we haven't had to adjust it much, but that really did cause a lot of fuss about upsetting people's lives they thought they had settled ten or fifteen years ago. That politically was very difficult. That nearly broke it.

the reason Housing Benefit expenditure exploded in the late eighties and early nineties was because of a policy of moving up rents in the social sector more in real terms so that they got closer to rents in the market sector, and also we lifted rent controls, which meant that obviously Housing Benefit expenditure was going to go up because rents were going up. Nevertheless, that was part of an overall policy which was to try and get a more market-orientated rent structure. Now there are also faults in the Housing Benefit system at the moment which are not compatible with the sort of Social Security model that we want, so we have gone about reforming Housing Benefit as well, and in fact in the last three budgets there have been changes to Housing Benefit and I don't suppose we're at the end of those either. Nevertheless, we recognize that Housing Benefit expenditure is going to level out, well we hope it does level out, at a much higher level in real terms than in the early 1980s, when we had rent controls in the private sector, and we had social rents which were deliberately subsidised.

In the Fundamental Expenditure Review, the Treasury identified the link between housing policy and housing benefit as one of the cross-cutting issues they needed to monitor. As we trace in Chapter 7, they were reluctant to accept the full financial implications of a policy they supported in principle, and continued to worry away at the details of the benefit, especially in the context of their feeling that it was susceptible to systematic fraud.

4 Jobseekers' Allowance

This was an important part of the Lilley programme: the introduction of this benefit was intended to reduce expenditure on the unemployed from £1.3 billion annually to £0.7 billion by 2000, by 'improving incentives to find and keep employment' – compulsory reviews of progress with the sanction of ending benefit. This had an interdepartmental aspect because of the involvement of the (then) Department of Employment. The Treasury interest here was threefold: to promote an integrated approach to support for the unemployed in which the Employment and Social Security departments would not dig in support of 'their' programmes; to promote employment incentives that would counter any behavioural instincts to withdraw from the labour market; and to avoid 'wasting' money on eligible recipients whose household income position was not too severe. Therefore the means-testing element of the benefit was made much more prominent.

It needs to be emphasized, though, that bearing down on the unemployed has not been a primary Treasury objective in recent years. Benefits like disability and housing, which seem to be more unstable and unpredictable, have seemed to repay more of the Treasury's time and intellect. Nor is the magnitude of spending on the unemployed relatively that large. Indeed, the Treasury was prepared in 1993 to allow unemployment benefits to be excluded from the control total as 'cyclical social security', accepting that they would rise in recession but preventing savings when unemployment fell from being applied to other benefits.

5   Fraud

Under Lilley this became an increasing preoccupation, not just because it provided the raw material for his populist conference performances but because a general impression had been allowed to develop that fraud was the most promising part of the benefits 'North Sea' for locating large deposits of potential savings. Both DSS and the Treasury were anxious to tap them and under Lilley's programme identification of fraud became a major preoccupation of the Benefits Agency. In 1994, an internal review suggested that the level of unemployment benefit and income support fraud might be running as high as £1.4 billion per annum and in housing benefit at about £900 000. Various measures were adopted to deal with this: the creation of the benefit fraud inspectorate, provisions for sharing information between local authorities and the Benefits Agency and a 'Benefits Integrity Project' specifically directed at disabled people in receipt of high-value awards of Disability Living Allowance. Lilley was eventually able to claim that in consequence of these actions savings of over £1.5 billion in public money had been achieved in 1996–7.

The Treasury's active sympathy with these measures was reflected in our interviews:

> the high priority that the government attaches to the anti-fraud effort, and also because of the good ratio of savings on programme expenditure for every pound you put into fraud expenditure we have deliberately given that priority. We have agreed with the DSS extra resources to go into fraud and we have ring-fenced it, which means that the deal is that they don't

divert any of that money that we've allocated to fraud to other things like marketing benefits *[laughter]*, and we exempt them from across the board running costs. I think it's fairly well known that there was a 5 per cent general swipe on running cost expenditure in the last Budget. We specifically exempted the DSS's expenditure on fraud on that, and it's agreed between us that that's a priority area, and we've always honoured those deals and the DSS have always honoured their part.

6 Pensions

Here, substantial economies had already been secured as a result of the Fowler review; but these were not due to come on stream until well into the next century. With the addition of the equalization of the pension age for men and women at 65 these measures would, the DSS estimated in 1995, reduce public expenditure by £10 billion per annum by 2030 – not exactly a 'big bang', more a distant report.

However, the problem of the flat-rate pension as a deadweight in the social security budget remained. It was perceived as the central contract in the National Insurance system, but its specific purpose was less and less clear – too low for pensioners without other provision, but too incidental to those with a good occupational pension. Putting anything in its place would take a long time to implement and possibly be expensive, as the difficult debates of 1985–6 made clear.

It is therefore noteworthy that in the final months of the Major government Lilley and the Treasury were able to construct a plan to abolish the state pension by remitting national insurance contributions into privately run pension schemes. This was to be financed by reversing the present pattern of tax reliefs on pensions – removing reliefs on payments into pension funds but making the pension when eventually payable tax-free. Although conceptually unsatisfactory this did moderate the up-front financial burden of the proposal. In the end, the suggestion of privatising everyone's pension arrangements fail to win acceptance and the proposals were a negative factor in the Conservatives' case at the 1997 election. Labour's own pension proposals of 1998 returned to the themes of voluntary take-up of stakeholder pensions and a flat-rate income guarantee. But at least the Treasury had been associated with bold thinking. Typically, the idea that the tax privileges of pension funds were a ripe target was picked up in Labour's first Budget, but this time without anything in return.

The cumulative effect of this whole programme of selective activity was to diminish the medium-term upward potential for growth in spending on social security. It also incidentally invalidated the alarmist forecasts published in 1993. But perhaps more important, the convergence of thinking between the DSS under Lilley and the Treasury helped to promote a common understanding on strategic objectives strong enough to survive a change of government. It was Labour that reaped the benefit in the form of a lower-than-expected outturn of expenditure in 1997–8.

Developing relationships after the FER

Social security was possibly the most demanding test case of how the 'New Treasury' approach of partnership with departments can work in practice. Our research suggests that what we have here may be two processes taking place simultaneously: convergence on strategic objectives and divergence on implementation (in terms of presentation and pace). The size of the budget and the significance of even small changes to the programme keeps pushing implementation back on to the agenda and with it conflict on details. It is here that the differences of perspective between the departments are revealed. In the telling words of an official who had worked in both the Treasury and DSS:

> when I was in the Treasury people used to say to me the Treasury doesn't understand about implementation, it thinks that once a decision is taken and announced in the Budget, that's it, you can get on to the next thing, but I have to say that until I came here I had no idea of the enormous effort which has to go in to the implementation of policy changes. On something as big as Jobseekers' Allowance, for example, which on the face of it at the Treasury looks fairly easy, you can actually see what has to be done on the ground, the high quality time people have to put in with the effort of making it work.

In this debate about objectives and their implementation, a central question is of what 'strategic' means and who has the lead; as a Treasury official put it to us:

> that sounds like a fairly second order difference, doesn't it, of degree and speed, and that 'But, oh yes, we're actually agreed

on the basic objectives', but when it comes down to negotiating with them how far we should go on restricting a particular benefit, these are the important issues, because this is what actually matters when it comes to the government producing a bill, for example, to reform Invalidity Benefit, and what is formally a difference in degree or a difference in the speed at which you wish to go, actually because of the size of the expenditure and the importance of it, they become fairly important matters on which there is disagreement, and therefore while we're partly agreed about the place we want to get to, you'll find our relationship over the last few years has been peppered with quite a lot of disagreements of the nature that I've described, and we get frustrated with them and they get frustrated with us for that reason.

or as put in a contrasting manner by another Treasury official, again in 1996:

There is a large measure of agreement between Peter Lilley and his Treasury colleagues on what the Social Security system should be trying to achieve. If there is any difference, it arises over the speed at which that can be achieved rather than on fundamental questions of what the objective is, so at any rate at Ministerial level there is not a great sort of argument about objectives. Now, DSS officials have shared this view because that's their Minister, but they also are aware that some of these things are more difficult to achieve in the kind of timescales that we are talking about, and because of where they are they are obviously much more sensitive to people out there who actually administer it . . . than we have to be. There is an element in the Treasury where . . . if you know too much it actually gets more difficult to do. A certain kind of brutish ignorance helps, because you're in a classic principal–agent kind of situation in the sense that there are tremendous asymmetries of information between us and them. You obviously rely a bit on whether they've said the same thing in the past and it hasn't turned out to be quite as bad as they've said, and whether other places seem to have done this and it hasn't all collapsed . . . some of the things that you [interviewer] describe as unthinkable are things which DSS have thought about and would regard as either politically difficult to achieve at all, or in the timescale we're talking about, but they're not mad.

Still, there is an appreciation in the Treasury of the way that the changing policy climate might open up possibilities of cost saving: as one official speculated to us while the Conservatives were still in office (and before the pensions proposals had been announced):

> Times change and attitudes change and we're aware of that. I don't think anyone is yet in favour of abolishing the state pension, but in ten years' time, who knows? But we've gone quite a long way. We've certainly greatly reduced the importance of the earnings-related pension, SERPS and so on, which might have been thought unthinkable ten years ago. Sickness pay is now entirely the responsibility of employers. Again, that might have been thought unthinkable many years ago. We're now expecting people to meet all the costs of their interest payments for mortgages and so on, so times change. But we try to stay within the boundary of what is feasible. You're always testing it, but some things that weren't feasible last year might be feasible this year. The climate has changed on lone parents, for example, and when the political climate changes and you say to yourself, well things that, where you mightn't have thought of taking money away from lone parents, you think about it seriously now because the Party is not very keen on lone parents.

Treasury concern for supply-side issues is also available as a rationale for intervention. As one official put it to us:

> I am a very firm believer that it is the Treasury's job, not only to control public expenditure but also to have a view about what that public expenditure is delivering, and that means, in Social Security, having a fairly clear Treasury view about what the balance of the benefit system should be between benefits, how the benefits should be constructed, not for the hell of it, not just because I enjoy interfering in these matters, but because these matters are fairly crucial to some of the other Treasury roles like our responsibility for macro-economic performance, because the balance of the benefit system affects the trade-off between work and leisure, the trade-off between consumption and saving, all of which are major influences on economic development, so I am a very firm believer that it is not just the level of spending but the make-up of it.

Problems in forecasting

Particular difficulties arise when policy variables often considered separately unite in a single issue. The poor forecasting record of DSS is a major point of intersection of political and technical matters. As Kenneth Clarke said in a briefing after the 1996 Budget, 'I am sick and tired of the way that DSS spending always overshoots the plan targets' (*Financial Times*, 28 November 1996). A Treasury official put their complaints to us in this way:

> To my mind the real problem with DSS forecasting is not that it's out. It's always going to be out with an aggregate of £90 billion, and we're never going to forecast it correctly. The thing that really bothers me about it is that we systematically under-forecast it. The reason is that the DSS's forecasting models for the medium term are not properly picking up the way that different bits of the benefit system are inter-related with each other and the way that certain social changes are pushing up benefit expenditure, so we have consistently underestimated the growth in lone parents and the proportion of lone parents who will be dependent on means-tested benefits. We have persistently underestimated the growth at which Disability Benefit expenditure goes up. We have persistently underestimated the number of Housing Benefit claimants. We are getting slightly better at it. We now have an explicit factor in the models for under-forecasting which is just, frankly, recognising that the models at the moment are not perfect, that they seem to have an under-forecasting bias, so we're making a block adjustment for them. That is one of the major technical, as it were, problems that we've got with Social Security spending at the moment, that we're still systematically under-forecasting it, and it is a major problem.

As we trace in Chapters 9 and 10, the single most important change in the context of public expenditure planning in the late 1990s was that the biases in the forecasting model swung in the direction of overestimation of spending, as the economy turned up and the greater rigour of benefit rules started to have effect.

The social security spending team

To understand the particular difficulties entered into the Treasury–DSS relationship in the 1990s we have to bear in mind the dual process described above: the underlying convergence of strategic objectives may be masked by a quite confrontational style and content to the relationship – and which both sides, for their different reasons, have no great incentive to defuse. The unusually long tenure of the social security team leader from 1993 to 1999, Joseph Halligan, is evidence of his grasp of the subject-matter and assiduous identification of ways that spending might be contained within government spending targets. For DSS, it marked a new level of critical scrutiny of both policy and operation, and of scepticism about its protestations of inability to meet spending targets. In the post-FER structure Norman Glass, Halligan's deputy director, was less available to DSS as a channel of communication and general policy manager than had his fellow deputy director Gill Noble been when she was exercising these responsibilities.

A theme of overachievement was suggested to us by several DSS respondents – that a Treasury team leader can be too assiduous and extend into themes that ministers find unacceptable to the point of losing credibility and even being something of an asset to the spending department. However, the Chief Secretaries we interviewed managed a wry smile when Halligan's name was mentioned. There are conveniences in having a 'rottweiler' on hand to deal with intractable areas like social security, both in securing a mastery of the technical detail and in putting the other side through their paces.

What DSS is searching for is a relationship that combines the intellectual quality traditionally associated with the Treasury with a willingness to defer to the spending department on the reasons for falling short on shared objectives. One DSS official who had worked in the Treasury put it like this:

> I do think that the Treasury does deal with us in a fairly adult manner; the complaints we've got about them are that they don't understand about the complexities of real life, that sort of argument. You can have a discussion with the Treasury and come away having learnt something, and that hasn't changed. What we'd really like would be to have people over there of the same intellectual quality as we have now, and that have also worked

over here, and therefore have a better than intellectual under-standing of problems. It really is genuinely difficult to know in advance exactly what is going to happen when you change policy and therefore to fail to deliver precisely as you were trying to is not necessarily a sign of incompetence; it reflects the reality of life.

Personal sensitivities also intrude on joint exercises, where there is a narrow line between getting the Treasury on board to facilitate later approval, and ceding hegemony to them. Various exercises went on in both departments with variations on whether person-nel from the other were involved and who they might be – staff who had worked in both departments being a particular resource. The Treasury does not have the staff to do large exercises, and it has to piggy-back on DSS for information, but it does look at policy; in 1996 it had 'a think about medium term policy on Social Secur-ity from a Treasury perspective'. At the heart of the DSS–Treasury relationship is the tactical manoeuvring based on differing resources of power and information. Power may derive from both hierarchy and reputation, and information depends on its quality, its timeli-ness and its proprietorship. The interaction between them is well described by a Treasury official:

> We know a lot, but they will tend to know nooks and crannies of the system that we don't fully understand, and very often what will happen quite often in the Survey is that we will be arguing about something which appears politically unpleasant for one reason or another, and not very acceptable, but we need the money, and they will say, 'right, well, actually we don't want do that, but we've got another way we can do it' which involves some obscure bit of the Social Security system and they will pull this rabbit out of a hat, but unless we go on arguing about the politically unpleasant ones, they'll never feel under any obliga-tion to pull the rabbits out of the hat. It's the asymmetry of information again, so that's the way you tend to argue. Very often we're arguing for things which we know in some sense will never actually run, but which, if we don't argue for them, we would never squeeze out the ones that may run.

In general, we should record that the Treasury officials in the line on social security were to our observation engaging and committed individuals. The dynamics of expenditure control in the field have to some extent shaped their approach and perhaps even changed their personalities. Much depends on how far Treasury officials can be expected to internalize the constraint variables of feasibility and acceptability rather than provide a critical counterpoint to them in the certainty that they will be pressed by DSS. Both Conservative and Labour governments seem to prefer the latter role in the over-all determination of the policies and it is this that has been shaping the behaviour of officials.

The emerging links in social security

The ideological convergence over the Lilley period did not lead to a smoother relationship, at least at the outset. The problem of knowledge about 'out there' – of knowing what was going on among client groups, and what political impact changes might have – was always a problem, which the Treasury was never able fully to surmount.

There were some moves towards the containment of pressures in the periods before the election, with a recognition that the two departments are bound together as the dominant players in their field – the pre-eminent policy ministry and the biggest spending department. This has been promoted by the transfer of staff - in one especially significant case, Chris Kelly, from the Treasury in a Grade 2 position to work on policy development in DSS, some-what off-line on spending negotiations. Moving on to Health as Permanent Secretary in 1997, Kelly was succeeded at DSS by his own successor at the Treasury's Budget and Public Finances Direc-torate, Paul Grey. The attractions to the Treasury officials of these moves seemed to be a combination of getting career credentials outside the Treasury, and of having hands-on a large budget. In the opposite direction came the Deputy Director of the non-social spending teams, Alice Perkins, with an emollient watching brief on relations with other departments, who eventually moved to a re-source job in the Department of Health in 1998. At politician level, this movement was confirmed by Alistair Darling's natural progres-sion from Chief Secretary to Secretary of State for Social Security in 1998, and even by Peter Lilley's spell as Shadow Chancellor in 1997–8.

Both sides think they have set the agenda for the other, on the broad lines of the Lilley programme as endorsed by Labour as part of Conservative spending plans, but the effect has been one of an association amounting almost to a colonization by the Treasury approach to these matters. As a result, welfare reform could never again be an exercise steered through from the DSS, even when Frank Field was appointed Minister of State for the topic. Field's exercise drew in many other government departments with interests to defend; but it was the Treasury's central role that eventually compromised his attempts to set the agenda. Despite promises Field was never allowed to drive the whole welfare reform process, with consequences that we describe in more detail in our concluding chapters.

7

More than Moving Money: The Treasury and Public Provision of Services

Seen from the Treasury perspective, there is a whole range of reasons why the activities of a particular spending department should stand out from the general run of public expenditure. In the case of social security, as we showed in the previous chapter, the sheer scale of expenditure compels attention and its cash nexus invites Treasury agenda-setting. In the case of other social spending departments, the mechanisms of strategic control are more complex but the need for economic and financial appraisal of policies by the Treasury has also become pressing in the 1990s.

In terms of the traditional concept of Treasury control, a tendency to stray outside spending limits or failure to manage resources efficiently will be sufficient to justify close attention. As we have seen, a department that acquires a reputation for being risk-prone will lose it only with time and much diplomatic effort. But in the case of the three departments whose relationship with the Treasury we explore in this chapter, there are other specific reasons for wariness on the Treasury's part. The eternal political visibility of spending on health and education provides a special context for discussion of spending decisions in those fields. Housing no longer possesses that special aura which it once enjoyed: but the conjunction between housing budgets, general local government spending and rent subvention through the social security system touches another area where the Treasury is especially sensitive.

As we have already shown, the Treasury can be taken to have a number of general objectives in its approach to the management of public spending: securing consistency with the current government's political priorities; forwarding the Treasury's own agenda; and securing the maximum degree of effectiveness in delivery. In addressing expenditure under these three headings, these general objectives may undergo some specific modifications: health and education may on occasion be examples of 'virtuous' public spending; education in particular calls up issues around the Treasury's 'Ministry of Economics' role, with its potential effects on the supply side; effectiveness in these fields may require a special emphasis on attracting private capital through the Private Finance Initiative.

In addition, the relationships with these departments make useful comparative test cases for the evolution of the 'New Treasury' approach after 1995 and the ways in which it has differed in these cases from the pattern now established in social security, which we discussed in the previous chapter. But it is important to recognize at the start that there are important differences in the structural context in which the relationships have developed.

The cash–services division

One fundamental division in public expenditure is between programmes that transfer money to recipients and those that are used to provide services, and they provide different control problems for the Treasury. In social security, as we saw in Chapter 6, there is a deceptively simple calculus of cost and entitlement that tempts the Treasury into designing its own preferred distribution of expenditure. In health, education and, to some extent, housing the consequences of pulling the levers of policy are more complicated. In terms of crude totals of public expenditure, these programmes are less significant than social security, though still substantial in relation to government expenditure as a whole and the potential gains that the Treasury can expect to make through their interventions are accordingly less significant. In recent years there has been a redistribution within these welfare state services as health has overtaken education and housing has fallen off in favour of housing-related transfers through social security and tax relieves (Table 7.1, which draws upon Glennerster and Hills's invaluable digest of recent data and policy detail).

As departments, Health and Education and Employment have certain characteristics in common that distinguish them from the Department of Social Security. They both have substantial capital building programmes; directly or indirectly, they have responsibility

Table 7.1   Public expenditure on services, 1980–95

£ billion (1995–6 prices)	1980–1	1985–6	1990–1	1995–6
Education	28.5	27.9	31.8	36.1
Health	25.9	27.8	33.2	40.7
Housing	12.3	6.5	6.7	3.9

Source: Compiled from Glennerster and Hills (eds) (1998: table 8A.1).

for the employment of staff, which raises questions around the setting of pay levels in the public sector. They deal with important professional groups, doctors and nurses in the first case, teachers in the second, one group occupying a key strategic position and the other wishing that it did. Health and education are also areas where there are significant levels of private provision. And health care provides the arena in which one of the UK's most substantial private-sector economic players – the pharmaceutical industry – operates.

Secondly, since both these departments operate in politically highly visible areas, the two secretaries of state have to become accustomed to acting in an exposed arena. Careful watch is kept by a variety of interested parties on the level of resources devoted to health and education; so their performance in the annual spending round can quickly make or break their Ministerial reputations. Because media attention is virtually guaranteed, especially in the field of health, progress is continuously under observation within government and particularly at both addresses in Downing Street. A 'seasonal scare' on the level of health spending is almost an annual event and has helped to produce a situation unique across the range of public finances: a public commitment (1992 and 1997) to increased spending on the NHS in real terms. Although through repetition this came to be seen as a Conservative ploy that Labour matched only with reluctance during the 1997 election campaign, once in office the Blair government was more than keen to exceed it.

Housing is in a different position because of its location in government alongside responsibility for local government and (sometimes) transport and its steady loss of salience since the 1960s. Once, housing was seen as a key social service, to be protected as a priority even at times of economic pressure. Now, housing is much nearer the model of a commercial, privatized service than either health and education. Housing provision has been redefined as an aspect of personal responsibility, to be financed from income or savings or if necessary from social security. The funding of the most important remaining interventions is now off the housing budget altogether: they are tax expenditure issues like MIRAS (mortgage interest relief, finally abolished in 1999) or Housing Benefit, paid from the social security budget. The residual housing budget shows the consequences of almost two decades of its use by the Treasury as a pot to raid for savings, as the government struggled to redefine the service itself as one that would operate in future through the market. However, housing still has its pressure groups (especially Shelter, the campaign for the homeless) and substantial economic interests (builders and mortgage lenders, who shade into the wider influence of the construction industry and the financial services industry respectively).

All departments operating in these areas have undergone fundamental structural reform in the recent past. The DH was split away from the DSS in 1988 and the DfEE is the product of the 1995 amalgamation of the Department for Education and the Department of Employment. The Department of the Environment, into which housing was submerged in 1970, lost Transport in 1976 but regained it in 1997 as part of Deputy Prime Minister John Prescott's new 'empire' of the Department of the Environment, Transport and the Regions (DETR).

Equally, if not more significant has been the fundamental reordering of the fields for which the departments are responsible. What amounted to the mass privatization of the public housing stock through the 'right-to-buy' scheme was one of the key policy initiatives of the first Thatcher government, followed by enforced increases in rent levels in the remainder of the council housing stock and housing association properties. In this process, DOE's concern to reconceptualize rather than run down the service was matched by a Treasury much less interested in the social impact of housing policy than in the potential of substantial savings to help balance the books.

The reforms of health and education are both products of the radical final period of the Thatcher administration. If he is to be taken literally (perhaps a questionable proposition) these two fundamental reforms were both initiated as a direct result of interventions made by Nigel Lawson when he was Chancellor. In both instances, according to Lawson's account, he was careful to exclude the two departments from initial thinking on the subject of the review, largely

reflected in the PRO documentation reviewed in Chapter 2. This can be put down in large measure to the effects of the market-driven reforms introduced at the beginning of the 1990s. More than the successive reforms of the health service that took place at regular intervals during the 1970s and early 1980s, which concentrated on restructuring the machinery of the service rather than cultural change, these later changes commended themselves strongly to the Treasury.

For example, commenting on the reforms, one official expressed themselves as being very satisfied with the new management structure of the health service, with its shift 'from being a service that was largely a command and control structure . . . to being a service that was designed to take most decisions at the periphery but within a strategic framework and not only that but the elements of a market as well, an internal market'. Another comment was that '. . . in some ways the NHS reforms and for that matter the Griffiths input in the 1980s [on management of the NHS] . . . has enabled us to exercise more direction on the health care environment'.

But this does not have to be the detailed direction previously thought to be necessary. Although the general principles of control of capital expenditure may not be different,

> what is different is our precise relationship with the department and the precise controls they have and the structure of delegated limits. The Department of Health is blessed with a relatively rational and detailed approach to capital spending and we have been working with them over a number of years. We've put particular emphasis on developing a manual of procedures recently and in doing so to strengthen and enhance the appraisal, approval and monitoring capabilities they have and so we've been able to review and where appropriate to raise the delegated limits in line with the strength of the systems.

This meant that by 1996 the delegation limit on the mainstream hospital programme had risen to £100 million, though those for private finance and information technology were still rather lower. But this does not signal caution on the extent of use of private finance; rather the opposite:

> We're great enthusiasts for the PFI . . . if you want to persuade yourself that this is not just creative accounting you only need

to go and see one or two of them . . . what they're delivering is a massive improvement in services to patients . . . we've reached the Holy Grail where everyone can be happy

– or as happy as any Treasury official has a reasonable right to be.

In effect, the Treasury Health team operated over this period as a defender of the internal market in the NHS and the separated functions of purchasers and providers, seeing its task as being to continue to reinforce the downward pressure on costs. The commitment to increased expenditure in real terms needed to be interpreted, in the team's view, as a shift of resources in the direction of more patient care, looking at labour costs and input costs as critically as possible as part of that process. An important tool was that of assumed efficiency savings, which was increased from 2.5 per cent to 3 per cent in 1995 and maintained at that level by the Blair government. This index is an example of a high-level indicator that the Treasury loves, and that they push to be applied further and further down the health service. DH argues with them, but an official close to these arguments was reconciled to their inevitability:

Certainly we are under pressure to aim for ever higher efficiency gains as any organisation is. I think it is always going to be an issue between ourselves and the Treasury whether a particular level is achievable or not. 3 per cent looks extremely ambitious given that the Health Service has seldom managed to achieve efficiency gains at that level – I think the long run trend has been under 2 per cent, slightly higher since the reforms, but it is quite difficult technically to rely on the figure for an individual year and we always argue in the Departmental Report that one should not take an individual year's figures, one should look at longer run trends. I think that points to somewhere nearer 2 than 3 per cent. . . . I do not believe that Treasury are unresponsive to arguments on this. I do believe that they want to press as hard as possible and I think they may have pressed us further in the past than we would have wished to go but I do not feel as though there is no point in us having these discussions because there is no room for manoeuvre.

The team used their participation in the FER on health expenditure, during which they participated between them in all twenty of the study groups set up, to get to the heart of departmental decision-taking. In making this attempt, the team had the additional advantage of a Chancellor, Kenneth Clarke, with a personal stake in the success of the NHS reforms, of which he was – in an earlier incarnation – one of the chief architects; as a health official put it, 'he has attempted to be a better Secretary of State for Health from the position of Chancellor of the Exchequer than he felt he was in all the particulars when he held the post itself'.

Officials in the health spending team at the Treasury tried to get out and see the NHS in action; from the departmental side that was laudable but at the same time risky:

> [the team leader] would ask me where I thought would be a good place to go about something and I would offer him advice on that but I wouldn't expect to be consulted, and I wouldn't expect to control where Treasury go. I have had problems on occasions when I have felt that Treasury have spoken to people who are excessively gung ho. The NHS is very ambivalent about this. On the one hand they have demonised the Treasury, and on the other they are deeply flattered when a Treasury mandarin arrives on their doorstep and there is an enormous temptation to roll out the red carpet and tell them how wonderfully they are doing, how well they are managing, and what efficiency gains they've made and if only the rest of the Health Service could be run like this they could save millions of pounds. It is a terrible temptation to these people who see a Treasury official once in a lifetime to explain how they could run the whole organisation much more efficiently.

DH's role in holding the ring between the Treasury and the NHS also becomes difficult in the presentation of spending outcomes:

> we have to use just the very same arguments that the Treasury were using against us to try to market the outcome to the Health Service. That is the nature of the business. It's one of the quieter gear changes in Whitehall when spending departments move from fighting the Treasury to presenting the outcome shoulder to shoulder with the Treasury. It's quite well rehearsed, but it's always embarrassing . . .

In general, some senior DH officials thought that 'the Treasury captured too much ground for their own good' because of their involvement and observation in health matters, and were at risk of losing their critical detachment. Departmental collusion in this development was cheerfully described as 'loving them to death'. But despite these cross-currents there seems to be little doubt that the relationship was functioning more satisfactorily. Regular meetings were better developed than in other departmental areas; quarterly stocktaking meetings were being held to ensure that there were no nasty surprises (on either side). There were regular awaydays to pick up any points outstanding after the public expenditure survey has been completed. This approach was preferred by DH to the formalization of relations in a concordat:

> It seems to me one of the objectives for us now in our dealings with the Treasury is as it were to have a less bureaucratic relationship, one which depends more on personal relationships, which depends more on talking with Treasury . . . I think some of the days or half days we've had with them, looking at particular themes and issues' have been more productive than spending time in any exchange of paper. A concordat may be helpful. I can't readily think of occasions when having a documented set of terms for our relationship would have been helpful in the last year [1995–6].

Some issues did remain outstanding – and there is always the risk in this field in particular of a sudden political storm either around funding levels or a specific case upsetting the smooth progress of the dialogue. And when resources are being publicly debated the department always has at the back of its mind the possibility of an appeal to highest authority – the backchannel to Downing Street can never be completely closed off.

One potentially difficult area that did not cause problems in the event was the decentralization of executive responsibilities. The Treasury declared itself happy with the division of tasks between the headquarters staff in London and the NHS Executive in Leeds, with policy and financial management functionally separate below the very top level. The Leeds operation, merging the previous Regional Health Authorities into the civil service apparatus, was congenial to the Treasury. If the occasion demanded it, Treasury officials were quite content to go to Leeds or use the new technology of videoconferencing. Nor was any significant concern expressed to us about the devolution of responsibility from the NHS Executive to Trusts. Rather, the Treasury officials portrayed themselves to us as eager to accelerate this process, so that the objectives set at the centre were confined to those of genuine strategic significance and their control over executive management – pay and conditions – enhanced.

One that did was the hardy perennial of the drugs bill, prominent in early discussion of health service expenditure, as we saw in Chapter 2. A very long-running theme has been the issue of whether to regard the pharmaceutical industry as a worthy example of British enterprise that deserves support and sponsorship or whether to try to cut down on prescribing, especially by GPs, whose expenditure is still not cash limited unless they are fundholders. Outside observation, focusing on hospital services, often misses the long-term salience of issues like this and their recurring place in Treasury–department relations; for instance, a health official noted that under the Conservatives

> the Clarke agenda has seemed to me to be quite a bit to do with the drugs bill and our relationship with the pharmaceutical industry, where he's been sceptical about the PPRS (Pharmaceutical Price Regulation Scheme) which governs the profits of the pharmaceutical companies and is the mechanism we use to try to make sure that they don't make undue profits to hold the balance between our wish to have a successful research-driven balance of payments-contributing, employment-generating domestic pharmaceutical industry, and fair prices for the taxpayer as far as the NHS is concerned – having as we have in this country virtually a monopsony so far as pharmaceutical products are concerned.

Another recurrent issue has been the role of the professional groups, especially the doctors and the legitimacy of their participation in policy debates. As Chancellor, Nigel Lawson commented that 'The National Health Service is the closest the English have to a religion with those who practice in it regarding themselves as a priesthood. This made it quite extraordinarily difficult to reform' (Lawson, 1992: 612). His successor, Kenneth Clarke, when responsible for the service was in turn bitterly sarcastic about the role of doctors and what he regarded as their blatant grandstanding in appealing for public support for campaigns that were as much about their own as the public interest. Distrust of pressure groups, in this as in other fields, is part of the Treasury official's mindset, sometimes justified by presenting themselves as the 'taxpayer's friend' (one theme in speeches by Terry Burns).

In sum, the relations between Health department and Treasury moved a considerable distance in the period up to the election of the Labour government in May 1997 and had defused many of the tensions associated with an area of expenditure that was an avaricious consumer of resources and could tug on the political heartstrings. This gave the Treasury the confidence to accept the wish of the Labour government for more health expenditure and to alert them to the needs of the service. As we shall see in Chapter 9, the result was a relatively generous treatment of health in the Blair government's first year and subsequently in the Comprehensive Spending Review.

The education case

The Treasury has for a long time nurtured a close interest in a number of issues in the field of education, broadly construed, and perhaps particularly in its potential linkages with questions of employment. This is felt at different levels in the department, from the team leader who saw it as the essence of the Treasury's developing 'Ministry of Economics' interest in supply-side issues to the former Chancellor, Nigel Lawson.

For all this, the Treasury has had a detachment from education as a process of teaching and learning. Until the 1970s, education policy was mainly a matter of keeping pace with expansions in demographics and entitlement, through building and teacher training. Then Labour's 'Great Debate' from 1976 articulated scepticism about the value of modern educational practice and started to recast educational professionals as selfish trades unionists. The Treasury picked up these points, but their approach had a resource allocation focus that did not engage directly with the debate in the 1980s on curriculum and qualifications. Their concerns were less focused on education policy *per se* than on the political economy of education. These included a continuing interest in the skills base of the economy – both basic literacy and numeracy and more advanced technical education, as related to the economic value-added of investment in different types and stages of education, a particular interest in programmes for the 16–19 age group and the different organizational arrangements and funding regimes applied to programmes. Here, the Treasury have acted in a 'vanguard role' in trying to sort out what they regard as anomalies generated by the structures of the public sector.

Further persistent themes have included a recurrent suspicion that individuals who participate have profited excessively from investment in higher education and that the subsidizing of this sector should take more account of social rates of return; an interest in market-type mechanisms like vouchers for nursery education and learning credits for 16–19-year-olds and anxiety about the physical infrastructure and efficient use of space. And the prominence of education in local authority expenditure and employment, combined with the weak financial levers for controlling it because of the block grant system, gave a further off-centre tilt to Treasury consideration of the issues.

Partly for these reasons, the FER flagged education as an area in which the Treasury should develop a closer and more systematic interest. The Review suggested that it might even be one of those selected for the rare compliment of advocacy by spending teams of additional expenditure, in their proactive role. However, up to this point – at least until the merger with Employment – the department was still seen by the Treasury as being largely dominated by the professional lobbies and with extended lines of control – the large programme budget largely spent by local authorities, the bane of the Treasury's expenditure control life. Reforms to the education system in the late 1980s have largely changed this, with further and higher education removed from the orbit of local authorities and the power of LEAs further diminished by the institution of independent grant maintained schools and introduction of local self-management for others.

The old Employment Department brought a different culture to the merger, based on a different approach to management. Since the return of mass unemployment in the 1970s it had developed a reputation for innovation, designing a series of new programmes intended to deliver training and job creation – though these were not always quite as novel as their packaging might have suggested. For the Treasury, 'innovation' came to be seen as a matter of bouncing ministers into hasty anti-unemployment measures and creating an 'alphabet soup' of small overlapping programmes whose greatest impact was often the political credit gained by their introduction. There were disputed frontier areas with education, especially in the vigorously contested 16–19 age group and the general issue of the rationale for skills acquisition – packaged by the department as 'lifetime learning'. There were other overlaps with social security on support for the unemployed and the first experimental 'workfare' schemes which led to the merger of the DE's Unemployment Benefit into Jobseekers' Allowance. The department and its satellite agencies enjoyed a reputation for a 'can-do' approach, but also poor quality and cost control. As one DfEE official formerly in Employment put it: 'the former DfE has a reputation for being very cerebral, very bright, but slightly detached', whereas DE was a '"roll your sleeves up" department'. DE had a less than impressive reputation for financial management, but there was a sense that this had been 'sorted out' by its former Permanent Secretary, Nicholas Monck – previously Treasury Second Permanent Secretary on the public expenditure side.

The merger with education was often mooted, but when it came in July 1995 was a surprise to the Treasury who had reckoned that John Major was not in a good enough political state to dispense with a Cabinet post in this way. It was accomplished with considerable speed and left surprisingly little resentment behind it. As one Treasury official put it to us, 'when the departments merged they had to stop their turf wars which they did with remarkable speed and efficiency'. Senior management reviews had been completed separately in the two departments just at the point of merger and resulted in a total cut of 30 per cent in senior staff posts. It did not go unremarked that most of the senior officials in the new department, including the Permanent Secretary Michael Bichard, came from DE and that the organizational design seemed to be employment-orientated.

After the merger of the departments, the two Treasury teams were also merged at the end of the 1995 survey. As with the departments themselves, so in the Treasury the approach of the two teams had been rather different: the education team more relaxed than the employment one, where there were constant problems of cost control. An additional complication had been that local authority spending on education was previously handled by the Treasury's local government team. After 1995 that changed, but this added a further layer of complication to an already complex portfolio.

The new team, with the support of their deputy director, set out from the beginning to develop an independent role – indeed they had been able to inject some of their more pressing concerns into the process of amalgamation and had therefore been well positioned to raise issues and comment on the new set of operational objectives that were produced by the joint department in 1996 (this was described to us as 'pushing our supply side interests'). These interests went back to before the merger, when, in at least one official's view, the Treasury helped to provide the necessary linkages between programmes:

> There has been quite a lot of effort to map and analyse – sometimes with a hidden agenda and sometimes with an overt agenda – to rationalise, improve and systematise, with quite a lot of effort put in to tackling the 16 to 19 year group, in particular.

Nevertheless, the team noted that there were still many anomalies, both in philosophy and working practices. With a deputy director concentrating on 'cross-cutting' strategy (and for much of this period holding the troublesome 'social exclusion' brief) there was a need at team level to devote much time and energy to getting to grips with the detail of implementation. Going beyond the new merged department out to the numerous quangos and agencies, one official commented that 'there's scope for all sorts of things going wrong. We are putting a lot of onus on the department to control its satellites in whatever shape they may be'. Closer inspection of the 'real world' of education provided occasions for surprise and sometimes concern especially in the perceived persistence of anti-vocational attitudes among staff such as careers advisers who had been represented to the Treasury in advance as lacking bias between vocational and academic routes.

Some of the anomalies that the Treasury was trying to address from this official's aspect were procedural ('the inspection, the quality control, the assessment exercise were so different in different age groups, sectors and departmental traditions'). Others related directly to the Treasury's relationship with the department. This was partly a function of the different ways in which the two former departments' finances had been organized:

> Here is the old Education Department, huge programmes, masses of money but by and large not penny packet individual programmes. There were people in [the old Employment Department] worrying about minute sums of money going on small business training programmes which cost three or four million a year, and there was a whole mountain of people at Sheffield managing contracts with Career Service providers on a very detailed basis – and that was replicated to an extent within the Treasury.

On the PFI, the Treasury's longstanding interest and concern about educational maintenance and buildings found a new outlet, better understood, apparently, in the further education than the higher education sector. Again, questions arose about the micro-management of this by the Treasury: there were PFI experts around Great George Street but in a separate unit and not in the spending teams. PFI links in with the Treasury's wish to turn aside from the intractable world of educational delivery to the less controversial ground of building and maintenance with its respectable supply-side connotations. DfEE has seen an opportunity here, in the words of one of its officials, to persuade the Treasury that the country has 'hopelessly underinvested' in its educational infrastructure.

In sum, the approach of the Treasury team seemed to be based on a notion of defining priority areas within which the Treasury's supply-side brief could be promoted and pushing along the internal integration process as part of a general drive for a better co-ordinated approach to the Treasury's concerns, defined as addressing the supply side in a more coherent way than had been done before, enhancing the role of markets, seeking to break up some of the vested interests, and all under the rubric of the Treasury's own objectives.

Seen from the other side, this approach could be problematic. Although the Treasury had conveyed regret about the major row that had broken out in 1994 in which in retrospect the Education department had suffered quite unnecessarily and used the technique we described in Chapter 5 of coupling a change of personnel with a spirit of turning the page on the past, a degree of wariness was apparent in our interviews on the 'other side of the street'. This was reflected procedurally in the tight grip kept by the DfEE Finance Division on contacts with the Treasury. Here, it has attempted to act as a gatekeeper: as an official put it, 'information leaves the department in a controlled way' – to the point of causing some exasperation on the Treasury side:

the Finance Directorate wants to be the gatekeeper for everything and they get tremendously excited if we ring up people in the policy directorates without telling them, and even more excited when the policy directorate rings us up and then tells them. And as a result things have slowed down and there is a lot of sludge in the system.

Reciprocally, there were DfEE complaints about delays caused by overstretched junior staff in the Treasury team. But behind these rather formal and 'correct' exchanges a less formal style of interchange had developed. Although a concordat document was discussed when employment was still an independent department, it was not pursued after the merger. Strategy papers prepared in the Treasury were not initially shown to DfEE, though subsequently the Treasury team showed their statement of objectives to their opposite numbers. This judicious mixture of formality and occasional use of backchannels seems to have allowed a working relationship to develop that has space for the interests of both parties. The evident interest of both the team leader and the deputy director in promoting the wider economic and organizational aspects of finding means of promoting a Treasury agenda remained a potential source of difficulty, but the debate was a constructive one and laid the foundations of the close working relationship necessary when the Labour government came to launch its 'welfare-to-work' policies, initially conceived in the Treasury but largely implemented by DfEE.

The housing case

Housing is worth studying because of its loss of salience in recent years as a main area of social policy – a process in which Treasury pressure has played a part – and its fascinating quasi-market position in which public and private supply, government and individual responsibility, economic and social pressures, and cash and construction programmes, are finely balanced. This loss of salience and alternative status as a potential fall-guy for expenditure cutbacks has made the field, and those responsible for it in government, a main target for Treasury attention.

Housing had been the setting for a Conservative 'project' to privatize a whole sector of social policy. The 'right-to-buy' programme of 1979 was a great boost to owner-occupation. Much public rented housing remained, but this was eroded by transferring most public housing investment (and later the stock itself) to titularly private housing associations and denominating the result as 'social housing' not intended for mainstream occupants. Council rent subsidies were reduced, and by the 1990s there was a conscious policy of forcing large rent increases and picking up the bill for those not in work via Housing Benefit. By 1993, Chief Secretary Michael Portillo had, in the words of a DOE official, 'a vision of the housing market in which the public sector did not own or supply housing'. But the concept of the market is a problem – whether, in the same official's words, 'you can have an efficient market when you have a 100 per cent subsidy'.

From the Treasury's point of view, housing policy issues interact with organizational reputations. The Department of the Environment has been cast at the other end of the spectrum as the most unreconstructed of social policy departments, wedded to unrealistic and obsolete notions of housing the nation. In the words of one Treasury official in 1996,

> in one or two areas of the DOE thinking is, shall we say, a little bit old fashioned still; about let's say housing policy, some people at the DOE have long hoped that a Labour government would come in and we could go back to the good old days, and really they haven't really caught up with the reality even under a Labour government that money's going to be tight . . .

This general perception inform the Treasury view of DOE's handling of specific policies: 'dreadfully slow' on the Private Finance Initiative; on social housing

> they've now got some ideas which they're coming up with, but really, I mean, given the experience of the last three years of the survey you'd think they'd have talked about this some time ago and they hadn't, partly because I think they were still hopeful of a change of government and change of policy.

DOE did not accept that, but told us that 'we don't agree with them about the nature of the issues to be addressed'. Conservative environment ministers were rather weak, not matching the position of Labour's John Prescott in his enlarged Department of the Environment, Transport and the Regions. (Prescott's personal position and the configuration of the new department as 'speaking for England' make it a potential Keynesian rival of the Treasury.)

There do seem to have been particular structural problems in the setting of housing expenditure in the 1990s, stemming from lack of communication and a forced time-scale for the final settlement. DOE was resentful in 1995 when three days before the expenditure Cabinet their Secretary of State was forced to come back from a concert to take part in a meeting from 11.00 p.m. to 2.00 a.m. at which DOE were presented with a piece of paper from EDX with figures they did not recognize. What had happened is that savings that DOE had thought they had been allowed to keep from lower than expected inflation in council rent subsidies had been reduced – only to the tune of £30 million, but that had to be found elsewhere very fast. As a Treasury official who came on the scene later appraised it:

> one of the reasons for the public expenditure survey working badly in terms of relationships is not just the result but actually the way we conducted ourselves during the survey. It was quite extraordinary that essentially neither the DOE nor the Treasury actually talked to each other for about two months during that process, not one piece of paper was exchanged, not one telephone call, nothing . . . and then the DOE was given its settlement seven days before the Budget. That's just not the way to handle people.

Following through the dwellings-to-occupiers strategy has not been easy even after an intensive review of housing policy under the Portillo exercise, leading to a major White Paper in June 1995. By definition, it is a matter of burden-shifting from housing providers to income maintainers (tax and welfare agencies). Savings from this shift can accrue very quickly as grant levels are reduced and rents raised; costs run up cumulatively and are lost in other budgets, especially social security. Therefore the art is one of dispassionate policy analysis – simply put, of knowing when to stop. As one DOE official put it to us, 'raising rents was not the minimum public expenditure cost option'.

Matters improved after 1995 through more emollient Treasury personnel and an effort to separate policy discussions from disputes over numbers. The loss of the on-line grade 3 seemed to be a particular problem in this area. A 40-page concordat was torn up and a document of a couple of pages put in its place. Differences of philosophy remained, but the personal level worked better.

The processes through which policy is made in housing are often very complex, and the Treasury can get into quite precise deal-making on, for instance, the rate of Housing Association Grant (which has been reduced in recent years leaving private mortgage finance to fill the gap), the formula for setting rent rises in relation to earnings, and the targets for stock transfers from local authorities to private landlords. Debates over these figures are carried forward from round to round and end up as a haggle between numbers. But acquaintance with the sector shows the limits of 'simple-minded beliefs', as a Treasury official put it: '[I] find that every time I have any views the thing is so intricately, so inter-linked that it's very difficult to have a sensible view about anything without having a terrible knock-on effect.'

This sense of risking unpredictable or unintended consequences has put a brake on enthusiasm for some of these incremental policies towards the end of the Major government. The rate of Housing Association Grant was held at 58 per cent in both 1995–6 and 1996–7 before being lowered to 56 per cent in 1997–8. The guideline rent for local authority housing, related to average earnings, was to be held at 1995–6 level for the 1995 Survey period. The allowance for local authority management and maintenance had been cut in 1995, but in 1996 was secured in cash terms for the following two years. Stock transfers were made less of a Treasury grab by allowing local authorities in 1996 to spend 25 per cent of the proceeds (in line with the rules on the sale of council houses), and ending the former levy on transfer receipts for the next three years.

The Treasury sought advice on this from a panel of experts appointed in 1995, including Duncan MacLennan from Glasgow University. This parallels another group of experts on social policy more generally, including Howard Glennerster of the LSE. The activities of these groups have taken the form of reaction to Treasury papers and responses to requests for information rather than a proactive policy role. But they do show a greater interest in learning about the levers of policy in the housing system as a whole.

Housing has also started to use the 'challenge' concept – where local authorities and other funders are invited to bid for money for capital receipts on the basis of their innovative nature and ability to leverage-in private investment. Urban policy was merged into a 'Single Regeneration Budget' and stock transfers were financed on a comparable basis by means of the Estates Renewal Challenge Fund. The attraction of the challenge concept is that it gets resource allocation away from ideas of need or fair shares and promotes conformity with central government's approach.

Fundamentally, the Treasury view of a service is based on their degree of confidence in the spending department's handling of it at an intellectual as well as a practical level. DOE made great efforts to develop its economic analysis, using an ex-Treasury economist, in order to have a methodology available for proposing the optimal public expenditure solution on various time-frames. There was also debate about the need for social housing and on the cheapest cost of providing it in terms of build, rent or sell options. A DOE official told us that 'our whole purpose has been to get the Treasury to share the basic analytical foundations of our policy' and that this had developed in the 1990s.

One result of this approach was that the Treasury did come to recognize that aggressive cuts had their limits and eventually 'wheezes' the figures would have to be tried:

> I think there must come a point actually where you can't cut housing by much more, even if you have a very hard line right wing. . . . I think (we're) coming into a situation where, you know, if you cut much more you really are beginning to ruin the stock, so wheezes will be looked at, will be required.

This is a change of strategy in line with Heywood, but it has its limits. DOE saw a rare Treasury proposal for increased expenditure – on energy efficiency – as less a supply-side matter than a reaction to the imposition of VAT on domestic fuel. One DOE official even said that the Treasury had 'wimped out' on housing market reform under the constraint of the 'hard men of the GEP making the numbers add up'. We can identify here two themes evident in health and education as well – guardianship of the physical stock of the welfare state, for supply-side pro-investment reasons and as a means of long-term savings, and deference to the tyranny of the aggregate numbers. The themes have been carried forward into the period after the election of the Labour government.

Branch plants or political heavyweights?

In the areas discussed in this chapter there is clear evidence of the Treasury spending teams developing their strategic agenda and using the new working environment produced by the FERs to push it forward. Some of those in spending departments view this development with apprehension. They see the emerging strategic role as potentially disastrous, leading down the road to the danger of eventually becoming 'branch plants' of a Treasury as central policy-determining agency, already clearly signalled in the Heywood report. This might be understandable in the money-moving field of social security, but is seen as more dubious in complex areas of service

8

The Territorial Departments and the Detachment of the Treasury

There are good reasons for not neglecting the non-English parts of the United Kingdom in any discussion of British central government, but in the Treasury there is a more general analytical point that they illuminate. This we may call the concept of 'permissible detachment' – if expenditure is small and geographically distant the Treasury may be prepared to 'let go' to a greater extent than if the magnitudes were greater. Traditionally, the Treasury has been wary of automatic funding mechanisms that set up an institutional barrier to its scrutiny of departments. The biggest concession on this front – the aggregated defence budget which was basically a single line in public expenditure plans, and for much of the 1980s was reinforced by a Nato commitment to increase defence expenditure by 3 per cent a year in real terms – has been clawed back in recent years. But at a lower level of expenditure, the Treasury has an interest in shortening its lines of control. Confessions of factual ignorance about a service are seldom a motive for Treasury withdrawal, but a desire to reduce workloads can be. The process of local authority grant consolidation in the 1950s and 1960s was a policy of the Treasury rather than the spending departments.

Centralization and devolution in the Treasury

By definition, the Treasury represents centralization in British government. It also represents a Whitehall-centred mentality in which the active parts of jobs are constituted by the political agenda and economic aggregates of government. The Treasury epitomizes the phenomenon of brain power being applied to problems in the interior world of the office. In England, recruitment to the civil service in London can also represent a move from provincial origins into the heart of the action. In contrast, the civil service departments in Edinburgh, Cardiff and Belfast offer non-metropolitan career paths. Their norms remain closely aligned with those of the London civil service, but there is a contrast of perspective and usually a sense of national identity way beyond that found in the English regional offices of government.

Devolution in its various forms is a difficult issue for the Treasury to handle. The economic management of a unitary country implies in their view centralized control of public expenditure. Their whole mentality is inimical to the approach commonly found in federal systems where the overall public sector finances are a statistical afterthought to the taxing and spending decisions made at all levels of government. Any attractions of distancing themselves from decisions tend to be outweighed by the perceived disadvantages of loss of control. As we have seen, the Treasury is wary of precedent-setting or uncontrollable activity by smaller parts of the government machine. Devolution adds a further element of nationalist politics, in which politicians seek to outbid each other on the fiscal advantages of whatever constitutional option they prefer – as in the long-running debate between Labour and SNP about whether an independent Scotland's balance of government income and expenditure would be better or worse.

From the social policy viewpoint, devolution tends to create a field of action which is left once the security and economic management functions of government are reserved to the centre. Within the United Kingdom, social policy devolution is reinforced by distinctive policies and institutions. This is particularly true in Scotland, where the education system was a product of the ecclesiastical and local government structures preserved in the 1707 Act of Union.

The non-English nations have had two long-running themes in social policy which the Treasury have tolerated:

(i) a rather more generous resource transfer justified by relative need, especially in housing (through house-building and rent subsidies), education (the large university sector in Scotland being a case in point) and employment-related schemes;

(ii) a capacity for policy innovation, including the more comprehensive and earlier integration of social work in Scotland (taking in the Probation Service) and the unification of health and social work in Northern Ireland (later allowing the purchase of social work services by general practitioners and other NHS purchasers).

The Treasury has sensed that money may be flowing too freely through these channels, but ultimately the small size of the non-English parts of the United Kingdom makes it politically and financially cheap to defer to their presumed special circumstances. The local detail of social policy is seldom of interest to the spending controllers. Added to that is sometimes, as we saw in Chapter 2, a genuine admiration for the administrative processes in Scotland (though less often in Northern Ireland and Wales).

Therefore the Treasury's default position is not to get involved in too much detail on non-English social policy business. Provided that the control procedures are seen as sound (again a variable on which Scotland scores best) the policy has been allowed to diverge. Social security benefits are identical throughout the United Kingdom, and any differences in the relatively few other direct financial transfers have been manageable – variations in local authority rents was a long-running issue, and the higher rate of housing association grant and a divergence in student support arrangements are more recent examples. It is clear from the difficulties this latter issue caused in 1997–8 that the system could not bear too many cases of this kind. With the coming of the Northern Ireland Assembly, the Scottish Parliament and the National Assembly for Wales in 1999 the spending debate, and the Treasury's role in it, moved to a higher level of abstraction from detail.

Our research took place in the last years of the pre-devolutionary system, when some of the comfort of the old system was beginning to break down. Public debate was looking ever more critically at the fairness of the distribution, and the Treasury was beginning to reflect the 'English backlash'. The territorial departments were correspondingly defensive, but the technical debates were now somewhat ritualistic. The move to devolution signalled by the Labour victory of May 1997 opened up new possibilities for the national bureaucracies of the non-English nations and the likelihood that working relations with the Treasury would take on the aspect of diplomatic negotiation rather than civil service partnership.

Processes of territorial spending determination

A few authors have added to our knowledge of the way that territorial public expenditure is determined. Pre-eminent among them is David Heald, who has contributed numerous articles and monographs as well as influencing public debate as a special adviser to the House of Commons Scottish Affairs and Treasury Committees (see especially Heald, 1994). Thain and Wright's (1995) book has a detailed chapter (chapter 14) on the territorial departments. The Treasury itself has set the tone of the debate by its long-running statistical series on identifiable expenditure in the four nations of the United Kingdom, and latterly in the English regions as well (published in the annual *Public Expenditure: Statistical Analyses*) and its more recent calculations of government revenue and expenditure in Scotland ('GERS'). Figures for 1996–7 published on 16 November 1998 appeared to show a deficit of £3.5 billion (4 per cent of GDP) even if 90 per cent of oil revenues were notionally allocated to Scotland (Scottish Office, 1998). But the status of these data is disputed: they exclude allegedly non-attributable expenditure and are generally deployed as 'proof' of an 'advantage' to the non-English nations (Scottish Office, 1998). The Scottish National Party has repeatedly questioned the methodology of these indicators, but their effort has dragged the issue into a sometimes unproductive political debate. Two points stand out:

(i) it is very likely that Northern Ireland, Scotland and Wales (in that order) have a relatively more favourable balance of expenditure over income than any region of England;
(ii) the source of their expenditure advantage comes above all (now that direct public expenditure on housing has much declined) from rather higher expenditure on health and (except in Wales) education.

Within the Treasury, Scotland, Wales and Northern Ireland have always been considered together, sometimes alongside other functions such as culture, media and sport (the Heywood report, at the suggestion of the then-incumbent, proposed that it should become a part-time post). The extent of the previous knowledge of the territories held by the head of the team is a potentially sensitive point. The posts tend to be allocated for career management reasons, and in any case it is unlikely that any official would be equally familiar with Scotland, Wales and Northern Ireland. One former team leader spent most time on Northern Ireland and used expertise gained in former postings to take through particular issues, like privatization, in detail. New occupants are quickly educated into the problems of the departments through visits and meetings, but in any case what they are valued for is their knowledge of the Treasury and the spending process. The goal, as put to us by one respondent, is to ask 'can we arrive at a sort of accommodation which both sides feel they can deliver the minister on' (precisely a point made by Heclo and Wildavsky, 1974: 19).

One important distinction is that the Scottish and Welsh Offices (but not Northern Ireland) dealt direct with the functional Treasury teams on matters concerning health, education, industry and so on when such matters have to be referred to the Treasury because of their size or wider implications. These teams do seem to vary widely in their wish to intervene in detail and their preparedness to respect the special position of the territorial departments. These differences have much more to do with the history and personalities of the relationship with the English department than with any territorial variables. As a result, it has proved very difficult for the territorial team in the Treasury to negotiate with their colleagues a coherent set of delegations of expenditure authorities. A theme in our interviews was that the territorial team were reasonable 'front men' but that above and beyond them in the Treasury were officials making less helpful interventions. As well as the spending teams, there are numerous other Treasury officials dealing with civil service-wide management and accounting issues that will involve the territorial departments – a further compromise of any exclusive relationship with the territorial officials.

The Principal Finance Officers (PFOs) of the territorial departments have a special status because of the multi-functional nature of their tasks, which encompass the responsibilities of several Whitehall departments. Because the Scottish and Welsh Offices allocate their staff in a common personnel pool across all their services, their PFOs are even less likely than in Whitehall to have specific financial expertise. Northern Ireland has a separate civil service, and a Department of Finance and Personnel which plays a mini-Treasury role much more explicitly than do the finance divisions of the Scottish and Welsh Offices; it has a Principal Finance Officer (Stephen Quinn) and two supply divisions. Scottish Office Principal Finance Officers are part of a senior echelon of officials very largely Scottish by nationality and education and with experience of a range of functional areas: during our research they were Eileen Mackay and (from February 1996 to July 1998) John Graham. The latter's successor, Peter Collings, came from a more specialized background in the finance post in the National Health Service Management Executive for Scotland. The Welsh Office has tended to have more senior officials imported from London, including the Principal Finance Officer until 1997, Richard Wallace, who was succeeded by his former deputy David Richards. In one sense they are the traffic cops of the system, preparing documentation and isolating issues for decision; in another they are influential advisers to ministers and senior officials, and their personal values and sense of priorities are significant. The territorial PFOs also play an important part in the working of the expenditure system as a whole as they need to keep track of Whitehall negotiations across a wide range of services. As one said, 'we are a very valuable source of information ... the only time of the year when anyone asks our opinion'.

To the extent that in British public policy a more economically determined agenda is associated with England (coupled with dislike of the 'bleeding hearts' culture in the periphery) and a more socially driven one with the other nations, the territorial departments usually do not go all the way with the Treasury agenda on economic competitiveness and a restricted role for the public sector. But with the lack, pre-devolution, of a separate source of political legitimacy, the territorials have been bound by the structure and practices of United Kingdom government, including the authority of the Treasury. It is the latter set of considerations that determines the way that the Territorial PFOs have done their job.

The block/formula system

Scotland, Wales and Northern Ireland have a unique and in many ways curious system of expenditure allocation well described by Heald (1994) and by Thain and Wright (1995: ch. 14). It is neither a system of hypothecated revenues in which the yields from certain taxes flow to intermediate government, nor a system of needs determination in which funding is transferred in line with assessed need. Nor does it amount to a freezing of historical differentials, with comparable rates of growth throughout the United Kingdom. Rather, what we have is a system of a 'block' whose size is generated initially by the English equivalent expenditure, service-by-service, but moves according to a fixed ratio of changes in English expenditure. Once set, the Secretaries of State have, in theory, the freedom to move expenditure between categories without requiring Treasury approval.

Why has this happened? It reflects two imperatives: to contain the growth of expenditure, and to construct a semi-automatic mechanism that would allow for the exercise of discretion by the territorial departments without giving them access to more resources.

The idea of the 'block' was introduced in 1979–80 to simplify relations between the Treasury and the territories and manage debates about expenditure in the light of devolution (for which purpose it will be required for the first time in 2000–1). The 'block' is the total of expenditure within the ambit of the territorial secretaries of state which is held not to have wider United Kingdom implications and so is available for internal reallocation without detailed Treasury sanction. By defining a shadow 'block' of corresponding English (or for Northern Ireland corresponding British) expenditure, it is further possible to operate the 'formula' that keeps marginal changes aligned between nations and so avoids the need for continued discussion on changes in the size of the block.

The formula was given by David Heald the name of the 'Barnett formula' after the Chief Secretary of the time, Joel Barnett (though his personal hand in it has become embellished over the years along with the name; in evidence to the Treasury Committee in November 1997 he saw the main motivation for it as 'nothing whatsoever to do with devolution' but rather 'to make life a trifle easier and have to handle only English departments' (House of Commons Treasury Committee, 1997: Q1)). The Barnett formula has antecedents in other attempts to set Scottish expenditure semi-automatically, especially the Goschen formula of 1889.

The formula had a twofold purpose: to remove the need for politically contentious dispute about the size of the block, and to ensure that the territories would not automatically retain their existing shares of United Kingdom public spending. The device was to relate Scottish, Welsh and Northern Irish spending changes to their relative population shares rather than to the historical pattern of expenditure. This implied that over time the totality of territorial spending would move closer to the population ratio and away from the historic ratio, and by implication converge with English levels of expenditure. This was liable to be – and in fact became in the 1980s – a barely perceptible process that could even be put into reverse if English expenditure declined and so the cuts exported to the territories were moderated to their population share.

There was regular Treasury pressure to make the formula less generous, even before it had started and regularly thereafter. In 1992 it was modified to take account of the precise population ratios at the 1991 census (as adjusted by 1992 estimates). The effect was, for the Great Britain formula, to reduce from 11.76 to 10.66 per cent

Scotland's 'take' from any higher English expenditure, while increasing Wales's from 5.58 to 6.02 per cent (Heald, 1994: 148). The modification was a reminder of the formula's defensive status to a Scotland whose population has been falling relative to England (and to Wales) for many decades, and whose relative expenditure in social policy fields has long been higher. Whereas Scotland's economic and social problems did for long appear to be worse than England's, this is no longer the case after the recession of the late 1980s which hit England relatively hard.

In autumn 1997 the Treasury Select Committee chaired by Giles Radice launched an investigation of the Barnett formula (House of Commons Treasury Committee, 1997). The evidence of John Gieve, Mark Neale from the Treasury and the Scottish and Welsh PFOs on 13 November 1997 was to a great extent unrevealing, because the formula is so straightforward, allowing the Treasury to present it as it a simple non-political exercise, but it did reveal:

(i) the Treasury do not have the evidence of the relation between the Needs Assessment study and the Barnett formula (Q99 and 190);
(ii) it is not possible to generalize about whether in-year English increases are passed on to Scotland and Wales (Q102);
(iii) 'there are no current plans' for a new needs assessment exercise (Q117);
(iv) Barnett has 'a tendency towards convergence' under certain conditions (Q138);
(v) The Treasury and the other departments 'have not fully reworked the 1979 exercise to take account of social policy developments since then. The Treasury has tried to update the calculation but without arriving at a collectively agreed conclusion' (Q172 note by witness; perhaps the most revealing point in the evidence).

The size of the block is determined by a mechanical process of identifying comparable English expenditure. The block is an aggregation of hundreds of sub-programmes which are 'tagged' in a complex but generally technical and uncontroversial exercise as described by a Treasury official:

> in May, June time ... we write out to the territories and say that we are aware of the ... list of the changes in the way that English departments have regrouped their sub-programmes and so on. We set out our view about the precise composition of the

block in the light of that, and we invite their comments and . . . by the nature of that sort of technical exercise it normally takes two or three months to sort itself out. One doesn't come to blows over that kind of technicality.

The block's biggest practical effect is to claim the territories' share of any new money resulting from policy initiatives or increased allocations in England. The territorial Secretaries of State issue press releases taking credit for this money, but they are not in a position to argue for it on points of substance. In fact, they may be in less 'need' of it than are many parts of England, but do not have to face down any contrary arguments on detail. Criticisms of the formula are voiced in terms of generalized suggestions of unfairness which may in fact do the territories an injustice or deflect attention from the allocation process in England.

An important feature of the formula is that it does not apply to in-year increases. As John Graham of the Scottish Office explained to the Treasury Committee, 'we have no entitlement. If we think we have a good case for an increase to match an increase in England, clearly our Secretary of State is likely to make representations about that' (Q202). Sometimes 'uniform general adjustments' are applied directly to the territories, not necessarily to their disadvantage – as when Northern Ireland was given a share of welfare to work spending in line with its share of long-term unemployed, not population (annex 2, para. 14). What we can say is that any characterization of the formula as taking out the need for day-to-day traffic between the Treasury and the spending departments is misleading. There are enough cases requiring Treasury approval, Treasury initiatives on the management side, and political issues with expenditure implications to sustain a constant interaction.

These matters do not much concern bids for extra money, which are 'severely discouraged' as one PFO told us: 'the last time we made a bid outside the Block I can't remember'. They are more a matter of the Treasury's seeking room for manoeuvre by imposing rules which the formula was not designed to anticipate. Hence in 1997 they were able to promote their view that relief of the high level of local authority debt should be a first call on local authority funding even though in principle this should have been a matter for the Scottish Office.

The territorial departments are also not exempt from referrals of matters outside delegation limits; these are not logically connected

to the block at all. They are built in to practice (and often to legislation) and the Treasury may take the view that their analytical
capacity is not capable of sustaining as high a delegation level as
the English department; for instance on hospital building, the Department of Health (England) was, after a large increase in 1995,
delegated to approve projects up to £100 million, the Scottish Office
£50 million and the Welsh Office £35 million.

Political considerations also constrain the full flexibility of the
block. The Treasury faces bilateral or trilateral relationships between
the territorial departments: while these may be seen as rivals (and
in the words of one PFO 'the Treasury has in the past played off
one against the other'), in practice they work together to defend
the formula/block system, especially Scotland and Wales since industry expenditure was included within the block in 1993 and so
was no longer an area for competition in winning more money for
inward investment from the Treasury. The Welsh Office were pleased
with the widening, for the pragmatic reason that 'we took it into
the Block at a fairly high level . . . it didn't become a huge drain in
the Block as it might have done'.

But in the end the unitary political context of the United Kingdom has proved decisive. As a Treasury official told us, if a policy
difference 'potentially has repercussions either for another territory
or for England, then . . . that's something that one would expect
to be thrashed out in collective discussions beforehand'. The
key is a good continuing relationship with the Treasury at both
ministerial and official level. If that is there, the formula can
promote responsibility on both sides. As one Treasury official put
it, over the years

> the length of the arm got a bit longer for Scotland and Wales
> long ago, and that was . . . added to by the fact that, since the
> money had to come from the block, one could actually rely on
> the department, in its centre, to hold its own priority because it
> knew that . . . apart from being an escape path through which
> one would expect it to be used extremely sparingly . . . they ac-
> tually had to manage within a total they were aware of, so they
> would take . . . more care to do their own priority setting and
> rationing and would probably take better decisions if it were
> actually left to them.

The 'internal survey' in the territorial departments

The block/formula system requires an 'internal survey' in the territorial departments that mirrors the debates occurring in Whitehall as a whole – with the exception that the Secretaries of State take a personal lead in making the allocations which combines Prime Minister and Chancellor roles. With the Comprehensive Spending Review process of 1997–8, and the new devolution arrangements from 1999, much of what we observed about the allocation of expenditure within the territorial departments is of historic interest, but it does reveal the modes of accommodation to a block budget system which will be the post-devolution starting-point.

The territorial PFOs have a delicate relationship with their policy divisions, and especially so in the Scottish Office, which remains divided into sub-departments whose Secretaries separately account for expenditure as accounting officers. These Secretaries will expect to put up their own submissions for consideration by the Secretary of State, and would not consent to a heavy editorial hand from a PFO junior in rank. For this reason, the territorial PFOs are in a different position from the others. They must help ministers arbitrate between a wide range of policies but, as we have shown, they are not responsible for negotiating the amount of money available for allocation. As one PFO put it, in Whitehall, 'there is no rational way for a spending department to behave except by bidding for as much as possible', but in the territories 'the real difficulty operationally is getting a forecast of what is the likely outcome . . . part of the job is to manage expectations down . . . to provide headroom for the Secretary of State'.

Correspondingly, the block/formula system means that the internal allocation within the territorial departments is of subordinate interest to the Treasury, because changes do not call for any more money. Therefore the Finance Divisions do play a 'mini-Treasury' role in laying out options for the Secretary of State. As one PFO told us, 'we feel very much that we are the equivalent of the Treasury, but with a greater interest in value for money than they have': 'we ought to get away from the culture whereby finance people say to departments in the line, "Sorry, we have to put you through these hoops, it's all the awful Treasury"' – this was 'vastly counterproductive'. The approach in this PFO's case was 'I'd brief the Secretary of State saying "you might want to ask them X and Y"', a process which takes the job one stage towards a more analytical approach such as was meant to happen in the EDX committee (see chapter 3).

The block/formula system means that the timetable for the 'internal survey' is delayed by the need for information on corresponding English expenditure. Under the Conservatives, the 4–6 meetings at which the Secretary of State for Scotland allocated expenditure did not take place until November. The process started in July with the initial instructions of the Secretary of State, and departments submitted their appraisal of the effect of various spending outcomes by early September. But much of the exercise was speculative until the relevant English departments settle with the Treasury, a process of which the Scottish Office was a spectator (although a literal one, with a right to attend formal bilateral meetings). Until November, the form of a spending debate took place without any command over resources, but this could be very useful to the Finance Divisions in exploring the pressure points on expenditure.

In Wales, the process was more corporate because there is no tradition of functional departments within the office and only one Accounting Officer. 'The finance division controls the process much more than the Scottish Office', one of them told us, saying that 'we are a microcosm of the Treasury centre ... centres always get the blame'. Naturally, the finance division sees itself as an honest broker in charge of the process but not of the policy, but in organizational terms it is well-placed to have its way. The Division tried to have a series of bilaterals with policy groups in May or June, the so-called 'internal review' in the hope that 'very little ought to come as a surprise' and meet the Secretary of State in September or October. But as in Scotland the timetable meant that the 'illustrative settlement' based on English equivalents could not be prepared until November. The Secretary of State then saw the heads of each policy group for 30 minutes before final decisions are made; significantly, running costs are treated as a programme under the Principal Establishment Officer.

Northern Ireland bears the legacy of a previous devolved administration which replicated many of the patterns of Whitehall, including the distinction between the Treasury (the Ministry of Finance) and the spending departments. Now even more powerful as the Department of Finance and Personnel, it has guarded its own right to approve expenditure in the Northern Ireland departments without reference to the Treasury. It sees itself as 'a sort of Janus department', assuming a Treasury-like demeanour to Northern Ireland departments but a bidding mentality to Whitehall, aided by its understanding of the particular circumstances of Northern Ireland.

An institutional issue in Northern Ireland is the existence of the Northern Ireland Office, part of the United Kingdom Civil Service. This controls law and order and also serves as the principal source of policy advice to the Secretary of State. Law and order is, in the view of one official, 'a demand-led area that looks to Treasury in the first instance' even though it is in the Northern Ireland block. It is an area of tension but works because of the personalities involved and because the Treasury 'are happy to let us meddle' for cost control reasons; it is convenient to let the various parts of the Northern Ireland administration keep an eye on one another.

The Northern Ireland survey also reflected the lack of information on the overall UK resource position until October or November. Earlier in the year there was a 'redistribution process', guided by a 'broad steer' from ministers, in which departments are invited to help themselves; this also allows a check that what are offered up are indeed the lowest priorities. The main determination took the form of bilaterals in which one junior minister acts as a Minister of Finance and has small meetings on each policy area with colleagues. One departmental finance officer's view of the ministers' roles was that 'he says the words his officials give him and ours say the words we give them ... they don't have the ability to carry out an informed dialogue with each other ... the idea is to get the questions asked, the answers given and to move on'. The Policy Co-ordinating Committee of senior officials discusses DFP recommendations before they go to a final meeting with the Secretary of State 'at the very tail', by which time 'we may have carved out a small amount of money to let [the Secretary of State] make decisions'. Unlike Scottish and Welsh counterparts, the Secretary of State for Northern Ireland was not a major player in the detail of expenditure decisions.

The evidence on relative need

Lying behind all of these debates is the notion of need. The only time this was examined systematically in Whitehall was in 1977–9, when the 'Needs Assessment Exercise' brought together officials from the Treasury and the territorial departments for a fraught piece of Whitehall in-fighting. Disagreement on the methodology of the exercise was as important as disagreement on substance. The task was to assemble indicators that were a legitimate sign of need, and not just an expression of a volume of service associated with high expenditure. The report notes the lack of consensus on this, especially on the status of morbidity and sparsity indicators and the 'catch-up' requirements of poor housing and infrastructure, but ultimately this is not a matter that can be resolved by analysis. In a paragraph that gets to the heart of the 'needs' issue, it notes that

> in practice, the definitional distinction between 'objective' and 'subjective' factors is not of overriding importance. In the final analysis, a more useful division may be between the objective information which it is agreed to assemble and to present in a particular way and all other considerations. On this basis, the latter category of 'other considerations' might include not only the subjective, or arguably subjective, factors but also any feature of the collection of objective information which is unquantifiable or which it is considered, on reflection, is inadequately reflected in the proposed collection. (HM Treasury, 1979: para. 2.21)

It is sometimes overlooked that the territories 'escaped' from this exercise in tolerable shape: in the six programmes examined, the need for Scotland, Wales and Northern Ireland respectively was assessed as 16 per cent, 9 per cent and 31 per cent higher than England (1976–7) against the actual spending advantages of 22 per cent, 6 per cent and 35 per cent (ibid.: 6 and 45). The apparent evidence that Wales was getting less than its needs has continued to inform the Welsh Office's negotiating position: when their PFO gave evidence to MPs he started to quote from, and then left for inclusion in the evidence, a four-page memorandum of Wales's 'need to spend' on a range of indicators.

Relativities between the English regions were excluded from the exercise, but are central to the debate, because 'England' is seldom a salient unit for political or economic analysis. If some English regions stood out in the way that the territories do, then the problem would not be related to political structures. In fact, once data on identifiable spending in the English regions became available in the 1990s it became evident that Scotland, Wales and Northern Ireland ranked higher than any English region other than London with its special urban circumstances and high costs. Table 8.1 is compiled by welding together the data for 1995–6 for the four nations

Table 8.1 Spending per head on social policy by nation and region, 1995–6

Index: (UK = 100)	Total social	Social security	Health & pers social services	Education	Housing
Northern Ireland	118	114	112	129	186
Scotland	117	107	120	129	176
London	115	101	130	118	201
Wales	113	115	111	103	166
North East	110	114	113	98	79
North West	105	110	98	99	103
West Midlands	95	96	93	96	89
Yorkshire and Humberside	95	98	88	96	89
South West	91	96	92	86	31
East Midlands	90	91	88	91	83
East	89	90	86	98	71
South East	87	90	83	89	8
(UK average £	3084	1565	826	613	80)

Note: The 5 per cent of social spending in England which cannot be allocated between regions has been apportioned in the same ratio as that which can.

Source: Calculated from HM Treasury (1998c: tables 7.5b and 7.10).

and the English regions and assuming that English expenditure that cannot be allocated between region is distributed in the same way as that which can; this will not be wholly accurate but does allow a reasonable comparison with the four-nation data. We can observe the solid advantages to Scotland and Northern Ireland in education and to Scotland in health. The position of London is a reminder that the principal variable at work is the perpetuation of historical patterns.

The unallocated expenditure will have an effect on the validity of the figures, but no one is quite sure in what direction. As explained by Treasury statistician Allen Ritchie to MPs: 'It is not a case of us withholding information; we do not have it. This is unallocated because we have not been able to allocate it. It is certainly our ambition to allocate more of the spending.' (House of Commons Treasury Committee, 1997: Q145)

Numerous caveats apply to the figures, especially the differences in housing tenure which depress tax expenditures which are not attributed regionally, and the relative amount of private medical care. As with the Needs Assessment exercise, careful analysis is likely

relative to England were excessive and were such as to threaten targets set for public expenditure as part of the management of the UK economy, and the Scottish Parliament nevertheless chose not to exercise its powers, it would be open to the UK Government to take the excess into account in considering their level of support for expenditure in Scotland. (Scottish Office, 1997: para. 7.24)

This is a small genie let out of the bottle, as it shows the lack of a flexible response to the edging-up of self-financed expenditure: there could only be a set-piece confrontation. But others are capped: in particular the transfer of council tax benefit and Housing Benefit into the block so that increased council tax and rent levels will not be financed for those eligible for benefit out of non-block sources (ibid, para. 7.25) (housing benefit is already in the block for Wales).

The only possible 'legitimate' revenue enhancement is through the right of the Scottish Parliament (only) to varying the basic rate of income tax by half-point increments up to a maximum of 3 per cent. This was again a product of the Scottish Constitutional Convention and it required some very awkward drafting in section 76 of the Scotland Act 1998 to ensure that the value of this power would be preserved if there were ever structural changes in income tax; it is not a Treasury-friendly idea. It seems unlikely that the power will operate as a smooth incremental facility; if used it is likely to raise fundamental questions about the level of support for Scottish spending and remove restraints on Whitehall action, including any moves to a new Needs Assessment formula. Amid evidence that the convergence potential of the Barnett formula was taking effect in the late 1990s, the Scottish National Party took Labour's bait and went into the Scottish Parliament elections promising to reinstate Labour's 1p basic rate tax cut announced for April 2000 in the 1999 Budget.

As a follow-up to the White Papers, the Treasury went public on the principles and practicalities of the Blocks in the Darling memorandum of 8 December 1997 (HM Treasury News Release). There was one important change: from 1999–2000 the formula ratios were to be updated annually in accordance with the latest population estimates; the possibility is floated of using 'another formula' for council tax and housing benefit. The White Paper text on self-financed local authority expenditure is largely reproduced, though with a perhaps significant omission of the link to the non-use of capping powers and the caveat 'over a period and in such a way' to describe threatening growth. Other cited examples of cases where the Block would not operate are unexceptionable (the clawing-back of trading surpluses) but the spectre of a 'uniform general adjustment to public expenditure programmes' remained. The process of transparency of the rules was taken much further in a detailed Treasury statement of funding policy of March 1999 (HM Treasury, 1999d). This confirmed the effect of the declining Scottish population ratio (10.45 per cent in 1996, 10.39 per cent in 1997) and set out the mechanisms for resolving disputes.

After devolution, the immediate impact will be on the nature of relations in civil service terms. The danger for the devolved administrations is that, given the antipathy towards their case in parts of the Treasury, they will lose day-to-day influence in the operation of the policy and will simply be the recipients of bad news about their budget – like local authorities have been for many years. There is also a risk of loss of consultation on the calculation of English-equivalent expenditure in the block. Difference in party control between Westminster and the territories might mark the breakdown of the formula/block regime as it lost its status as a technical mechanism within a common political majority.

In terms of expenditure, the action is likely to involve attempts by the devolved administrations to escape the constraints of the assigned budget at the interface of devolved and non-devolved areas, especially in social policy (housing benefit, community care, higher education). Spillover into social security has been addressed in the Scotland Bill arrangements, but we can expect an exploration by the Executive of 'wheezes' in the areas of charging, write-off of debt, and public-private deals.

Wider implications of devolved budgeting

Our research on the territorial departments sought to establish how far they involved exceptional arrangements for anomalous cases, and how far they could serve as a model for a more detached approach to the affairs of other departments. Our first conclusion, reinforced by the Treasury committee report, is that the Barnett formula is an extremely rough-and-ready system which coped for a time with the dilemmas of territorial disparity, but did not solve – and was not meant to solve – the underlying issues of need and cost. It is an adjunct of English expenditure and relies on the fact that the latter is determined by political decision and is not an automatic flow: as one Treasury official said, 'the block only works because you have a comparator'. Similar difficulties can be observed in the 'real terms' commitment to health and defence under the Conservatives. The department claims the formula as a right, but eventually the Treasury becomes unhappy with the lack of substance in the spending negotiations. No formula can be negotiated precisely enough to cope with evolving circumstances, and over time the lack of a full debate on spending detail becomes unacceptable. Game-playing and tactical awareness between the Treasury and the spenders are fraught enough anyway, without introducing intellectual dances on the pinheads of formulas that were not designed to bear them.

The consolidation of some of Whitehall's English regional offices (especially Environment and Trade and Industry) into 'Government Offices for the Regions', joined by Regional Development Agencies in 1999, has implications for territorial budgeting. The development of 'challenge funding' (allocation of funds on the basis of competitive detailed bids by local authorities) has tended to decentralize the appraisal of projects. One PFO said 'you could envisage a model in which more and more of these decisions were shifted to regional offices so they eventually became rather like the Scottish Office – and then became subject to calls for local democratization'. But this devolution is not consistent. In health, as we saw in Chapter 7, the tendency has been to centralize administration, and recent trends in public management have made it harder to define a set of functions for a putative tier of English regional government. What is likely is that more attention will have to be given by the Treasury to English regional issues, but as a political exercise rather than as a technical search for an 'English Barnett'.

The other angle is the Treasury's letting go of small spending items – a matter of *de minimis* magnitudes rather than the principles of control. The Treasury has been notoriously reluctant to abandon its rights of control simply on account of the small magnitudes of sums involved. It has done so rather more in the territories than for other departments, but it has not altered the concept of Treasury approval of, in the government accounting phrase, 'novel and contentious' items. The most interesting case is Northern Ireland, where the Department of Finance and Personnel acts as a sub-contracted Treasury with its own departments to supervise. In turn, the Northern Ireland departments have had some protection from interference even when the Treasury has registered concern (as on some spending on training programmes). The same sort of practice is likely to develop in post-devolution Wales and Scotland, with the new channel of accountability protecting the Treasury from accusations of indifference or of not standing up for the taxpayer. We have the same approach in vestigial form in England, where over the years sensitivity about quangos seems to have subsided. But in general devolution will reinforce the divide in practice between England and the other nations.

Devolution throws into relief the accusation that the Treasury is ignorant of non-metropolitan detail and circumstances – or even colonial and anti-democratic. We may ask how far the Treasury is a product of the unitary United Kingdom and as such is an obsolescent institution (especially as both the European and the regional tier are strengthened). As part of the 'get out of the office' syndrome, we detected an interest in learning about local circumstances and social policy delivery (with, for instance, the health team visiting Northern Ireland and the education one Scotland although neither had any major responsibilities there). The difficulty is that of maintaining the Treasury's famed grasp of detail over a geographical span. Present practice is a fusion of three 'imperial' traditions: the ability to monitor circumstances from a distance by correspondence; the notion of the grand tour of the provinces; and the ability to get an accurate bearing through brief personal observation. The Treasury has seen no need for any regional offices at all, and plays no part in the Government Offices for the Regions in England. Unless the Treasury is careful, its unitariness may become part of the critique against it by territorial interests in Whitehall, now institutionalized in the Department of the Environment, Transport and the Regions.

In the end, technical systemization cannot be the answer to any qualitative defects in the system, which depends on personal relations between officials. Given the political stakes involved, it is not possible to 'chill out' problems by arithmetic or procedures. As John Gieve of the Treasury told MPs,

> you can collect an awful lot of data about numbers, ages and so on and so forth and conditions, but at the end of the day it is a matter of political judgment. Balancing those many factors must be a matter of political judgment. (House of Commons Treasury Committee, 1997: Q134)

A strong feature of the British system is that all parts of government, including the territorial departments, have been bound by both the same culture and by tight administrative rules enforced by the Treasury. This has applied even to the Northern Ireland Civil Service, separate in a way that the Scottish and Welsh administrations will not be. Techniques of parliamentary accountability were supplemented by the annual public expenditure procedure within government, and recently by the enforcement of managerial processes and Treasury-driven objectives. Whatever the fissile elements in the United Kingdom, its unique pattern of autonomy in some fields, especially civil society, but centralization in the operation of the political economy remained the rule. It is this uniformity that may be called into question after devolution.

9
The Treasury in Labour's First Year

We traced in Chapter 4 the way that the Fundamental Expenditure Review, and later the 'Kids' Paper' asserted the legitimacy of the Treasury's overall role in policy-making across government in all issues that affect the operation of the economy. As one public expression of this process, the Treasury started to publish its aims, mission and objectives in its annual report. These definitions were first worked out under the Conservatives; but they left no doubt that the Treasury has views of its own which go beyond pursuing the economic policy of the government of the day (Figure 9.1). The Labour Treasury team modified the Conservative objectives underlying the operation of the FER system – employment opportunities are in, promoting the efficiency of markets is out, and the statement is more concise – but the view of the world they embody shows a consistency of outlook in a recognizable line of direct descent from one administration to the next.

The Conservative objectives were not so much a party political statement as the Treasury's expression of what they took to be a consensus, capable of surviving a change of government, on the market-based nature of the economy. The fact that without fundamental adaptation they could be made compatible with Labour's policies was the outcome of a process of policy review that began in Opposition, when Labour fundamentally reappraised its approach to the economy and public spending.

The party's summary 1997 manifesto objectives (Labour Party, 1997: 4), showed a concordance of language and approach with the Treasury's: 'we will provide stable economic growth with low inflation, and promote dynamic and competitive business and industry at home and abroad'. This is flanked by 'we will help build

Figure 9.1   Treasury objectives relevant to public expenditure

---

1997 (Conservative – Kenneth Clarke)

Aim: to promote rising prosperity based on sustained economic growth

Objectives for expenditure:
> *maintain a stable macroeconomic environment by*
> delivering permanently low inflation;
> maintaining sound public finances;
> keeping public expenditure to a level that is affordable
> pursuing tax policies which generate sufficient revenue, while

doing the least damage to the economy and encouraging enterprise
> *strengthen the long-term performance of the economy and*
> *the outlook for jobs, in strategic partnership with others, by*

promoting policies and public expenditure priorities which improve
the use of resources and the efficiency of markets throughout the
economy, within an affordable level of total public expenditure

maintaining a financial control system which delivers continuing
improvement in the efficiency of government

maintaining a framework for government accounting which makes
clear how resources are used and provides effective accountability to
Parliament

promoting greater use of private finance in support of services
currently provide by the public sector and the privatization of those parts
of the private sector which do not need to remain in public ownership

---

1998 (Labour – Gordon Brown)

Aim: to raise the rate of sustainable growth, and achieve rising
prosperity, through creating economic and employment opportunities for all

Objectives for expenditure: achieve long-term stability by maintaining
sound public finances and open, accountable and effective arrangements
for delivering price stability

set levels of public expenditure which can be financed by a fair
and efficient tax system that promotes incentives to work, save and
invest

secure high quality, cost-effective public services which deliver
expenditure priorities and policies, including partnership between the
public and private sectors

Source: HM Treasury (1997b chart 1A; 1998d chart 1A).

strong families and strong communities, and lay the foundations
of a modern welfare state in pensions and community care', but
the spending pledges imply redistribution rather than increase: 'we
will increase the share of national income spent on education as
we decrease it on the bills of economic and social failure' and, for
the NHS, 'reducing spending on administration and increasing spending on patient care'. Leaving to one side the implicit conceptualization
of social security as 'the bills of economic and social failure' (a

very Treasury-friendly idea), we can note a tone which implied a radical departure from the party's traditional distrust of a heavy-handed, unreasonable Treasury. How had this change come about?

Labour's Treasury past

A long-standing Treasury theme of rational choice politics suggested that new governments could not enter office without making spending pledges which would then be promoted by both departmental ministers and their civil servants. Of Labour's pre-1964 Chancellors, two (Philip Snowden and Stafford Cripps) were austere figures who fitted easily into the mould of the Treasury. Of the others, Hugh Dalton was too constrained by the world economic context in the immediate post-war period and Hugh Gaitskell was in office too short a time to make much of a difference. But in 1964 Labour, too, under a rather tentative Chancellor, James Callaghan, without economic experience and outflanked by a flamboyant rival in George Brown's Department of Economic Affairs, started to conform to the Treasury's pessimistic model of political behaviour, previously associated with Conservative governments.

The Labour governments of both 1964 (as we documented in Chapter 2) and 1974 suffered similar experiences – initial manifesto-driven plans (especially in respect of pensions and housing) pursued for two painful years before financial orthodoxy was reasserted. The 1964 Labour government, recaptured vividly in Alec Cairncross's Treasury diaries (Cairncross, 1997) was the final flourish of the attempt to manage the economy and manipulate domestic demand by levers in a context of fixed exchange rates and vulnerability to balance of payments crises. As we noted in Chapter 2, in 1974 the Treasury and its ministers became detached from the rest of the government but eventually prevailed in 1976. The latter periods of both governments were in fact the most successful recent periods of containing public expenditure in real terms. The post-devaluation squeeze of 1968, managed by Roy Jenkins, and the cash limits of 1976, overachieved their purpose and left the overall record of the governments on public spending as an uncomfortable roller-coaster. As a result, in the Labour Party, Treasury 'capture' became a possibility to be feared – and to be planned against by working out a left-wing economic strategy while in opposition. This line of thought was dominant in the party for most of the 1980s, so it was an important change of course when, under Tony Blair and his shadow

Chancellor Gordon Brown, the Labour leadership seemed to be drawing upon the same kind of analysis about the position of the public sector that had informed the Treasury in the FER.

Here we must address the role of personality in the performance of Labour's Treasury. Edmund Dell and Roy Jenkins, in their slightly overlapping accounts of 'The Chancellors' (1996 and 1998) emphasize the unpredictability of the conjunction of personality and circumstance in this office. Nor has the Chancellorship been a frequent stepping-stone to party leadership: in recent years incumbents have tended to be political heavyweights, but their reputations have usually not been enhanced in the office. All of this context casts its shadow on Gordon Brown, Labour's Treasury chief since 1992.

Gordon Brown's progress

Despite two recent biographies (Routledge, 1998; Pym and Kochan, 1998), Brown remains an enigmatic and even secretive figure. In a formal sense he is among the best-trained of Chancellors (in politics and economics at Edinburgh University, with a doctorate), but his career has been in the presentational side of politics, with his major non-political job in television journalism. Working his way up in student politics and the Labour Party in the 1970s and 1980s, Brown had to tack to the left, of which process there are traces like his statement in 1983 (in a collection edited with Robin Cook, a team unlikely to re-form) that 'the first prerequisite for eradicating poverty is the redistribution of income and wealth from rich to poor' (Brown in Brown and Cook (eds), 1983: 20). Later, as a protégé of John Smith, Labour's leader from 1992 to 1994, Brown shared the collectivist philosophy of the Labour movement's Scottish base, which had some modernizing elements but was sensitive to trades union concerns and to the traditions of the party.

From the policy point of view, Brown's concern is located in the political economy – the translation of economics into real-world outcomes, especially the improvement of employability through education and training. The needs of the teenage unemployed unite most characteristically Brown's concerns and explain why this area was chosen for study while in opposition. This concerns also explains Brown's personal wish, trailed in the 1997 manifesto, to withdraw universal child benefit for over-16s in favour of targeted help for those who would make best use of it. Brown has also seemed to be more realistic than some about the position of families on benefit, their income needs and the disincentives to move from benefit into work. All of this concern has produced an interest in the possibility of a Treasury-driven social policy, using especially its fiscal instruments, unusual in recent Chancellors.

From the process point of view, Brown has introduced something new among British politicians who are not party leaders – a small-scale personal entourage of a chief of staff and chief policy adviser (Ed Balls, a former financial journalist), a younger researcher (Ed Miliband, brother of Tony Blair's policy chief David, again a pair of young achievers from the left-wing intellectual milieu) and a hardened media manipulator (Charlie Whelan, from a smoke-filled room trades union background, whose style lost Tony Blair's patience and prompted his departure in early 1999). This team was assembled in opposition and featured in the pair of television documentaries filmed by Scottish Television before and after the 1997 election and transmitted in October 1997. Not surprisingly, Tony Blair features little in these films, but there is also a curiously subdued role for Brown himself – seeking advice on 'the line' and tactics but generally passive as he seeks to manoeuvre past potential traps in the party and the media. The prime objective in his tactics seems to be surprise and ground-gaining, with the entourage used as advance guards in the manner of American presidential politicians.

The Treasury's Permanent Secretary, Terry Burns, reported in his account of the transition to Labour in 1997 that most of his pre-election meetings were with Ed Balls rather than Brown himself (Burns, 1997). After the election, officials often found their main channel of briefing to be to Balls rather than the Chancellor – not necessarily unfruitful, since Balls has both economic ability and political awareness, but not the Whitehall style. A further problem was Brown's habit of working on decisions in private settings, typically involving Paymaster-General Geoffrey Robinson, a rare example of a Labour politician with experience of business deals who was forced to depart in late 1998. All this contributed later to a Treasury unease, expressed most eloquently not in disloyal gossip but in praise for the 'correct' working style of Chief Secretary Alistair Darling.

As with all recent Chancellors, the cornerstone of Brown's position is his relation with the Prime Minister. Ever since 1994 the suspicion had lingered that Brown still saw himself as superior in intellect, experience and Labour credentials to Blair and was not reconciled to being overtaken by his once-close younger colleague. The publication of Paul Routledge's semi-authorized biography in January 1998 gave fresh impetus to these suggestions. In both public statements and in the reported frequency of private meetings, Blair's praise for his 'Iron Chancellor' and deference to his economic judgment was clear. But Brown's dislike of committees and preference for unminuted one-to-one meetings with Blair has always put a premium on the resilience of their personal friendship and mutual respect. Brown's instinct has been to position himself as an available, left-wing, authentically Labour contrast to Blair, but the Treasury brief, whether in government or opposition, is not the easiest base for this.

The provenance of the 'tax and spend' pledge

We can now trace how these characteristics of Brown's style and approach have worked themselves out in opposition and into government. All Treasury ministerial teams conduct a wary battle with their spending department colleagues. What is remarkable is the way that Gordon Brown started his while in opposition. In a speech in April 1996 he announced that

> my Treasury colleague Andrew Smith [then Shadow Chief Secretary] has written to Shadow Cabinet members to say there will be across the board efficiency reviews on public spending.
>
> So the same discipline will be applied to all departments as applied to our post-16 review: meeting our objectives by securing the best value for money within existing resources, and we will do so by laying down rules, promoting value for money and cost effectiveness.
>
> We must identify benefits to front line service delivery from re-ordering our priorities and making savings from any waste.
>
> First a strengthened programme review will be built into the public spending process so that waste and inefficiency in existing public spending is stamped out. (Brown, 1996: 4)

In autumn 1996 Alistair Darling (an able Edinburgh advocate with a cool style, who successfully retained equidistant respect from Blair and Brown) became shadow Chief Secretary and Labour prepared its manifesto position on taxation and spending. To the 'reordering of priorities' theme was now added the attempt to gain leverage for Labour's Treasury team by declining to put into play any review of some important parts of Conservative strategy.

Labour's election mantra was that it had no uncosted expenditure commitments and was approaching these matters from a businesslike rather than political perspective. As the manifesto put it:

> New Labour will be wise spenders, not big spenders. We will work in partnership with the private sector to achieve our goals. We will ask about public spending the first question that a manager in any company would ask – can existing resources be used more effectively to meet our priorities? And because efficiency and value for money are central, ministers will be required to save before they spend. Save to invest is our approach, not tax and spend. (Labour Party, 1997: 12)

The seven 'economic pledges that follow are: fair taxes; no risks with inflation; strict rules for government borrowing ('over the economic cycle' not borrowing to fund current expenditure and maintaining a 'stable and prudent' level of public debt); stick to planned public spending allocations for the first two years of office; switch spending from economic failure to investment (by spending reviews); tax reform to promote saving and investment; a 'welfare-to-work' Budget within two months after the election (it was actually a day late). These are cautious approaches but they did leave some room for manoeuvre. What was not flexible was the acceptance of Conservative departmental plans until 1999, and the provenance of this pledge reveals much about the approach of the Labour Treasury.

A pre-election statement on taxation was inevitable. While there had been some interest in raising the top rate to 50 per cent, the announcement by Gordon Brown on 20 January 1997 that the rates would not be increased during the first Labour term was in line with the worldwide downward pressure on headline income tax rates, and left vast scope for revenue enhancement through indirect taxes and removal of tax reliefs. What was surprising was the decision to accept Conservative spending plans by department as well as in aggregate and for 1998–9 as well as 1997–8. The wording bears reproduction in full:

> our first budget will not reopen spending allocations for the 1997–98 financial year. These are figures upon which departments are

already planning, and should continue to plan . . . each departmental minister will want to use their first year to work out
with their departments and permanent secretaries how they can
overhaul existing spending so that, within already announced
departmental budgets, spending is reordered to meet Labour's
priorities in the 1998–99 financial year.

So, instead of departments spending the first year of a Labour
government debating how to spend more money, they will use
their time examining how they can reorder existing budgets to
meet our priorities. (Brown, 1997: 7–8)

This approach had the effect of neutralizing policies made across
the government as a whole and turning the expenditure task in-
wards towards departments and their presumed own resources. Brown
later went further in an interview with John Lloyd:

People haven't grasped the importance of what we've been saying. In effect, we'll abolish the public spending round this year
and next. If we come in May, the April–April commitments have
already been made; next year I will be asking my cabinet colleagues to do the most rigorous review of the assets their
department have instead of the usual bidding. That's the context in which privatisation is not ruled out; it's getting the best
value for money. (*Financial Times*, 12 April 1997, p. 9)

Therefore the primary intention of Brown's strategy may be seen
as not so much to stick to Conservative plans, but to find some
device for neutralizing the natural tendencies of any new left-of-
centre government to use public expenditure in pursuit of its
objectives. It was like the closing down of a biological system, and
was subject to the same strains.

The inheritance: the context of public finances

On coming into office, Labour inherited a drought in the midst of
plenty – a basically favourable economic climate but a Conservative proposition (held but not usually implemented during their 18
years of government) that the public sector should not encroach
any further on the economy. This posed two control problems: that
an 'overachieved' control of expenditure would cause government
social policy to contract as a share of the economy, especially dur-

Table 9.1   Social policy expenditure as % of GDP

	1978–9	1995–6	1996–7	1997–8 (estimate)
Social security	10.0	13.1	12.9	12.4
Health	4.6	5.5	5.4	5.3
Education	5.4	5.0	4.9	4.6
Housing	2.6	0.7	0.5	0.4

Source: HM Treasury (1997a: table 1.4) and HM Treasury (1998c: table 3.4).

Table 9.2   Additions to the Control Total in the present and upcoming year in 1995–6

Additional expenditure in £ million and as % of previously announced departmental control total

		Conservative		
	Nov. 95	Nov. 95	Nov. 96	Nov. 96
	on 1995–6	on 1996–7		on 1997–8
Social security	+1 160	+1 040	+570	+600
	(+1.6)	(+1.4)	(+0.7)	(+0.8)
Education and Employment	−10	−430	+250	−1 020
	(−0.1)	(−3.1)	(+1.7)	(−7.3)
Health	0	+120	+130	+470
		(+0.4)	(+0.4)	(+1.4)

Source: HM Treasury (1997c: table 6.6).

ing times of rapid private sector economic growth; and that poor forecasting or political changes would undermine the stability of plans and require injections of funds, sometimes at the last minute, in response to unanticipated changes. Tables 9.1 and 9.2 illustrate the effect of these variables across the change of government.

Table 9.1 shows how a squeeze relative to the economy has borne most heavily on education and health. By the mid-1990s they were falling as a share of GDP, and education had suffered a long-run decline in share. Labour's manifesto said that 'over the course of a five-year Parliament, as we cut the costs of economic and social failure, we will raise the proportion of national income spent on education', a more expensive pledge than the one to 'raise spending on the NHS in real terms every year' (Labour Party, 1997: 9 and 21). In contrast, social security had shown strong underlying growth which with the impact of the recession had taken it from

10.2 per cent in 1990–1 to 13.1 per cent in 1995–96. However, the economic recovery and changed policies had started to reduce this share even before Labour took office; and Table 9.1 shows the perceptible fall in shares of GDP from the effect of tight inherited plans and a healthy economy in the first year of the Labour government.

Table 9.2 shows how often health and social security had received an injection of funds during or just before financial years, and how in contrast education was often the target for cuts under the Conservatives. Social security needed injections because of consistent underestimates in the cost of benefits on unchanged policies. This led to the 'autumn surprises' we mentioned in Chapter 6, in which the Treasury was confronted by the Department of Social Security very late in the Public Expenditure Survey process with the need to find additional money. As we discuss later, with an improving economy and more cautious forecasting, the 1997–8 plans proved resilient and eventually too pessimistic. Given the magnitudes involved, this has been the main source of the room the Chancellor has had to direct more resources into health and education. We trace later how Gordon Brown in several steps supplemented social expenditure, even within his self-imposed constraint, and was able especially to concentrate the additions on health and education. In the process, he has illustrated the way that the Treasury can concede flexibility where this is opportune – and especially in favourable economic circumstances. Small cyclical swings in the social security budget can either force painful cuts or permit useful increases in the smaller health and education budgets. This phenomenon lies behind the conceptualization of social security as a 'problem' which derived from experience in the later Conservative years and lies behind much of Labour's Treasury thinking.

Labour's initial impact and the July 1997 Budget

For his first months, Brown's style swept all before it. The Labour Treasury made a dramatic start when on 6 May it transferred power to set base interest rates to a new monetary policy committee of the Bank of England. Then on 22 May it announced the transfer of the Bank of England's role on financial services supervision to an enlarged version of the former Securities and Investments Board. These decisions had no direct bearing on public spending, but they did reveal a strategic vision of the place of a modern finance ministry, inspired by American and German models, where the central

will in effect subsidize or displace existing jobs have been understood since the 1970s and also creates a risk of an imbalance, with
funds being released fairly freely for 'welfare-to-work' but constrained
tightly elsewhere in the public finances. A further embarrassment
is the rapid fall in youth unemployment, which made the ratio of
the £700 million budgeted for this in 1998–9 against the £100 million
for the older long-term unemployed look misplaced (this imbalance was partly corrected in the 1998 Budget, as the figures in
brackets show).

The notion of 'funded from the windfall tax', as a justification
for exemption from the rigours of the spending regime, turned out
to be somewhat cosmetic. It was just another tax (£2.6 billion in
each of 1997–8 and 1998–9) and when defined with legally secure
detail proved to be a general tax on privatized firms rather than an
expression of monopoly or windfall status. Moreover, the tax was
used not just to fund welfare to work but also the so-called New
Deal for Schools, an extra £300 million a year of schools capital
expenditure designed to correct the chronic lack of funding for
this in the normal education budget. The March 1998 Budget further broadened the New Deal 'brand' into deals for partners and
communities. What is significant is that 'welfare-to-work' spending
financed by the windfall was not counted in the Control total (nor
was local authority housing spending under the capital receipts
initiative). This enabled the Treasury to avoid embodying 'welfare-
to-work' as a normal part of departmental entitlements to public
expenditure, and to retain it through to 2001–2 as a separate item
available at its own discretion.

The Government had to deal with a so-called 'Lilley overhang' –
various social security proposals built into the spending plans for
1998–9 but not yet fully implemented. After much interdepartmental debate the Treasury won a clear victory on these points.
The one major reversal, as a result of intense concern by many
ministers, was of the proposed extension from age 25 to 59 of only
paying shared accommodation rates to single persons on Housing
Benefit. Familiar stratagems were used to finance this: higher de-
ductions for non-dependant residents in the dwelling, reducing the
backdating time limit for claims for Housing Benefit and Council
Tax Benefit from three months to one month, and accelerating Social
Fund loan recoveries. But some important Conservative proposals
were accepted, especially the withdrawal of the lone parent premium in Income Support from April 1998 (already done by regulation)

and the lone parent rate of Child Benefit (requiring legislation to take effect from June 1998). The Government's Social Security Advisory Committee expressed many reservations on this latter policy (Social Security Advisory Commitee, 1997) and the need to get it through the House of Commons was later to provide a focus for the doubts of some Labour MPs about the social policy strategy of the Government.

Underlying the Budget was a fairly optimistic picture of the public finances which confirmed that the hard-to-forecast variable is income, not expenditure. The pursuit of fiscal stability was facilitated by a more rapid contraction of the deficit than had seemed likely before. The control total for 1996–7 came out at £260.4 billion, £0.2 billion less than forecast in the November Budget, and receipts were £286.3 billion against a forecast of £280.9 billion (by March 1998 these were further improved to £259.8 billion and £286.4 billion). The income tax yield was £76.5 billion against the £71.8 billion forecast, showing how buoyant it can be when the economy is doing well.

The turnaround by March 1998 was even more marked. The estimated Control Total for 1997–8 (£264.1 billion) was £1.7 billion down from the pre-Budget estimate and cyclical social security (£13.0 billion) was £0.9 billion down (HM Treasury, 1998a: table B11). Public expenditure had already fallen to under 40 per cent of GDP by 1997–8 (table B24) and was set to remain there through to 2002–03 (table B12). With such favourable aggregates – and social expenditure falling as a share of national income (Table 9.1) – Gordon Brown was in a position to be generous and creative in his development of policy.

The Pre-Budget statement of November 1997

The strategy of not having a spending round created a data gap. Because the 1997 Budget did not alter departmental control totals, they were implicitly read over from the 1996 Clarke Budget: the Red Book did not publish departmental totals at all, nor did it update the estimate of the plans in real terms. Moreover, Brown abolished not just the 1997 spending round but also the 1997 unified Budget, replacing it by a return to a spring Budget on 17 March 1998. Instead, he produced a version of the Autumn Statement on 25 November a 'Green Budget' (akin to the consultative 'Green Paper' but officially called the 'Pre-Budget Statement') designed to serve as a consultation document. On 10 December (apparently reluctantly, and in a written Parliamentary answer), updated estimates of expenditure by department in current prices and in real terms, were published and even they were altered by Budget time.

The Pre-budget statement continued Brown's penchant for launching low-cost social policy, notably a plan for a national network of out-of-school child care clubs financed partly from the National Lottery, and trailed Brown's idea of a working families' tax credit to reduce the economic disincentive of taking on work. Two departures from spending plans occurred at this time, cosmetically financed by savings from non-welfare areas. On 14 October money from defence and the nuclear industry was used to provide £300 million of extra health spending in 1997–8 (the first breach in the resilience of 1997–8 spending plans in order to avoid a 'winter crisis' in the NHS); and on 25 November in the pre-budget statement an extra £190 million in both 1997–8 and 1998–9 was produced to provide pensioner households with extra money (intended, but not mandated, for fuel bills) through savings in net contributions to the European Union. This latter was a Brown surprise that breached arrangements for implementing benefit changes which had been agreed between the Treasury and the DSS. Brown's caution on spending was emphasized when he launched a consultation exercise on a 'Code of Fiscal Stability' designed to take a perspective over the whole economic cycle, and later published with the March Budget.

The March 1998 Budget and the use of fiscal instruments

By 1998 the Chancellor was able to begin promoting his own social policy objectives, using the Treasury's fiscal instruments and its unique ability to innovate over the whole range of policy and drawing upon outside economic advice. The Budget drew upon a task force exercise on work incentives and taxation set up under the (then) Barclays Bank chief executive Martin Taylor (HM Treasury, 1998b). This was the main exhibit in a series of 'business friendly' initiatives, including changes in the rules on national insurance contributions (burdensome to firms with highly-paid staff but generally a convenience and a downward pressure on wages – and notable for the way that the Treasury let the Taylor group fix tax policy), the transfer of the Contributions Agency to the Inland Revenue, and in the lack of compulsion to extend occupational welfare, especially pensions.

The main policy innovation in the Budget was a shift of resources into families with children, especially working families, at a cost of over £2.5 billion a year when fully implemented in 2000–01. £1.35 billion was for the new Working Families Tax Credit and £1.22 billion for a so-called child support package (HM Treasury, 1998a: table C1). The Working Families Tax Credit, a tax expenditure replacing Family Credit from 2000, was a more generous benefit than many of the initiatives of recent years, because of the level of the credit and the low (by social security standards) taper of withdrawal as income rises (55 per cent above £90 a week). The package was set to reduce income tax receipts by about £5 billion, offset by the more than £3.5 billion saved by the ending of Family Credit (HM Treasury, 1998a: para. 3.36). The child support package included a rise in Child Benefit, further boasted for Income Support recipients, that rectified much of the losses to lone parents by the 1997 changes, but on a basis of parity of treatment of parental structures. The relief to the Treasury of a long lead-time on the announcements, now an increasingly common Budget ploy, was that the Child Benefit increase would not come into effect until April 1999. There was a further boost of £500 million to health and £250 million to education in 1998.

The Working Families Tax Credit was Brown's declaration that the Treasury, not the Department of Social Security, was the politically acceptable source of income transfers to those on the margins of work and poverty. In the process, some inefficiencies were built in: the Social Security Committee criticized it (House of Commons Social Security Committee, 1998) and as Frank Field pointed out after his resignation it spreads work disincentive more widely if less deeply throughout the lower-paid workforce. But the political advantage to the Treasury within Whitehall was clear, and there was an institutional reinforcement as well in the secretariat to the working groups which bcame the 'Work Incentives and Poverty Analysis Unit', a strikingly activist title which expressed the Treasury's immersion in both strategy and detail on these issues. By March 1999 Brown was happy to launch from the Treasury a detailed study of the extent of poverty and inequality and use it to justify the government's 'welfare-to-work' strategy as the most effective policy response (HM Treasury, 1999b).

Table 9.4 Labour supplementation of Conservative plans, 1997–9

£ million (% change)	Jul. 97 on 1998–9	Nov. 97 on 1997–8	Nov. 97 on 1998–9	Mar. 98 on 1998–9
Social security	0	+190	+190 (+0.2)	+330 (+0.4)
Education and employment	+835 (+6.0)	0	0	+210 (+1.5)
Health	+1000 (+2.8)	+268 (+0.8)	0	+417 (+1.2)

Note: Excludes new expenditure for 1998–9 outside the Control Total (see Table 9.2).

Sources: HM Treasury (1997c: table 6.6); HM Treasury (1998a: ch. 5); departmental press releases 2 July 1997, 14 October 1997 and 17 March 1998 (education and health England only; Labour 'headline' UK increases education £1 billion and £0.25 billion, health £1.2 billion, £0.3 billion and £0.5 billion).

Brown's injections of social policy funds

Gordon Brown's strategic victory in 1997–8 was to gain credit and leverage from his respect for Conservative spending plans, while supplementing them on his own terms when he saw fit. Nearing the end of the two 'no-change' years, we can compare Labour with Conservative plans for the main areas of social spending. Table 9.4 shows the scale of the three boosts to social spending in the two Budgets and the pre-Budget announcement. Table 9.5 shows the relationship between Labour's plans and the ones they inherited.

The most striking fact in the Control Totals is Labour's shift of spending from 1997–8 to 1998–9: a shortfall in the former year was applied to the latter, accommodating some significant additional social spending, especially in health. Even after the 1998–9 financial year began, a further £750 million was shifted into the control total because of a shortfall in 1997–8 expenditure (HM Treasury, 1998f: table 3A.1). The control total for 1997–8 was planned to be £265.6 billion as late as March 1998, fell to £262.3 billion in the June 1998 estimate, but by March 1999 ended up at £263.2 billion (Table 9.5). Various fancy pieces of Treasury footwork seemed to be at work here, to the despair of commentators seeking to interpret the statistics.

Social security, coming out under target in 1997–8 on both cyclical and non-cyclical elements, for a long time seemed to require more on 1998–9 because of higher inflation, but in the event that

Table 9.5   Conservative and Labour spending plans, 1997–2000

£ million Con March 97/**Lab Jun 98**	1997–8	1998–9	1999–00
Education & Employment	13 876	13 945	13 977
	13 892	**13 072**	
		14 170	**15 470**
Health	34 938	35 372	36 113
	35 291	**37 170**	**40 230**
Social security (DSS total)	79 843	83 100	86 350
	79 223	**83 621**	
		98 330	**103 830**
CONTROL TOTAL	266 500	273 700	280 900
	262 635	**274 900**	
MANAGED TOTAL		**333 600**	**351 600**
Social Policy Expenditure outside the Control Total:			
Cyclical social security	14 100	14 300	14 700
	12 800	**13 000**	
welfare-to-work (incl childcare)	0	0	
	100	**890)**	
		)	**1 330**
'New Deal for Schools'	0	0)	
	100	**300**	

Note:
i) education and health England only. The final row for each service gives figures on a comparable basis for 1998–9 and 1999–2000 from the Comprehensive Spending Reviews. Previously notified figures for 1998–9 (in the row above) have been affected by a 'reprofiling of student loan debt sales' (Department for Education and Employment) and the now-widened scope of the total and its social security element. Managed total for 1999–00 includes £1,330m welfare to work/New Deal money;
ii) later estimates for the outturn on the control total were given in the 1999 'Red Book' – education and employment 1997–8 14 290, 1998–9 14 360; health 1997–8 35 320, 1998–9 37 640; social security 1997–8 79 230, 1998–9 81 740; control total 1997–8 263 200, 1998–9 273 400.

Sources: HM Treasury, 1997a: table 1.2; 1998a: table B18, 1998c: tables 1.1 and 1.2, 1998f: table 1, 1998g: tables 1 and 2; 1999a: table B19.

year too fell beneath the Conservative plans. The education line is an artefact of transfers between headings and of receipts; the notional education standard spending assessment was to rise from £18370 million in 1997–8 to £19 380 million in 1998–9 (HM Treasury, 1998a: table B18) in line with the £1 billion provided in the 1997 Budget. On top of all this was the expenditure financed from the windfall tax, and local authority spending on building and repairing of housing of funded from capital receipts.

Expenditure strategy under Labour revealed a familiar Treasury combination of incremental adjustment to circumstances and a 'smoke-and-mirrors' effort on some of the figures. What should be observed is the inconsistency between this flexibility and the rhetoric of rigidity and toughness which has informed the Labour Treasury approach. This approach was built on assumptions about the right level of the public sector in the economy and of transfers from government in household incomes which had informed the Treasury's strategic thinking throughout the 1990s.

Much of what was done in Labour's first year in office was presented as a prelude to the Comprehensive Spending Review (CSR) exercise. In theory, this was to produce an authentically new set of plans derived from a sense of Labour's own priorities. Before it, there would be no spending round, no departure from Conservative plans (except where conceded by the Chancellor), public spending falling to under 40 per cent of GDP, no argument in the ministerial public expenditure committee, and a demarcation of spending on 'New Deal' Labour policies from those that were inherited. Afterwards, there was to be a zero-based reconstruction of public expenditure on Labour principles based on full spending reviews and Cabinet discussion and constrained only by a commitment to a low public sector deficit and no increases in income tax rates. Managing this process depended on a successful 'end-game' of the comprehensive spending reviews, which reached a climax in July 1998 and was intended to settle the main issues on expenditure for the rest of the Parliament. We trace in Chapter 10 how the motif of comprehensive review was played out through the CSRs, and also through Frank Field's attempt at a reappraisal of welfare as the Minister of State for Welfare Reform.

10
Spending Reviews, Fiscal Strategies and the Treasury in Labour's Core Executive

As we have seen, the concept of a 'strong Treasury' can be seen as shorthand for approaches at ministerial and official level which go much wider than the Treasury itself and permeate government as a whole. A strong Treasury in this sense – not just a strong Chancellor – was therefore a necessary condition if Labour wished to combine tight overall control of public expenditure with changed priorities and getting more out of available resources. In order to translate the priorities as summarized in the manifesto fully into action on expenditure, it is essential to find a tool-kit that will work. The stratagems used in Labour's first year produced some success; but the need remained for a longer-term approach which would provide stability for at least one parliament.

The Comprehensive Spending Reviews

Labour's Comprehensive Spending Reviews (CSRs) were a continuation of the well-established Treasury technique of fundamental review to gain leverage over policy and provide long-term stability in overall objectives. They can also be seen – in a narrower view – as a repetition of the Treasury's itch to expose what is still seen, despite the drive to improve relations, as the complacent and self-interested approach of spending departments. The previous major episode of this kind, the Portillo FERs from 1993 and the associated senior management reviews, let the Treasury into policy debate within departments, sitting on working parties and scrutinizing trends. Yet despite the subsequent move towards a more collegial style of working and in some cases the identification of robust common objectives, it is evident from the interviews reported in our central chapters that mutual suspicion had not entirely dissipated.

It is difficult to see how the identification of issues and spending demands could have been much different under Labour, even if the conclusions drawn might be. The Labour approach was a rather naive echo of the 1970s approach of zero-based budgeting, in which spending plans are built up in line with objectives, rather than as adjustment to the inherited pattern that has developed. The 1997 *Financial Statement and Budget Report* stated what the reviews were meant to achieve, but gave little credit to the difficulties of these exercises:

> departments will examine their objectives, and each item of spending with a view to setting new plans for 1999–2000 and beyond. The review will explicitly look to the medium term. Each department will set out clear objectives which they will have examined to ensure that they contribute to the top level objectives of the new government and complement the objectives of other departments. Each department will examine every item of their expenditure from a zero base, to ensure that each item is necessary for the achievement of the Government's objectives and is being spent in the most efficient way possible. (HM Treasury, 1997c: para. 1.62)

There were also to be 'a number of cross-departmental reviews' (including one on young people steered by the Treasury under the personal interest of deputy spending director Norman Glass) and finally 'an examination of the allocation of resources across government as a whole, leading to a complete set of new departmental spending plans from 1999–2000 onwards'. Alistair Darling in his statement of 11 June 1997 ruled out straightforward publication of them – 'the fruits of the reviews will be announced in different ways and at different times' (House of Commons Hansard, vol. 295 col. 1147). When the terms of reference of the reviews were announced on 24 June 1997 they were not to a consistent format – there was a mention of a zero-based approach in some but not all, some quotes from the Labour manifesto (as in health), much mention of government priorities but few giving many clues about how these would be analysed into reality (housing perhaps being the best of the bunch on this). The idea of single output document and a common structure came later.

The push for welfare reform

Frank Field's appointment as Minister of State for Welfare Reform was highly significant since his knowledge of the field and the sense of a non-partisan imagination at work, which he had displayed as chairman of the House of Commons Social Security Committee, had made him a figure to be taken very seriously. As we have already seen (Chapter 6), key officials in the Treasury were among his admirers. Field, unlike his Secretary of State Harriet Harman, was put on the Cabinet expenditure committee (PX, formerly EDX), the first non-Cabinet minister to be a member. The expectation was that Field would produce the blueprint for the whole welfare reform process, not merely in social security but extending across the whole range of all the activities of government.

But Field's capacity to determine events was fatally limited. From the outset, he did not have the support for which he asked: the welfare reform unit established to provide a departmental basis for his work functioned in isolation. His authority within the department was undermined by the decision to run his exercise alongside the CSR for the DSS and another review of pensions chaired by DSS junior minister John Denham. Outside the department, his ability to impose a new pattern on other social policy departments came into question, despite the Prime Minister's initial strong personal support for Field's assigned task of 'thinking the unthinkable'. And the Chancellor's own lack of enthusiasm for the project was palpable.

Events in autumn 1997 showed the political risks of making policy through a multitude of overlapping reviews. In an initiative coinciding with the Labour Party conference, 54 social policy professors including one of the present authors wrote to the *Financial Times* to criticize the Government for setting up a dichotomy between 'welfare-to-work' and redistribution of income through social security (1 October 1997). This put into play a discussion which flared up in December 1997 because of the conjunction of two events. The interim conclusions of the CSR on social security were being produced, but with the involvement of departments like Education, Environment and Health, which had a self-interested opposition to cuts in the social security budget, they tended to leak. Furthermore, the vote to restrict lone-parent premiums was imminent, and the government declined to compromise (partly because the parallel changes in Income Support which in fact attracted more criticism were already legislated and under way).

On 8 December, a memo leaked to *The Times* was alleged to give the fullest picture yet of Treasury ideas: flat-rate housing benefit, taxed or means-tested child and disability benefits, the inverse relation of pensions to national insurance records, and the privatization of industrial injuries insurance. This overshadowed the launch of the new Social Exclusion Unit on the same day. On 10 December, 47 Labour MPs voted against the government and welfare reform moved to the top of the political agenda.

On 21 December a letter from David Blunkett to colleagues was published in full in the *Sunday Telegraph* and revealed Blunkett's reservations about some of the ideas emanating from the sickness and disability steering group of the CSR, including reducing the value of Disability Living Allowance and Incapacity Benefit.

Meanwhile Field had produced a draft of his Green Paper on welfare reform but the evident political sensitivity of the subject meant that it was drawn into the Downing Street machine and publication was postponed. Instead, Tony Blair himself took a position of leadership on welfare in order to further emphasize the magnitude of the policy decisions the government was hoping to take. In December 1997 Blair decided to form and chair a new ministerial committee on welfare, on which Field sat; but the Chancellor's attitude seemed to remain unenthusiastic. In January 1998 welfare roadshows were started (the first one by the Prime Minister himself to Labour members in Dudley), supported by DSS 'focus files' covered by a 'case for welfare reform'. With the aid of extensive press coverage, public opinion was being softened up, but the political outcome remained problematic.

Frank Field's Green Paper finally emerged on 26 March 1998 (Department of Social Security, 1998a), but its impact had already been substantially diminished by the policy changes just announced in Gordon Brown's Budget earlier the same month. Although the Green Paper boasted a preface by the Prime Minister which surveyed the whole terrain of welfare, the actual content was surprisingly thin. Although lengthy, it contained little that was new; rather, the emphasis was on moral exhortation, historical discussion and a largely theoretical list of criteria for evaluating the benefits of welfare policies. There was little policy content beyond that already contained in the Budget, and some cautious drafting that barely alluded to the discussions of late 1997, let alone face the issues raised then head-on. Where the possibility of new policy directions was raised – compulsory saving for second pensions, the relating of Housing Benefit to housing policy, a new work criteria for incapacity benefit claimants, a new gateway to disability benefits, and a reform of the Child Support Agency – the difficult decisions were left to be taken later.

The whole episode illustrated the difficulty of making fundamental policy shifts on issues affecting Whitehall as a whole from a location outside the Treasury, without the explicit and sustained support of No. 10. The main personal casualties were the Secretary of State for Social Security, Harriet Harman and Field himself, who both departed from office after the July 1998 reshuffle – Field voluntarily, after his bid for the top job had failed (in his interpretation as a direct result of Brown's hostility).

The political end-game on the Comprehensive Spending Reviews

Just as Gordon Brown had been able to present a Treasury-based solution to 'reform of welfare' policy dilemmas in his March 1998 Budget, he was able to conclude the CSRs in a presentationally successful way. This was done by 'bouncing' an announcement of the outcome in two stages. On 11 June, the day of his speech at the Mansion House, Brown announced to the House of Commons a medium-term framework for expenditure, the Economic and Fiscal Strategy (HM Treasury, 1998e). He confirmed that the annual spending round had gone, and that departmental totals would be fixed for three years. He continued the fiscal stability themes of not borrowing to finance current spending and of running surpluses at some stages of the economic cycle in order to reduce the burden of debt interest. He then announced that public spending was to allowed to grow on the high side (up to 2.75 per cent a year in real terms). This allowed a spin to the media that the apparent rigour of Brown's approach was concealing a significant rise in spending on public services (*Financial Times*, 12 June 1998). In fact, the containment of expenditure at around 40 per cent of GDP was confirmed and the relaxation was only by comparison with previous plans.

The most plausible interpretation of the new framework is as an attempt to unpack the aggregate of spending, previously an icon of control, into its components in three ways:

(i) *cyclical and non-cyclical expenditure*: this distinction had been attempted to rather small practical effect in the case of social security, but the Labour Treasury promoted it in an attempt to explain why it was not using the favourable state of the public finances to spend money on public services. The response was that at the present stage of the economic cycle it was necessary to run surpluses. This well-worn reasoning was also used to explain that Britain could not yet join the single European currency as her economy was out of synchronization with the rest of Western Europe. In the June 1998 statement, the cyclical argument underpins the distinction between services which are to have a three-year budget and those (especially social security) that are to be managed annually. This attempt to single out the normal from the exceptional is a rationalist approach that lay behind PESC but has not proved robust in practice;

(ii) *capital and current expenditure*: Brown's decision that all departments were to have distinct capital budgets was the most explicit acceptance yet by the Treasury that recent budgetary approaches had failed to take full account of long-term returns from capital spending and so are biased in favour of current. This has been coupled by a growing Treasury awareness of the negative effects of past failures to replenish the capital stock of the public services. The progress of Treasury thinking on this matter had been facilitated by the Private Finance Initiative, now embraced enthusiastically by Labour (under the guise of 'getting it to work'). The PFI requires a talking-up of the attractions of projects in order to induce private participation and also leaves in its wake some projects which for social and political reasons have to be financed in the conventional way. The result is a more positive atmosphere for public sector investment that goes some way to redressing the evident imbalance with the private sector that had grown up in recent years;

(iii) *resources and cash*: after some initial doubts, Labour endorsed the resource budgeting and resource accounting proposals that are to come into effect in 2000 (see Chapter 3). It was not certain even to those most closely associated with the project whether politicians could be persuaded to adopt the new format as the basis of their deliberations, but at least it introduces a new, and in principle technically preferable, analytical approach. More realistically, it will replace the old cosmetic devices for dressing-up the figures with new ones associated with private sector results and balance-sheets. Since these devices often serve to flatter performance and to conceal the cost implications of what has been done, they may be helpful to a positive presentation of public expenditure.

The conceptual basis of public expenditure is now presented as 'fairness between generations'. This principle implies that 'those generations that benefit from public spending should also meet the cost' (HM Treasury, 1998e: para. 3.2.3). The Economic and Fiscal Strategy relates this to the 'golden rule' that 'over the economic cycle the Government will borrow only to invest and not to fund current spending'. This rule is in fact neither golden nor axiomatic, but it is used to solve the problem that 'in the past, governments set limits for total spending without distinguishing between current and capital spending. This led to bias against investment, which often constituted an easier (though short-term) target for spending cuts' (ibid.: para. 3.2.1).

The Government left itself room to back away from the full rigours of its approach. The Strategy recognized that 'some aspects of current expenditure may also transfer the fiscal burden in ways that can not easily be quantified; long-term fiscal projections still under development will take account of demographic change; and 'generational accounts' which roll forward each generation's prospective tax and benefit position for the rest of their lives are to be calculated (ibid.: para. 3.2.3). Through these devices the social spending departments were given a foothold for a less schematic approach in different political circumstances.

The June 1998 strategy marks a break with the idea of 'cash is cash' dominant since the 1980s, in the same way that PESC tried to do in the 1960s. The question is whether the system will survive the strains on it any better than PESC did. The introduction of cash limits in 1976 was similar to an emergency control on a firm with a sudden cash-flow crisis but a sound underlying position. Brown the rationalist was happy with the necessity for, and even socialist credentials of, the new framework he had set up, but doubt remained on whether it could survive economic difficulties that might bring into play another set of Treasury tools.

The outcome of the Comprehensive Spending Reviews

The report on the CSR eventually published on 14 July (HM Treasury, 1998g) is a thin document which reports what the Government has done rather than setting out analytically how it made its choices. Entitled 'Modern Public Services for Britain: investing in reform', it presents a picture of 'prudence with a purpose', ensuring greater stability in the public finances but permitting significant investment in reform, with an emphasis on those areas where the government has made manifesto commitments, principally education and health. This is presented as an increase over the three year period in education of 5.1 per cent and in health of 4.1 per cent, compared with an increase of only 1.8 per cent in other services (HM Treasury, 1998g: chart 1).

As usual, the move to a new system is an opportunity for statistical confusion, and many of the data in the CSR report are not directly comparable with previous plans, especially in social security (ibid.: table 2). 'Total managed expenditure' is very close to general government expenditure and is broader than the control total; the implications is that no expenditure is to be left unmanaged, whether on an annual or triennial basis. Table 10.1 shows the pronounced jump in expenditure between 1998–9 and 1999–2000 as Labour's own plans supersede the Conservative hangover. Real increases are not confined to Labour's priority areas, and the expectations for social security again look optimistic even though they are held down by the hiding of Working Families Tax Credit as a tax expenditure. Contrary to scenarios suggested in Brown's two Budgets, spending plans again floated above the level of 40 per cent of GDP.

The CSRs as they emerged fell short of the 'big bang' zero-based reconstruction of public expenditure on Labour principles based on full spending reviews and Cabinet discussion and constrained only by a commitment to a low public sector deficit and no increases in income tax rates. In fact, the outcome was much closer to the traditional public expenditure survey system's compromise between incremental and zero-based budgeting which was realistic about the unpredictability of events, Cabinet politics and the limitations of budgeting on a multi-year basis. In particular, it represented a clearer victory for the proponents of real growth in Labour's priority areas than had seemed likely when the exercise was launched.

Going into 1999, the Chancellor's line was that the CSR figures would be able to withstand the downturn in economic growth facing the British economy during the year. Brown's Pre-Budget Statement was brought forward to 3 November in order to present a rosy picture of growth still exceeding 1 per cent. CSR plans remained intact, but an overall budget surplus was predicted to be only a one-year phenomenon of 1998–9. It emerged that yet again net expenditure room could be declared in the form of higher revenues and lower expenditure than previously estimated for 1998–9. Social

The two policy announcements were incorporated in a Welfare Reform and Pensions Bill introduced in February 1999, with personal media contributions by the Prime Minister using 'toughness' rhetoric. The idea of the single work-focused gateway to benefit was reinforced in the presentation of the bill, and speculation that the gateway interviews would lead eventually to an extension of the number of benefit recipients required to seek work was not discouraged. Alistair Darling's term of office as Secretary of State for Social Security was showing striking evidence of convergence with his Conservative predecessor Peter Lilley in his further reinforcement there of the Treasury orthodoxy of means-testing and targeting.

The Public Service Agreements: contracts reappear

As part of its agreement to a three-year expenditure framework, the Treasury set up the notion of contracts with departments – the 'Public Service Agreements' – to specify their objectives and how they were to be achieved, in the light of manifesto priorities and other statements. These were published in December 1998, and monitored by a Cabinet Performance Review committee (PSX) chaired by the Chancellor. This committee is to be serviced by the Treasury and by a Performance and Innovation Unit in the Cabinet Office, headed by former Treasury official Suma Chakrabarti, one of the rising stars in our narrative (see Chapter 5). We can see these agreements as a fusion of two traditions:

(i) the performance review motif promoted by Blair's No. 10, in which the service of the manifesto becomes a means of breaking down departmental interests and the newly identified pathology of 'departmentalitis';
(ii) the contract/codification motif as first set out in the FER to express the Treasury's preparedness to devolve control if stated terms are observed by the spending department, but not otherwise; the personal link here is Jeremy Heywood, since 1997 in the No. 10 Private Office.

The text of the Agreements (HM Treasury, 1998h) suffers from the same problem as much of 'new Labour speak' – it conflates statements of what has been done, aspirations, performance indicators, and tests of whether the government has succeeded in its first term.

The Treasury's 33 performance targets (ibid.: 114–16) are an impressive statement of its broad concern about social and economic policy, but they are compromised by the use of phrases like 'continue to develop' and 'put in place policies'. One of the most explicit social policy targets, to 'reduce the number of households facing marginal deduction rates over 70 per cent by 2001–2' is a modest statement of a policy direction already addressed in more ambitious detail by the Working Families Tax Credit. The DSS's PSA was only an interim one with a concentration on administrative processes rather than outcomes. When the full agreement was published in March 1999 (HM Treasury, 1999c), it did get some way into targets which mixed policy rules and their economic and social context, such as reducing the number of lone parents dependant on Income Support by 10 per cent by 2002. The Department of Health, building on its earlier clinical and management work, was a pioneer in this area and its PSA offered the clearest output-based targets of operational value.

The spending control aspects of the PSAs are limited, the White Paper stating that 'should a target not be met there is no question of money being deducted from the budget for that department. Nor will additional funding over and above that already allocated be made available simply because a department is failing to meet its targets, but support and advice will be given by the [Cabinet] committee' (ibid.: 2). The phrase 'no question' is a striking example of a phrase usually associated with the Treasury, the department whose business is to say no, being turned against it. With some equivocal language on the status of the targets – they are intended to be met, but they are stretching, and progress towards them will vary – the White Paper defers much of the action on the use of the PSAs. It provides a framework for the continuing debate between the Treasury and the spending departments, but does not determine the outcome.

Central mechanisms for developing social policy

The CSRs had also represented an opportunity for the Treasury to become directly involved in making social policy through taking responsibility for the cross-departmental aspect of some of the reviews on the Criminal Justice System and Provision for Young Children. The latter, known as 'Sure Start', was led in an open and informal style by Deputy Director Norman Glass, and took the

Treasury to the centre of social policy innovation. Presentation of the programme has been coy about the Treasury role – the ministerial lead was from health, and the budget and staffing is based in education – but 'Sure Start' undoubtedly represents a prototype of Treasury social policy: the identification of a cross-cutting issue based on research evidence; its conceptualization as a 'brand' under which a number of policies can be promoted; the 'ownership' of this brand by the Chancellor (as in the Sure Start Maternity Grant announced in the 1999 Budget); and the identification of new money that is not held under normal departmental arrangements.

One subject to which the Treasury had initially laid claim was social exclusion (in contrast to its lack of interest in joint approaches to social policy pursued by the Central Policy Review Staff in the 1970s). This perplexing issue had been the focus of an earlier attempt to co-ordinate approaches throughout Whitehall, through discussion at Permanent Secretary level. The topic had then become the responsibility of a Treasury spending directorate task force (also chaired by Norman Glass), which formally listed social exclusion as a cross-cutting issue that it was monitoring. It might therefore appear that the creation of the Social Exclusion Unit in December 1997 in the Cabinet Office reporting direct to the Prime Minister was a loss of turf by the Treasury.

However, the Unit as established was very small (about 12 people including secondments from outside Whitehall), it was given no budget and it was placed under a former Treasury official, Moira Wallace, who had initially moved to the Private Office at Downing Street. In a speech to the Social Policy Association in July 1998 she emphasized that the Treasury still paid her (and fed her in its canteen).

The Unit initially concentrated on individual items of educational, criminal and housing policy, not high-spending programmes like social security. It identified the lack of 'joined-up solutions to joined-up problems' and 'initiativitis' in social policy. These were limited exercises, based on exhortation, not expenditure, without much impact outside the specialized policy areas concerned. However, the Unit was responsible for something of a policy coup in September 1998, when its work on poor housing estates and neighbourhoods initiated an action programme, sponsored personally by the Prime Minister.

The new funding for this programme had been foreshadowed in the CSRs (HM Treasury, 1998g: para. 3.26) and involves £800 million of money branded as a 'New Deal for Communities' and announced by Gordon Brown in his July statement (although not financed from the windfall tax). Procedures for allocation of these funds to a limited number of pilot areas will be based on a re-formed Single Regeneration Budget approach operated on the 'challenge' principle which informs so much of present-day spatial resource allocation. The real innovation consists not of this pro-gramme but rather in the declared intention to develop a comprehen-sive approach to the regeneration of all such areas, based on a programme of work by 18 task forces chaired by junior ministers, with interlocking briefs co-ordinated by the Unit itself to demanding timetables.

John Prescott, the Deputy Prime Minister, was put in charge of this initiative; natural enough in view of his departmental respon-sibilities, but also an expression of prime ministerial confidence in someone other than the Chancellor. In practice, though, the Trea-sury is a major player in the exercise. It is represented on ten of the 18 cross-departmental teams and chairs two of them (through the Financial Secretary). As an initiative across government, the social exclusion approach raises the same questions about institu-tional checks to the Treasury, as do the performance review mechanisms. Is Treasury power still driving the system, or has its institutional position in the core executive been compromised under Labour – despite Gordon Brown's personal primacy over economic policy?

The Brown Chancellorship: an interim assessment

Gordon Brown is the first Chancellor since Lawson to have a clear sense of a wider role for the Treasury in setting priorities for the government as a whole. His first Budget had as its centrepiece the ambitious 'welfare-to-work' proposal, presented by the Treasury under the rubric of 'modernising the welfare state'. As a friendly critic, John Lloyd, put it in *The Times.*

> he conceives of the Treasury as the headquarters of an industrial conglomerate, with subsidiaries quaintly entitled the Departments of Education, Health, Social Security, Trade and Industry. He shares the view of his fellow countryman Adam Smith that the economy is an interrelated matrix of activities (4 July 1997).

Brown's aim is still to secure a new paradigm of welfare based on a self-reliant ethical socialism in a society nourished by the notion of inclusion through hard work – as John Lloyd puts it, a belief that 'only through work of hand and brain can the individual fully enter into the civic state' (*The Times*, 4 July 1997). Lloyd's 'holding company' image is one previously, and critically, put to us by some respondents in spending departments (Chapter 7).

Brown has a welfare agenda that has become a first-order concern of the Treasury and reinforces the sense of the inevitability of a 'strong Treasury' and need to give it analytical strength. His agenda is based on work but has broadened to include rectitude, individualism and sensitivity to business needs. Rectitude comes through the Code of Fiscal Stability and the Economic and Fiscal Strategy, which tries to codify a renunciation of making hay from a sunny fiscal picture – self-denying for the Treasury, but also an instrument for checking other departments. Individualism comes from various initiatives on reintegration into work (partners making themselves available for work, and counselling under the New Deal) which seem designed to prevent sheltering from the labour market by virtue of being a parent or partner. This spirit is evident in Martin Taylor's report on Work Incentives, perhaps the most systematic Treasury-based review of the purpose of welfare that we have seen, with its statement of liberal individualism: 'I believe that wherever possible Government should avoid framing special rules for categories of people based on their social and family arrangements' (but not the framing of rules to prevent lifestyle choices about remaining outside work) (HM Treasury, 1998b: para. 1.34).

Brown's use of the income tax system to conceal and dignify welfare spending is an old ploy, as theorists of the social division of welfare have pointed out. But there are good reasons why a separate regime for benefits has been established. British social security has been based on either need or contribution record, and relates to the household not the individual. Income tax relates to the present work status of individuals, recognizes marriage but not other relationships, and allows something of a manipulation of the realities of household budgeting, as in the independent taxation of husband and wife. Negative income tax proposals have previously been rejected as too inflexible, inefficient at directing help at those most in need, and promoting a distribution of household income unfavourable to women. The move from child tax allowances to Child Benefit in the 1970s expressed this line of thinking. Now

Brown has driven a tax-based social policy through (despite the anxieties of the social policy experts) and put the Treasury in the lead on policy-making in this sensitive area.

The Comprehensive Spending Review exercise provided a device for continuing, by other means, the 'fixed goalposts' approach of the manifesto and having only one decision-point – in April 1999 – when the expenditure course was set by the government collectively rather than the Treasury. But we can detect a considerable ambivalence in the presentation of the CSRs. Even since the election, Gordon Brown had promoted a rhetoric of stringency and constraint, and this informed his presentation of the Economic and Fiscal Strategy in June 1998. But along the way it became clear that in terms of Labour's own sentiments and the needs of the services there was no enthusiasm for bringing public expenditure below 40 per cent of GDP even further and faster than the Conservatives had hoped to do. Therefore in press briefings more positive themes about public spending were presented – even to the point of talk about spending sprees – which the spending departments and indeed the Prime Minister were glad to promote. Brown himself has always been prone to use formulae which serve as satisfactory interview or debating points but are disingenuous about his real intentions – such as the talk during the election campaign of the need for more investment or to end the wasted resources of unemployment. Replacing his discourse of frugality by one of generosity was an uncomfortable transition, suggesting that the Treasury were not sure how far to make a virtue of having found real new money to fill the space the pot of gold obtained from zero-based reallocation should have occupied.

Many commentators in the world of social policy had found it particularly difficult to express enthusiasm for Gordon Brown's policies during Labour's first two years. He seemed to be building-in to British fiscal policy the principle that public expenditure should grow at a slower rate than the economy as a whole, and that the maintenance of 'real terms' expenditure linked to the retail prices index is a sufficient response – indeed a concession – to services and individuals dependent on the state. In fact, the index-linking approach tugs these clients behind the general expansion of the economy and evades the specific cost pressures they face. The CSR outcomes addressed these issues and did provide an injection of additional resources in real terms, but Brown's past rhetoric deprived him of much of the credit for it.

As with Nigel Lawson, the last creative Chancellor who claimed to have fixed the British economy and in so doing asserted the Treasury's central role on policy, Brown has also left himself vulnerable to malfunctions in it. More precisely, with spending now under fairly successful aggregate control, the problem is in the large and poorly-predicted surges and shortfalls in tax revenue which have become evident in the last ten years. It is easy to foresee a scenario where the three-year spending totals prove too generous in the Treasury's terms, especially on the current expenditure side, and either the performance review process or the recalibration in 2000 when resource budgeting is introduced are used as opportunities for further thoughts. The demarcation of capital budgets, the traditional easy targets during cuts exercises, may be a pre-emptive bid to protect them.

But after the March 1999 budget, the strategy – and the luck – remained intact. What had seemed like optimistic predictions of economic growth in the pre-Budget statement were confirmed, though many forecasters still judged them ambitious. The Chancellor was able to predict a surplus in the public finances for 1998–9, though for that year only, with later surpluses confined to the current account. Once again, the tendency to underspend was evident, with debt interest and social security the main contributors (Table 10.2). The social security element in the control total for 1998–9 was estimated to be £1920 million less than had been forecast in March 1998 (HM Treasury, 1999a: table B19). With receipts still predicted to rise by £20 billion a year, the rate dipping only in 1999–2000, the Chancellor was able to build a pleasing edifice if it were accepted that the economic scaffolding on which it was placed was secure.

Along the way, Brown was able to carry through more of his social policy strategy, building on the Treasury's own instruments of tax credits, income guarantees and alignment of income tax and national insurance contributions. MIRAS was finally abolished, Child Benefit was increased and the 10p starting rate of tax introduced. The sweeteners to health and education were continued and became more precise: £100 million for school technology, £60 million for new school books (presumably with a portrait of the Chancellor inside the cover), £500 million to upgrade every accident and emergency unit 'that needs it'. These supplements were becoming almost addictive, and they did not in most cases embody new expenditure, conveniently being drawn from the Reserve and the Capital Modernization Fund.

Table 10.2   The public finances after the 1999 Budget

£ billion	1997–8	1998–9	1999–2000	2000–01	2001–02	2002–03	2003–04
Current receipts	315.7	334.2	345	364	385	405	425
Current expend.	304.3	313.5	329	346	362	379	398
Investment less asset sales	18.0	17.9	20	22	25	28	31
Total managed expenditure (change from July 98)		331.4	349.2	368.8	387.3		
	–1.8	–2.4	–1.2	–2.4			
Net borrowing incl. windfall tax	9.1	–1.0	3	3	1	3	4

Source: HM Treasury (1999: tables 2.3 and B13).

But in terms of overall welfare strategy, Brown's approach looked more opportunistic. His one previously clearly stated aim – to tax Child Benefit and replace it for the older age-groups – was tacitly abandoned. The new children's tax credit represented a reversion to the pre-1977 approach of putting child support in the pay-packet rather than the purse. Technical uncertainties about the Working Families Tax Credit remained. Brown's final fling – the promise of 1p off the main rate of income tax in 2000 – seemed a reckless move at a time of economic uncertainty, and was perhaps related to his attempt to present the Budget to the Scottish media as 'made in Scotland' and a 'Holyrood handout' in preparation for the election campaign for the Scottish Parliament – a deferred pay-off for not embracing nationalism. Like other Chancellors before him, Brown seemed to be something of a gambler, becoming overcommitted to his policy direction and expanding the Treasury's reach into the policy activities of government.

The central choice: 'beefing up' or 'choking off' the Treasury

Brown altered some of the Treasury's institutional objectives, but in general his approach harmonized well with the philosophy of the Treasury, as it developed over the years of recovery from the humiliation of Black Wednesday in September 1992. Both have an interest in a strong Treasury which sets the framework on the generalities in a way that allows selective intervention on the specifics. Brown's Budgets are testaments to the triumph of Treasury dominance in the framing and presentation of economic policy and its social implications. But has this dominance extended to the control of the policy-making process in the core executive, and is this a notion that should be embraced or resisted?

At the start of our research, we were agnostic about whether the Treasury's role in British government had been in general heroic or villainous. We were influenced to some extent by the body of social policy and left-wing economics literature that saw the Treasury as a brake on growth and redistribution. We were also conscious of the need for central steering in a bureaucracy that inevitably caused power to gravitate to organizations with responsibility for resource allocation – making the question not one of keeping power away from the financial centre but knowing what to do with it once it arrived there.

After finishing our research we became convinced that prescriptions which sought to resolve problems by making the Treasury weaker were likely to fail. The history of the Department of Economic Affairs and Civil Service Department showed the futility of promoting countervailing forces within government. The latest attempt – to promote an enlarged Cabinet Office as the co-ordinator of government policy, promoter and evaluator of innovation and filter for new policy ideas – risks running into the same problem as it gets into Treasury business, as it will certainly do if the new Performance and Innovation Unit set up by the Prime Minister in July 1998 discharges its brief to 'complement the Treasury's role in monitoring departmental programmes' (House of Commons Hansard, 28 July 1998, written answer, vol. 317, col. 133) too enthusiastically.

To understand why the Treasury would seek a leadership role in social policy, we need to locate its interest in social topics within its wider conception of its task. Our conclusion is that the Treasury's interest proceeds from, and is sustained by, its sense of its responsibilities as the manager of national economic and financial policy. This sense encourages it to intervene in several orders or levels of policy.

The Treasury's *first-order* concerns remain the economic aggregates – growth, inflation, tax yields, spending control totals, the budget deficit. These are not perfect expressions of the reality of the economy, but they need to be right in order to preserve the political credibility of ministers. As their definition may be changed, some of them – particularly on the budget side – are susceptible to technical ingenuity. The 'search for savings' is a predominant and surprisingly crude theme. Failure to achieve targets is seen as a weakness of control rather than an expression of unexpected, entitled demand. The Treasury's *second-order* concerns are with the efficient functioning of market mechanisms. Goods and services worth producing are seen as having a price, implicit or explicit; the generation of these prices cannot be controlled, but the protection of the incentives to do so in a non-distorted way is a realistic objective. In the sphere of public policies, this takes the form of concern with work incentives, with the separation of customer and provider interests, and with the balance of individual and social rates of return. It is often summarized as the 'supply-side' or 'Ministry of Economics' function of the Treasury. Frequently, it takes the forms of a perceived correction of the pattern of influence bearing upon spending departments – promotion of the consumer interest *vis-à-vis* the producer, or of the national economy against a presumed alliance of staff in the service and the beneficiaries they present as deserving. At its most developed it might imply the advocacy of additional expenditure in some fields, especially where there are long-term costs of deferral; this was foreshadowed by the FER, but regularly described to us as an unnatural function for the Treasury and unlikely to become a normal technique.

At the *third order* are concerns about the outcomes and impacts of policies, especially when they seek to bear upon multi-faceted problems like poverty, crime, disability and lack of employment skills. Here the Treasury has traditionally lacked expertise. It has long employed economists, but mainly on the appraisal of individual projects rather than the evaluation of overall policies. It has not had the mix of disciplines desirable for good policy analysis. It has observed in a very partial way, through consideration of difficult projects and some isolated acquaintance with delivery systems. It has relied heavily for its information on the departments it sometimes distrusts.

The result of these different orders of priority is that the Treasury faces a particular gap between its wish to intervene on social policy and its ability to do so. The important variable is its willingness to defer to colleagues in another department and accept their objectives and priorities. Upon examination, these objectives – as set out, for instance, in departmental annual reports – often imply a level of public provision and intervention greater than the Treasury would feel comfortable with. Therefore the acceptance that departmental ministers are responsible for the definition and pursuit of government policy in their areas becomes difficult to concede. The controls may be much less detailed and continuous than in the past – especially in the field of departmental running costs – but they constrain policy and require compliance. In response, departments may concede Treasury points about which they are unconvinced in order to meet savings targets. What is weakened is a sense of shared responsibility for the social policy of the government as a whole. Not surprisingly, the review process in the CSRs and PSAs made a particular attempt to align objectives and targets in ways with which the Treasury would feel comfortable, but over time departments are liable to drift away in the direction of their own preoccupations and clientele.

We found much concern about social policy among senior Treasury officials, an interest in observing it on the ground, but also a certain detachment from the measure of real experience of social services. This applies particularly to complex, multifaceted issues, where the supply of money and services is used to influence individual behaviour. The Treasury finds it difficult to separate their conception of spending departments' expertise from their assumed interest in the present structure of production and consumption. There is a tendency for Treasury officials to seek to generalize from their own very partial exposure to detail rather than accept a position of ignorance, which would imply a deference to the spending departments.

Our general conclusion is that the Treasury does not have a separate first-order social policy, but does have a strong sense of the direction social policies need to be going in order to fit in with the economic objectives of the government. The Treasury is going to promote this direction, and it has the position inside government to do so effectively; and so to our mind the most important issue is the quality of understanding the Treasury brings to its task.

The Treasury's role in social policy

To understand what the Treasury's role might be, we need to locate it among several options for the central steering of government. For social policy we suggest, certainly in British circumstances and probably more generally, that there can be three possible locations which represent in turn a focus on the economy; on society and social programmes; and the government system in its politico-administrative sense (Figure 10.1):

(i) the Treasury in its capacity as both the economics and finance ministry, giving it a concern about the cost and effectiveness of social programmes and their impact on economic performance; as well as the spending teams covering each social department, it also has a capability to address cross-cutting issues, and in some cases a special unit like Work Incentives and Poverty Analysis can be set up to take the lead on policy-making;

(ii) departments or units with an explicit social policy function, especially if they are more than the organising mechanism for a single service or client group – the former Department of Health and Social Security was an unsuccessful attempt at this from a needs-based perspective; the Department for Education and Employment has a politically more robust focus on skills acquisition and integration into the labour market; the newly restored 'big' Department of the Environment, Transport and the Regions has a less prominent but still important social policy contribution through the housing market and urban regeneration. It is also possible to locate in a social department a unit charged with integrative reform, notably Frank Field's ill-fated welfare reform effort in 1997–8;

(iii) the support system for the Prime Minister and the Cabinet and its committees, represented after the July 1998 announcement by the integrated Cabinet Office (including the Office of Public Services, the Performance and Innovation Unit and the new Centre for Management and Policy Studies), and by the continuing Social Exclusion Unit and the Prime Minister's domestic policy staff. The intention is to make the Cabinet Office operate as the corporate headquarters of the Civil Service, with the Secretary of the Cabinet establishing a team, including a number of permanent secretaries, to function as a Management Board for the Civil Service.

Alongside this 'horizontal' division about organizational turf is a 'vertical' demarcation of levels of intervention based on competing objectives. These driving forces for change can include a motivation that comes from political philosophy (morality, even); a concern with cost; the need to secure satisfactory policy processes and outcomes (and present them convincingly) or a push for more efficient management of delivery. There is often a lack of engagement between these general motivations and an interest in social policy, and they are seldom integrated into a coherent intellectual apparatus. The usual model is of sudden surges of interest by the Prime Minister

Figure 10.1 Aspirants to the leadership role in social policy

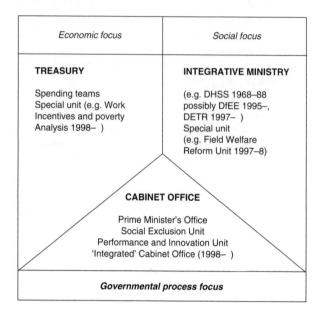

or Chancellor, especially when more than one level of intervention comes together. Mechanisms for co-ordination need to account of these motivations for political involvement, even when they appear to lack predictability or rationality.

We see the greatest need in central policy-making as a broader analytical capability on the interface between social and economic policy, going beyond the processes of expenditure allocation, with its inevitable bias towards short-term tactical considerations. We are conscious of the failure of detached units like the Central Policy Review Staff to influence policy outcomes directly. The Treasury is the default mechanism for policy analysis in the government, and it will resist any institutional alternatives that might weaken the Chancellor's position in the Cabinet – including the building-up of the Domestic Policy Staff at 10 Downing Street in the Prime Minister's capacity as First Lord of the Treasury.

On balance it may be best to locate the analytical centres within the Treasury, so long as it can embrace the degree of consultation and information-sharing promised in the FER. We see a need to supply some correction to the current position where the dominant intellectual perspective is overwhelmingly that of economics, the main discipline of specialist advisers and – more importantly – of generalist administrators. One possibility is to appoint seconded officials to pursue cross-cutting issues identified for attention. We feel it is also important to locate the offline, reflective 'spare persons' not just at the deputy director level set in the FER but also lower down the hierarchy at the former Assistant Secretary and Principal levels.

We were impressed by the efforts made to implement the Treasury's own 1994 reviews; but such a major retooling combined with a severe loss of staff at senior grades and a continuing search for public expenditure savings imposed a heavy burden on the remaining key actors, especially at team leader level. Our hypothesis that in these circumstances it would be difficult to combine the active and passive roles the Treasury is seeking has been largely confirmed. This suggests that senior management's wish after the FER to take on new strategic functions on a lower staffing base may have been too ambitious. Such is the importance of clear thinking about social policy in the core executive that a fuller texture of staffing, with secondments to and from departments and the wider policy and academic worlds, would be amply justified.

Events in 1998–9 seem to us to lend weight to our analysis. The Treasury was strengthened by the evidence-based consideration of policy options in the Work Incentives and Poverty Analysis Unit and around the 'Sure Start' programme. At the end of the spending reviews, the Treasury was driving and making policy and was imposing its own social policy priorities – in particular, for investment-based supply-side spending that could be justified as a national retooling, rather than unmandated transfers to individuals. The 'welfare-to-work' agenda was run from the Treasury, and the Working Families Tax Credit embodied an unapologetic use of tax expenditures and transfer of clientele from the Benefits Agency to the Inland Revenue. The Treasury was glad to advertise its involvement in the social CSRs (as in its 1998 *Annual Report* (HM Treasury, 1998d: para. 1.2.20)) and was taking an important role in the New Deal for Communities.

Against this is the enhanced capacity of Cabinet Office after July 1998 and the declared determination of the Labour government to drive through coordination from that office, in order that policy, in the Prime Minister's Commons statement of 28 July 1998, meets 'the corporate objectives of government as a whole, rather than just the objectives of individual departments' (ibid.: col. 134). The White Paper on the civil service, *Modernising Government*, launched on 30 March 1999, reaffirmed the need for 'joined-up government' but was again ambivalent on how the various mechanisms at the centre would relate to one another. Whether by accident or design, the Treasury is remarkably absent from the White Paper, not being mentioned at all in the chapter on policy-making (Cabinet Office, 1999: ch. 2), and the Performance and Innovation Unit is given the task of examining the 'system of incentives and levers', which might include 'pooled budgets across departments, cross-cutting performance measures and appraisal systems which reward team-working across traditional boundaries' (ibid.: 2.9). Treasury turf is well in play here. Just as the Budget was Gordon Brown's policy system, this White Paper is Tony Blair's.

Conclusion

In terms of Figure 10.1, what we see under Labour is the failure of any attempt to steer social policy from within the social depart-mental framework. Frank Field's story encapsulates the frustrations of a minister in the department with by far the largest social spending budget (social security) attempting to make social policy, even with the explicit sanction of the Prime Minister to do so. Of the re-maining contenders for the central role, the notion of the Cabinet Office as a focus for integration and development of policy devel-oped fast in 1998–9; but, in both financial and philosophical terms, it is likely in the long run to lack the grip on policy which the Treasury is able to assert.

We hope that our research has given some substance to the econ-omic aspect of the academic debate about governance, fragmentation and hollowing-out. As we saw in Chapter 1, the thrust of this de-bate was to suggest that problems had arisen through a failure by government to steer the network-based delivery mechanisms it had brought into being. The implication was that the threads of con-trol had been lost and would have to be recreated (albeit in a sociologically more modern form). As we noted, the Treasury tends to get left out of this debate. Even Foster and Plowden, two highly Treasury-aware authors, leave their thoughts on this hanging, not developing the implication that some form of Treasury activism will have to be reconstituted:

Crossman, R. (1977) *The Diaries of a Cabinet Minister: Vol III, Secretary of State for Social Services*. London: Hamish Hamilton and Jonathan Cape.

Deakin, N. and Parry, R. (1993) 'Does the Treasury have a Social Policy?', in R. Page and N. Deakin (eds), *The Costs of Welfare*. Aldershot: Avebury.

Deakin, N. and Parry R. (1998) 'The Treasury and New Labour's Social Policy' in E. Brunsdon, H. Dean and R. Woods (eds), *Social Policy Review 10*. London: Social Policy Association.

Dell, E. (1996) *The Chancellors*. London: HarperCollins.

Department of Social Security (1993) *The Growth of Social Security*. London: HMSO.

Department of Social Security (1998a) *New Ambitions for our Country: A New Contract for Welfare*, Cm 3805. London: HMSO.

Department of Social Security (1998b) *A New Contract for Welfare: Principles into Practice*, Cm 4101. London: HMSO.

Department of Social Security (1998c) *A New Contract for Welfare: Partnership in Pensions*, Cm 4179. London: HMSO.

Donnison, D. (1982) *The Politics of Poverty*. Oxford: Martin Robertson.

Dunleavy, P. (1991) *Democracy, Bureaucracy and Public Choice*. London: Harvester Wheatsheaf.

Foster, C. and Plowden, F. (1996) *The State Under Stress*. Buckingham: Open University Press.

Fowler, N. (1991) *Ministers Decide*. London: Chapmans.

Garnham, A. and Knights E. (1994) *Putting the Treasury First*. London: Child Poverty Action Group.

Glennerster, H. (1997) *Paying for Welfare: Towards 2000*. London: Prentice Hall.

Glennerster, H. and Hills, J. (eds) (1998) *The State of Welfare*, 2nd edn. Oxford: Oxford University Press.

Heald, D. (1983) *Public Expenditure*. Oxford: Martin Robertson.

Heald, D. (1994) 'Territorial public expenditure in the United Kingdom', *Public Administration*, 72(2), 147–75.

Heath, Sir T. (1927) *The Treasury*. London: G.P. Putnam's.

Heclo, H. and Wildavsky, A. (1974, 2nd edn 1981), *The Private Government of Public Money*. London: Macmillan.

Hennessy, P. (1989) *Whitehall*. London: Secker & Warburg (quotes from revised Fontana edn, 1990).

HM Treasury (1979) *Needs Assessment Study: Report*. London: HM Treasury.

HM Treasury (1984) *The Next Ten Years*, Cmnd 9189. London: HMSO.

HM Treasury (1991) *Competing for Quality*, Cm 1730. London: HMSO.

HM Treasury (1994) *Fundamental Review of HM Treasury's Running Costs: A Report to the Chancellor of the Exchequer by Sir Colin Southgate, Jeremy Heywood, Richard Thomas and Suzanne Cook*. London: HM Treasury.

HM Treasury (1996) *Departmental Report of the Chancellor of the Exchequer's Small Departments*, Cmd 3217. London: HMSO.

HM Treasury (1997a) *Public Expenditure Statistical Analyses, 1997–98*, Cm 3601. London: HMSO.

HM Treasury (1997b) *Chancellor of the Exchequer's Smaller Departments: the Government's Expenditure Plans 1997–98 to 1999–2000*, Cm 3617. London: HMSO.

HM Treasury (1997c) *Financial Statement and Budget Report*, HC 90. London: HMSO.

HM Treasury (1998a) *New Ambitions for Britain: Financial Statement and Budget Report*, HC 620. London: HMSO.

HM Treasury (1998b) *Work Incentives: A Report by Martin Taylor*. London: HM Treasury.

HM Treasury (1998c) *Public Expenditure Statistical Analyses 1998–99*, Cm 3901. London: HMSO.

HM Treasury (1998d) *Departmental Report of the Chancellor of the Exchequer's Departments*, Cm 3917. London: HMSO.

HM Treasury (1998e) *Stability and Investment for the Long Term: Economic and Fiscal Strategy Report 1998*, Cm 3978. London: HMSO.

HM Treasury (1998f) *Public Expenditure 1997–98 Provisional Outturn*, Cm 3988. London: HMSO.

HM Treasury (1998g) *Modern Public Services for Britain: Investing in Reform. Comprehensive Spending Review: New Public Spending Plans 1999–2000*, Cm 4011. London: HMSO.

HM Treasury (1998h) *Public Services for the Future: Modernisation, Reform, Accountability. Comprehensive Spending Review: Public Service Agreements 1999–2002*, Cm 4181. London: HMSO.

HM Treasury (1999a) *Economic and Fiscal Strategy and Financial Statement and Budget Report*, HC 298. London: HMSO.

HM Treasury (1999b) *Tackling Poverty and Extending Opportunity*. London: HM Treasury.

HM Treasury (1999c) *Public Services for the Future: Modernisation, Reform, Accountability. Comprehensive Spending Review: Public Service Agreements 1999–2002. March 1999 Supplement*, Cm 4315. London: HMSO.

HM Treasury (1999d) *Funding the Scottish Parliament, the National Assembly for Wales and the Northern Ireland Assembly – A Statement of Funding Policy*. London: HM Treasury.

Holland, G. (1995) 'Alas! Sir Humphrey. I knew him well', *RSA Journal*, November, 59–91.

House of Commons Public Accounts Committee (1995) *Child Support Agency*, HC 31. London: HMSO.

House of Commons Social Security Committee (1998) *Tax and Benefits: Pre-Budget Report*, HC 423. London: HMSO.

House of Commons Social Security Committee (1985) *Review of Expenditure on Social Security*, HC 134. London: HMSO.

House of Commons Treasury and Civil Service Sub-Committee (1995) *HM Treasury's Fundamental Expenditure Review*, HC 435-I. London: HMSO.

House of Commons Treasury Committee (1997) *The Barnett Formula*, HC 341. London: HMSO.

Howe, G. (1994) *Conflict of Loyalty*. London: Macmillan.

Jenkins, R. (1998) *The Chancellors*. London: Macmillan.

Jenkins, S. (1995) *Accountable to None: The Tory Nationalization of Britain* London: Hamish Hamilton (quotes from Penguin edn, 1996).

Labour Party (1997) *New Labour Because Britain Deserves Better*. London: Labour Party.

Lawson, N. (1992) *The View from No. 11*. London: Bantam Press.

Likierman, A. (1988) *Public Expenditure*. London: Penguin Books.

Likierman, A. (1995) 'Resource Accounting and Budgeting: Rationale and Background', *Public Administration*, 73(4), 564–70.

Likierman, A. (1998) 'Resource Accounting and Budgeting – Where are we Now?', *Public Money and Management*, 18(4), 17–20.

Lowe, R. (1989) 'Resignation at the Treasury: the Social Services Committee and the failure to reform the welfare state, 1955–57', *Journal of Social Policy*, 18(4), 505–26.

Lowe, R. (1993) *The Welfare State in Britain since 1945*. London: Macmillan.

Lowe, R. (1997a) 'Milestone or millstone? The 1959–61 Plowden committee and its impact on British welfare policy', *Historical Journal*, 40, 463–91.

Lowe, R. (1997b) 'The core executive, modernisation and the creation of PESC, 1960–64', *Public Administration*, 75(4), 601–15.

Monck, N. (1997) 'The Need for a Strong Treasury, and how to make it Work' in D. Corry (ed.), *Public Expenditure: Effective Management and Control*. London: The Dryden Press.

National Audit Office (1997) *Audit of Assumptions for the July 1997 Budget Projections*, Cm 3693. London: HMSO.

Parry, R., Hood, C. and James, O. (1997) 'Reinventing the Treasury: economic rationalism or an econocrat's fallacy of control?', *Public Administration*, 75(3), 395–415.

Pliatzky, L. (1989) *The Treasury under Mrs Thatcher*. Oxford: Basil Blackwell.

Plowden, E. (1989) *An Industrialist in the Treasury*. London: Unwin Hyman.

Prior, D., Stewart, J. and Walsh, K. (1993) *Is the Citizen's Charter a Charter for Citizens?*, Belgrave Paper No. 7. Luton: Local Government Management Board.

Pym, H. and Kochan, N. (1998) *Gordon Brown: The First Year in Power*. London: Bloomsbury.

Richards, S., Smith, P. and Newman, J. (1996) 'Shaping and reshaping market testing policy', *Public Policy and Administration*, 11(2), 19–34.

Ridley, N. (1992) *My Style of Government: The Thatcher Years*. London: Fontana.

Roseveare, H. (1969) *The Treasury: The Evolution of a British Institution*. London: Allen Lane the Penguin Press.

Routledge, P. (1997) *Gordon Brown: The Biography*. London: Simon and Schuster.

Scottish Office (1997) *Scotland's Parliament*, Cm 3658. Edinburgh: HMSO.

Scottish Office (1998) *Government Expenditure and Revenue in Scotland 1996–97*. Edinburgh: The Scottish Office.

Smith, M.J. (1999) *The Core Executive in Britain*. London: Macmillan.

Social Security Advisory Committee (1997) *Lone-Parent Benefits*, Cm 3713. London: HMSO.

Thain, C. and Wright, M. (1995) *The Treasury and Whitehall: The Planning and Control of Public Expenditure 1976–93*. Oxford: Clarendon Press.

Theakston, K. (1999) *Leadership in Whitehall*. London: Macmillan.

Timmins, N. (1995) *The Five Giants: A Biography of the Welfare State*. London: HarperCollins.

Walker, A. (1982) *Social Planning*. Oxford: Basil Blackwell.

Wass, D. (1984) *Government and the Governed*. London: RKP.

Weir, S. and Beetham, D. (1999) *Political Power and Democratic Control in Britain*. London: Routledge.

Weller, P., Bakvis, H. and Rhodes, R. (eds) (1997) *The Hollow Crown: Countervailing Trends in Core Executives*. London: Macmillan.

Wright, M. (1995) 'Resource Budgeting and the PES System', *Public Administration*, 73(4), 580–90.

Young, H. and Sloman A. (1982) *Yes, Minister*. London: BBC Publications.

Young, H. and Sloman, A. (1984) *But, Chancellor*. London: BBC Publications.

Index